OUTSIDER, INSIDER

�È◈◈◈

OUTSIDER, INSIDER

AN UNLIKELY SUCCESS STORY

◇◇◇◇

The Memoirs of

ANDREW HEISKELL

WITH RALPH GRAVES

MARIAN-DARIEN PRESS
NEW YORK

First North American Edition

Published in the United States by Marian-Darien Press

Picture Credits

Page 44: New York Public Library for
the Performing Arts
Pages 89, 128, 131, 206: Time Inc.
Pages 149, 151: John Olsen, *Life*
Page 210: Carl Mydans, Time Inc.
Page 221: Amy Davis, *Baltimore Sun*
Page 224: Enterprise Foundation
Page 226: Martha Holmes, Time Inc.
Page 259: Norman Mintz

All family pictures are from private collections

10 9 8 7 6 5 4 3 2 1

PRINTED IN THE UNITED STATES OF AMERICA

To my wife Marian,
who made this book possible
— as well as many other good things

CONTENTS

◇◇◇◇

FOREWORD
BY VARTAN GREGORIAN

◇◇◇◇

In 1980, after my decision not to accept the Chancellorship of the University of California at Berkeley, and my subsequent resignation as the Provost of the University of Pennsylvania, I came to New York for an interview with the Presidential Search committee of New York University.

While I was in New York, a national recruiting firm asked me to meet the leaders of the New York Public Library. My "interview" with the late Richard Salomon and Andrew Heiskell was an amazing event, indeed a happening. I was in the presence of two extraordinarily successful, decisive New Yorkers. Dick Salomon was the CEO of Charles of the Ritz. He had revolutionized Madison Avenue with his imaginative marketing of the perfume and cosmetic industries. He was outgoing chairman of the board of the New York Public Library. Andrew Heiskell, the incoming chairman, was the outgoing CEO of Time Inc. and a member of the Harvard Corporation. The two men were trying to interest me in the presidency of the New York Public Library. Without exaggerating, 20 minutes into our interview, both men got up and, with great excitement, declared, "You are *our man*! We *want* you to be the President of the New York Public Library. You *must* be our next leader!"

Their decisiveness, their vision, their passion overwhelmed me. Within that short span of time we had established an amazing rapport. Thus began a unique, wonderful and enduring friendship with Andrew Heiskell.

After some soul searching and intense consultations with my wife, family and several friends, I decided to accept the challenge and to head the New York Public Library. I knew about the central role of the Library in the educational and cultural life of the City and the nation, but I did not know about its history, structure, finances, organization and governance. I accepted the presidency with great trepidation but with a clear view. I reasoned that if I succeeded in rejuvenating the Library and restored its central role in the cultural and educational life of New York, it would be considered to be a miracle; if I failed, it would be a worthy yet public "martyrdom." Either way, I could not lose by serving this extraordinary institution. Many of my friends had grave misgivings about my decision. Indeed, one trustee of the University of Pennsylvania told me I should see a psychiatrist.

The New York Public Library, along with other cultural and educational institutions, was hard hit in the late 1960s and the decade of the 1970s. There were projections that the Library would soon lose its entire endowment and accumulate a $50 million deficit.

The Library's extraordinary and unexpected renaissance is due to the leadership of a unique troika of Andrew Heiskell, Brooke Astor and Richard Salomon. Under Heiskell's leadership, we forged a new partnership with the City and the State of New York. We launched a major capital campaign that netted $327 million. All in all we raised some $400 million and received at least $100 million in collections as well. The main building and many branches were renovated and air conditioned; the hours were extended, and even a new library for the blind was built. Andrew, Brooke and Dick were also responsible for recruiting an extraordinary board of trustees for the Library—one of the best boards in New York City.

During my eight years as president of the New York Public Library and nine years as president of Brown University, I have come to know Andrew as chairman, as a leader and as a friend. I have come to know Andrew the private person as well as Andrew the public persona.

He is a fascinating man, a unique and complex man, a man of remarkable intelligence and culture, a man of passion and deep convictions. To me, he symbolizes vigor, zest for life, tenacity and optimism.

To me, Andrew was the perfect chairman of the board. Having served as chairman and CEO of Time Inc., he knew the difference between leading and managing. He helped set guidelines and policies and extended generously his time and emergy to me, but he never micromanaged. To the best of my knowledge during his chairmanship and my presidency at the New York Public Library, we never disagreed. To come to think of it, that is not true. We did disagree on several occasions when he wanted to raise my salary and I kept declining it. From the very beginning, our relationship assumed the character of friendship. The irony that both of us were born abroad— Andrew in Naples, Italy and I in Tabriz, Iran—and that we were trusted with the fate of the New York Public Library did not escape us.

In many ways I can describe Andrew as an Italian WASP. He has all the good attributes of an ideal WASP: he believes in tradition, in honor, dignity, integrity, fairness and fair play. He still believes that one's word is one's bond. Unlike Owen Wister, a 19th Century Philadelphia WASP, who jokingly said that in Philadelphia even moderation should not be excessive, Andrew is a passionate WASP. He is a proud man. Even though he is a very private person, often a man of few words, sometimes taciturn, nevertheless this introvert has been known to exhibit the full passions of an extrovert, especially when it comes to the causes he cherishes, his family, democracy, our Constitution and America's role and responsibility as a world leader. I have seen his anger when dealing with issues of racism, injustice, discrimination and assaults against the First Amendment.

I have witnessed many of Andrew's other triumphs: the salvaging and restoring of Bryant Park, the awesome work of the Enterprise Foundation, his contributions to the National Urban Coalition, his satisfying tenure as a member of Harvard University's Corporation, and his untiring efforts, amongst others, on behalf of the American Academy in Rome and People for the American Way. A perennial devotee of social, cultural and educational causes, he never brags about any of his major accomplishments. He has always shared his successes with others, building teams and teamwork. A very generous philanthropist, he has never highlighted his giving. As a WASP, he gives without drama. He is quiet about money. And what impresses me most, he is never impressed by the wealth of other individuals. He is only impressed with the *quality* of individuals—their intrinsic values and their position and long-term commitment to the public good and our democracy.

Andrew Heiskell is *sui generis*, always reinventing himself. He gives "re-

tirement" a good name. Both psychologically and socially he can never retire. He is an activist par excellence. A firm believer in the First Amendment, a fanatic defender of the Constitution of the United States, he is not
afraid to express his views, both popular and unpopular. This impatient
patient man cannot accept no for an answer. He ardently believes in life as
a sphere of possibilities, not limitations. He believes firmly in the adage
that when there is a will, there is a way.

As you read his memoirs, you will enjoy the journey of this uncommon
man. He epitomizes the character and the spirit of the 20th Century. I
count myself among those who have been fortunate to work with this leg-
endary CEO of Time Inc., who helped shape so much of our national and
international agenda, who since his "retirement" has helped so many great
institutions and so many worthy causes.

I will always relish my association with Andrew, our many triumphs, our
many struggles. I will always remember our first formal reception at the
New York Public Library for public officials (only two of them showed up),
and our early morning appearances before the City Council and the Board
of Estimates.

I will remember our frequent trips to Albany. I will remember, now with
fondness, our interminable appearances over some eight years before in-
numerable public agencies, community boards, the Parks Council and the
Municipal Arts Society, on behalf of the restoration of Bryant Park. This
tested our faith in the complicated legal and democratic processes of the
City of New York, compounded by rigid and inflexible mindsets. But given
the outcome, every bit of that effort was worth it. Bryant Park is now one
of the gems of our City.

I remember one late night Andrew and I were testifying before a community board on behalf of our plans for Bryant Park. The community
board had many "radical" proponents of the public sector who fought
against its "contamination" by the private sector. On that occasion we carried with us two editorials. One was written by Lenin in 1913 in the pages
of *Pravda,* extolling the virtues of the New York Public Library (he had read
the first annual report of the Library). The second one was an editorial in
Literaturnaia Gazette describing Bryant Park as an endless public urinal, an
ideal place for drugs and prostitution and therefore a "befitting" gathering

place for dissident Soviet writers. The board was impressed. We won a small battle that night, one of the many such battles that were won during Andrew's tenure.

All of us who know Andrew are grateful to him for the battles he fought, for the battles he has won and for the battles he will win. The beneficiaries have been our own city, our country, our society and our democracy. Thanks for the memories.

PREFACE

◇◇◇◇

A dozen years ago, with no thought of ever writing these *Memoirs*, I agreed to participate in the Oral History program of Columbia University. I was persuaded that the program was an important way to preserve personal reminiscences of people who have lived through significant experiences, and that my own reminiscences might well be of interest to others. I still think that today. I don't know how many hours I spent being interviewed, but the tape recordings made over a six-month period resulted in a transcript of 824 pages. The conversation is casual, sometimes disorganized, often incomplete, and it ends a decade ago, before many important events in my life took place. It is all it was intended to be: an oral history, not a finished piece of work. Columbia gave me several copies of the transcript.

Some members of my family read parts of it and were frequently surprised by what they learned about me — their own husband, their own brother, their own father. They insisted I should do my life as a book, and I finally agreed.

This time I needed not just an interviewer but a full collaborator. I chose Ralph Graves, a former managing editor of *Life* and editorial director of Time Inc., and the author of five novels. We both had long careers at Time Inc., and 32 of our Time Inc. years overlapped. We had both experienced many of the same events and the same people, although always from different angles. Our memories frequently jogged one another's.

Graves interviewed me at length, especially about my personal life, which had scarcely been touched on in the Oral History. He also interviewed other people who have played a significant role in my life: my wife Marian, my sister Diana, my stepdaughter Susan Dryfoos, and Robby Lantz, Ralph Davidson, Charley Bear, Bill Frey, Joe Kastner, Arthur Rosenblatt, Dan Biederman. I am grateful for their generous contributions to this book.

Our longtime chief legal officer at Time Inc., Gabe Perle, read the manuscript to protect me from libel and invasion of privacy. I appreciate his assurance, as I always did at Time Inc., that I am innocent.

My marvelous assistant Barbara Widmayer helped both Graves and me throughout the long writing process. She then took on the chore of removing pictures from their frames, having them copied for publication and then putting them back in their frames, where they look as good as ever.

I especially want to thank my old colleague and buddy at the New York Public Library, Vartan Gregorian, for writing such a flattering Foreword to this book. I will try to live up to it.

Despite my 42 years at Time Inc., including 20 years as chairman, this is not another Time Inc. history. This is a personal history of me. Many books have been written about Time Inc., including an excellent three-volume company history by Robert Elson and Curtis Prendergast. I have drawn on it repeatedly for facts and dates and names.

A very large part of my life, especially in the last 20 years, has been devoted to nonprofit organizations. Many articles have been written about the nonprofits I have helped to shape. But again, this book is not a history of those nonprofits. It is a record of my own personal involvement.

We stopped writing these *Memoirs* several years ago for a variety of reasons. We started up again at my wife Marian's urging. She was convinced that we had to finish and publish this book. That is what Graves and I have now done.

I had another personal motive, aside from Marian's strong conviction. As I neared 82, I felt the toll of age. I did not like it, but I had to acknowledge it. In terms of health, it had been a bad year for both Marian and me. She suffered a very serious ailment and a critical operation. I had at least two ailments (not counting arthritis) and one operation. For the first time in my life I would wake up in the morning and feel that maybe I would rather stay in bed than get up and tackle whatever matter was on the top of my agenda. If you have been as active as I have, for as long as I have, this is a surprising and unacceptable development. But it told me it was now or never if I wanted to finish these *Memoirs*.

I am mainly writing for my family, my many friends and my colleagues in countless endeavors. Most of them have been exposed to only one facet of a life that has had many, many facets. I trust they will find the other facets interesting.

Given my career, the title *Outsider, Insider* will strike many as puzzling. Yet as I look back, I am aware of always being alone in the midst of an endless series of *milieux*. Most people "belong" to a group, adopt its standards and are supported by its members. I did not belong. I was forever on the outside, looking in. I was forever aware not only of being "different" but of being looked on as "different." My youthful peregrinations and my rapid career rise kept me from being part of any group. Perhaps during my seven years in France I could have belonged. But of course the French rarely take a "foreigner" into their home life or social life. Wherever I was, whatever I was doing, I always felt like a foreigner.

Of course I am not a "loner" in the usual sense of the word. In fact, I enjoy my many friends, most of whom date from my retirement years. On that score I have been extremely fortunate.

But in my heart I know I'm a loner.

OUTSIDER,
INSIDER

◇◇◇◇

MY NOMAD CHILDHOOD

◇◇◇◇

I WAS BORN IN NAPLES, AN APPROPRIATE BEGINNING FOR my weird childhood. I had no business being born there. Neither of my parents was Italian and they did not even live in Naples. They were American expatriates living on the island of Capri, 20 miles across the bay.

In 1915 Capri had no hospital, no medical facilities of any kind, so my mother sailed across the bay to deliver me at the Naples hospital. Fortunately my birth was registered at the U.S. consulate there. Otherwise under Italian law I would have been considered an Italian citizen and, as an adult, could have been drafted into the Italian army. During the early years of World War II, I stayed totally clear of Italy. I thought it quite possible, in spite of my birth registration, that Mussolini might decide I should become an Italian soldier, a role I would have found extremely uncongenial.

I was christened Andrew, with no middle name. My parents were stingy with names. My sister Diana, five years older than I, also has no middle name. But after christening me Andrew, a much-used name in her family, my mother decided that was too much for an infant, so she called me Bobby, a nickname she simply pulled out of a hat. I remained Bobby or Bob until I was past 30, when my wife decided she liked Andrew better and changed it. For a number of years thereafter I was called both Bob and Andrew — confusing to everybody, including me.

As a little boy I lived on Capri in the Villa Discopoli, a house my parents had rented when my sister Diana was born. It was a sprawling place with big rooms, built in the Moorish style around the turn of the century. In the garden my father grew cactuses as a hobby. My parents gave large parties in our villa, because Capri was very social and sociable in those days. There

1

My father Morgan Heiskell holds me at a very tender age.

were waves of invaders: Swedes, Germans, Brits, writers, homosexuals —
everybody came to Capri and went to parties.

But I remember very little about it. I have vague memories of the beach
and of the *Faragliones,* the spectacular rocks that rise several hundred feet
out of the water at one end of the island. I left Capri when I was only six

and never returned except for a brief visit 70 years later. I was told our villa is still standing, but since it had been turned into a condominium, I did not want to see it.

My first language was Neapolitan because the servants were Neapolitan. Neapolitan is a *patois,* quite different from Italian in flavor and pronunciation, just as Provencal French is very different from Parisian French. My second language was Italian. But apparently I was rather stubborn about speaking English, so my mother finally hired a British nanny to correct this. British nannies are known for one thing — namely, they will never learn a language other than English. So I succumbed and learned. My accent is still a bit strange. I suppose it's the combination of the English nanny and all the other languages I learned in succession while I was growing up all over Europe.

My father Morgan Heiskell and my mother Ann Hubbard were born and raised in Wheeling, West Virginia, a dull third-rate town by historical accounts, rundown, rather crooked, known for its red light district. My father's father owned a wholesale business there, and my mother's father ran Wheeling Steel. Her father was decidedly upper crust. My father's father was sort of middle crust.

My own father's education was erratic — and so was he. At an early age he took off and went around the world, partly working his way on a boat. This made him quite distinctive in the sense that, unlike other people in Wheeling, he had seen the world.

When he returned to Wheeling, the inevitable occurred. My mother was a raving beauty, and he was a good-looking, glamorous young man who had traveled abroad. My mother's father strongly disapproved of the marriage because he did not think my father was stable, but they got married anyway.

On their honeymoon they visited Capri and liked it so much they decided to live there. That's quite a big jump, if you think of it, from Wheeling to Capri. This was 1908, and people simply didn't do that in those days. But my father thought Wheeling was a pretty terrible spot, and I guess my mother went along with it. Neither of them ever went back to Wheeling except for a brief visit.

My father was a tall man, about six-feet-two, and he remained slim all

This traditional naked baby picture of me looks better than most such pictures.

his life. He had a strong face, not pretty or handsome but strong. His first thought for a profession was to be an artist. He had a big studio at the villa and painted in the Impressionist style. My sister Diana, who would become a real artist, was intrigued by his painting. She remembers that one time when he was away from the studio, she took up his brush and palette to "improve" the painting he was working on. This was not well received by our father.

All Diana and I have left of his work are two small paintings, one landscape and one Venetian canal. Near the end of his life, he sold all the rest of his paintings at auction, probably for about what the frames were worth. He was a pretty good painter, in my opinion, but not good enough to make a profession out of it.

He could afford to live in Capri only because his parents gave him money. And the parents went a good deal farther than that. My grandmother adored her son Morgan, and she couldn't stand to be so far away from him. She persuaded her husband that he was working himself to death, that he should sell his business and retire so that they could move to Capri and be near Morgan and the grandchildren. My mother was less than delighted to have her in-laws right on her doorstep, even though they were paying the bills.

She was devoted to her own father, but because he had objected so strongly to her marriage, she was too proud to ask him for money. Even in the later years when she was moving around Europe, alone with two small children, she never asked him for help.

My sister Di and I have never known for sure why our parents broke up. There may have been other women involved and we think our mother had an affair with the British writer Compton Mackenzie, who lived on Capri. Whatever the reason, they certainly did not tell us why.

My father was away a lot, and I'm sure that contributed to the split-up. He gave up painting to become a photographer — a very good one. During World War I he was a photographer-observer in France, shooting pictures of enemy positions out of the side of a small airplane while the enemy was shooting up at him. At the end of the war he went to Rome, where he served in Rome as a fourth-rank diplomat.

The family broke apart during those years. In 1920, when I was five and Di was ten, my mother took us off to Varangeville, a lovely little village on the Normandy coast. This was not a resort but a true village, inhabited only by local French. I can't imagine how our mother found Varangeville, but she rented a cozy, comfortable house, and we lived there for half a year. Obviously this was a trial separation from our father, though probably not called that at the time. We took long, long walks every day. I remember the beach, and I remember that in the autumn we walked through layers and layers of fallen leaves, shuffling our way through the deep piles.

After Varangeville, my mother decided to pay an unheard-of visit to Wheeling. This, too, must have had something to do with marital problems. We spent two or three months there with my maternal grandfather Hubbard, an imposing man with lots of thick brown hair. It was my one and only visit to Wheeling, and the only thing I really remember clearly is that Di and I went roller skating, and she had a bad fall.

We returned to Capri very briefly, and I suspect that was when my

My father and I share a thoughtful talk on Capri. Not long after this, he and my mother split up, and I did not see him for another 35 years.

parents finally decided to split up for good, although they were not divorced until a long time after that. I was six years old when we left Capri to begin a strange nomadic life.

We spent the next eight years living in one hotel or another, in one country or another. We lived in Austria, Germany, Switzerland and France, with occasional side trips to Italy. All this moving about had something to do with favorable exchange rates for the American dollar, but I'm sure my mother also got recommendations from other hotel guests about pleasant places for us to live. Although I learned a number of languages, I had no formal schooling at first, just tutors here and there. The whole experience of being brought up in a succession of foreign countries can be either a superb education or a disaster. I was lucky.

The obvious question is, why did we stay in Europe? The natural thing for a lone woman in her thirties, saddled with two small children, would have been to go home to her family in Wheeling. I suspect that because her father had disapproved of her marriage, she did not want to run home to him in defeat. Or perhaps she just preferred Europe to West Virginia. It seems a defensible position.

We lived on money from our father's parents and later, when he went into business, from our father himself. We lived comfortably but not luxuriously, always in two hotel rooms, never in a suite. My mother had one room, my sister and I shared the other. It was always cramped, but I didn't mind. We were, after all, living in rather nice hotels, benefitting from the exchange rate. Wherever we were, we ate all our meals in the hotel dining room, so our behavior had to be excellent. One's manners were expected to be good, and they were.

I recently asked Di, "Didn't we have a lot of trouble meeting new people all the time?" She said, "Sure, but when you have such an attractive mother, everybody's nice to you." The easiest way to get a beautiful woman's attention is to admire and praise her children. Indeed, my mother was stunningly beautiful, with a superb, classic profile. She was tall, about five-eight, with a slim figure and a wonderful carriage. She wore her thick brown hair piled high on top of her head, Gibson Girl style. With a jaunty white boater hat perched on top of her coiffure, she was a delectable sight. But she was always a little reserved, sedate. She never threw herself at peo-

My mother Ann Hubbard Heiskell was the perfect Gibson Girl, with a boater, high-piled hair and a lovely face.

ple, there was always a slight distance. She was meticulous about her appearance. Even when she was an old lady in her nineties and in failing health, she still wanted her clothes and her hair to look just right.

In our hotel days in Europe, she wore long, full-length dresses, because our lifestyle was highly conventional. Each evening the three of us would enter the hotel dining room. My mother would be in the lead and I, neatly dressed in a jacket and tie, would be right behind her. I'm afraid I was always a terribly good little boy. Di would usually be trailing a bit behind me, because in those days she was always in revolt against whatever was supposed to be proper. She was a good-looking, athletic tomboy with a strong face that matched her independent outlook. We used to fight, and she beat up on me until I got too big for her. Then the fighting stopped.

Our first hotel homes were in Austria, where we spent two years in Salzburg and a little town called Zell am See, where Di and I caught whooping cough at the same time. We whooped and whooped and whooped. We were extremely unpopular, two children whooping loudly and incessantly in a quiet residential hotel. My mother had to take us out every day, take us as far away from the hotel as possible, to maintain some semblance of consideration for the other guests.

In Austria I started to learn German. When we moved to Bavaria, to another hotel in a town called Feldafing about 40 miles south of Munich, I became fluent. I also learned to count, and to count very well, because the German mark went from something like par to the dollar to a billion to the dollar in a short period of time.

I saw people going into stores carrying the bundles of marks, or even pushing the bundles in front of them in little carts. The three of us were reasonably well off because we had dollars, but when we changed them into marks, we had to spend them immediately because by next morning they might be worth only one-tenth as much. Right after going to the bank, we would buy what we needed, spend all the money and take the purchases back to our hotel. I learned to count in millions and billions at an early age.

In Feldafing I had my first lesson in politics. It was 1923 and people would talk about this crazy fellow Hitler, who ranted about Communists, Jews and capitalists. All proper people said, "Don't pay any attention to him. He'll just go away." I have been very wary of extremists ever since.

My sister Diana and I stand on some hotel parapet in some hotel overlooking some lake in some European country. In our nomad childhood they all began to look alike.

Our Feldafing hotel was on a lake. We used to steam around the lake on those elegant old power boats, all beautiful, shining mahogany. Di, who was always trying to cause trouble one way or another, would sit on the deck overhanging the outdoor dining room, dangling her bare feet on top of the people having lunch.

I think I must have learned to love food soon after I was born, and I loved everything — bratwurst, bauernwurst, sauerkraut, usually washed down with beer. All children drank beer in Austria and Germany, just the way all French children drink wine.

Our hotel had a wonderful vegetable garden, and I used to steal carrots, just pull them out of the earth and eat them raw. Nothing better than a carrot right out of the ground with a little taste of the earth. I still try to get carrots that haven't been washed, but in America you can't get an unwashed carrot. Feldafing also had marvelous venison, and they knew how to hang it. You should hang venison for a month. Today most people kill it, chop it up and eat it right away. That is not proper venison.

During these years my mother never talked about our father, and for reasons I don't understand at all, I never asked questions. I never said, "Hey, why don't I have a father?" Of course, I hadn't known him very well or for very long, and he had been away from home a good deal of that time, so his disappearance from my life was not the shock it might have been. Still, my attitude was odd. And my mother's attitude was extraordinary. In most separation cases one parent makes nasty cracks about the other on a fairly regular basis. My mother never did that. She just never mentioned him. My sister, being five years older, did miss our father and in later years she visited him. But I never saw him again until I was 40, and then I saw him only a few times before his death.

One reason the father question was not important to me in my boyhood was that I never lived with other families. If you live in one society, one neighborhood, and everybody else has a father and you don't, it sticks out. But living around Europe the way we did, we never had family friends, only acquaintances.

As far as I was concerned, my mother was it. Our life totally revolved around her, and as far as I could tell, she devoted her entire existence to us. She made sure I did my homework, first with tutors and later at various schools. She did not set goals, but she had definite expectations for us, more for me than for Di. She wanted me to grow up like her father and be very successful in business. Di, being a girl, was only expected to grow up and get married — which she never did. My mother read aloud to me, but she did not tell me stories — that would have been out of character. She was even-handed with us. I can't remember her ever getting angry and losing her temper.

When I was ten, my mother decided it was time Di and I went to proper schools instead of studying with tutors. So we moved to Lausanne — two rooms in a hotel, of course — and I entered a Swiss school. Swiss education is tough. They start doing algebra and Latin at an early age. I was not only behind all my classmates, but I also did not know the language. So I had to learn French-Swiss along with algebra, Latin and soccer. I even had to learn about being with boys and girls, because until then I had had very little contact with other children.

Our hotel was on the downhill side of Lausanne, and the school was up at Chailly, at that time almost a suburb of Lausanne. Every morning I had to ride a bicycle half an hour uphill. In the spring term school started at 7:00 A.M., so here I was, a ten-year-old bicycling at 6:30 A.M. and getting back at 5:00 in the afternoon, and then doing three hours of homework. My mother made certain I did it all. Eventually I got to be third or fourth in my class, but it was hard work.

The school had uniformly good teachers, and in the three years we lived in Lausanne I caught up with all that I had missed before. During this period my mother had an affair with a Colombian gentleman named Maldonado who lived in our hotel with his two daughters. He was charming, courtly, very South American in his appearance. My mother was so discreet that I didn't find out until 35 years later — and then in a bizarre way. I ran into one of the daughters in Paris, we had a brief affair, and she told me that many years ago our parents had done the same thing.

The other children in my school were perhaps 80% Swiss, with only a sprinkling of girls. The school was strict academically, but it also believed in athletics, so every afternoon we had an hour or more of soccer or some other strenuous exercise. I learned to ski — by far my favorite sport. All in all my Swiss education was happy but tough. After three years

I was really well grounded, not quite with a whip, but almost.

All this time we lived in a hotel, and why I didn't think this odd is beyond me. One of the end results of my bizarre education is that while I never felt that I belonged anywhere, I never found anybody else very strange. For me, all people were different from one another to begin with. I had no basis for comparison or contrast.

I was not brought up in Peoria. If you are brought up in one town, you tend to think that the mores of that town are *the* mores, and all other mores are strange, impossible, disgusting. I was brought up to live with a whole series of different mores, and it obviously had considerable impact on the kind of person I became.

I never thought of myself as American. I didn't think of myself as anything. I was always in transition from this place to that place, always having to adjust to a new set of circumstances, a new language, new people, new friends, new everything. When I think back, I have to say to myself, well, it's probably the best education you could have if you survive it. For a lot of kids it would probably have been destabilizing to move that much, but somehow my sister and I took to it. My mother deserves the credit for making it work. Ours was a small menage but a strong one.

In 1928 when I was 13, we moved from Lausanne to Paris. Now for the first time we lived in an apartment like other people. We finally made it! My mother found a fifth floor apartment in the 16th Arrondisement on the rue de Marroniers, between the Seine and the Bois de Boulogne. We each had a bedroom of our own — and even a living room and a dining room. However, I got only a fraction of the benefits of apartment living because I was immediately sent off to boarding school, to the Ecole de Montcel.

On the first day when I was asked to recite, the entire class burst out laughing — an explosion of laughter. I was shocked and embarrassed. What in God's name had I said that was so terrible, that made them all laugh? It was just my accent, my French-Swiss accent. Kids are very quick to let you know that you are "different."

I was always different. Wherever we lived — Italy, Austria, Germany, Switzerland, France — I was always an outsider. I never belonged.

My cosmopolitan upbringing did have advantages. Although I was an American, I learned many other languages, and I learned to adjust quickly to new settings and especially to new people. But I was always a little strange to them. I was always the new boy, arriving from some other place.

The Ecole de Montcel was set in a beautiful park near Versailles, about a dozen miles south of Paris. The school was originally a 19th Century chateau. All the rooms were odd, never intended to be used for classrooms or dormitories. Some classrooms were large with tall French windows, some were tiny with only a single pane of glass. The bedrooms were whatever you lucked into. The johns were those terrible stand-up French contraptions, one of the major blots on French civilization. We all ate together, 120 students plus faculty, in a basement dining room in the main building. The main dish we looked forward to was French fries, all cooked in a huge wire basket.

Each day began with a shower and dressing, and then we all lined up in front of the chateau and jogged through a beautiful park for ten minutes until we got to the place where we did our regular calisthenics. Then we jogged back to the chateau for breakfast and classes.

I had two great teachers and one who was almost great. If you have had two great teachers in your entire life, that is all you are entitled to. One was Polish, a man named Zabriskie, who taught math and algebra with such verve that I was excited to go to his class. In my last years there I had a brilliant teacher of philosophy named Fernandez. (Unfortunately he turned out to be a Nazi sympathiser and was shot during the war.) We also had an outstanding literature teacher who had won the coveted Prix Goncourt for one of his novels.

The Ecole de Montcel was as rigorous as my Swiss school. My whole memory of European schools is that they were tough and demanding, much more so than American schools. I was usually first in my class, partly because of my excellent Swiss schooling, partly because of my mother's encouragement, partly because of my own ambition. Meanwhile my sister Di attended the Parsons School of Design in Paris, her first serious training for her later career as an artist.

The school administration appointed me a captain in the student disciplinary system, and in my final year I became the chief captain. Many years later a bald-headed man ran into me at the New York restaurant "21" and said, "Oh, I remember you. You used to beat me with your shoe." It was the actor Yul Brynner, then starring in *The King and I*. I didn't remember beating him with a shoe, but I guess his memory on that subject would be better than mine.

I was always tall, much taller than the Swiss and French kids. In fact, by the time I was 15, I was as tall as I am today, six-feet-five-and-a-half. The kids called me "Carnera" after the giant heavyweight boxing champion Primo Carnera. I was indeed very tall but much skinnier than Carnera and not much of an athlete.

In the French education system, the climax of all your studies is the *baccalauréat*, the examinations marking the end of high school. Your whole state of mind for several years is fear and dread of the *baccalauréat* — or *bachot*, in slang. If you don't pass it, you are *nothing*. I suppose there are people who became successful after failing their *baccalauréat*, but they would be the exception.

In those days the *bachot* was done in two stages, a generalized first year and then a specialized second year. I decided to specialize in both science and philosophy, which was rather ambitious — too ambitious, in fact. To my surprise I flunked science, which I thought I was good at, but I passed the philosophy, and that was enough to pass my *bachot*.

After I passed, I was invited to stay on at the Ecole de Montcel as a teacher. I was 18. I taught geology and arithmetic to the younger children, teaching about six hours a week and making a thousand francs a month, pretty good pay, enough to make me self-supporting. You have to put out a lot of effort to keep kids interested, but I enjoyed it. The challenge in teaching is not how much you know but how interesting you can be. I had one unusual talent that I used to stimulate my students' interest in arithmetic. I would ask one to give me a four-digit number, which I wrote on the blackboard. Then I would ask a second boy to give me another four-digit number. I wrote it under the first one, like this:

$$4234$$
$$\times \underline{3671}$$

Then I went into a trance, stared out the window, concentrated hard. Finally I would turn and write the answer on the blackboard:

$$15,543,014$$

I would ask the whole class if that was the correct answer. It always was, because in those days I could imprint the successive multiplications in my mind, placing each in its own separate, staggered position, add up the columns and produce the right result. The stunt taught my students multiplication and addition — as well as showmanship.

(When I tried to duplicate my feat for this book, I found it impossible. I had to work out the above example on paper, and got it wrong the first time. Today I would have trouble doing this exercise mentally with two-digit numbers.)

While teaching, I enrolled at the University of Paris. I traveled back and forth by motorcycle and almost got myself killed until I could afford a used car. At the university level the whole French system changes. You really don't have to go to class. All you have to do is take exams at the end of the year. "Going to the university" in those days consisted of buying the transcript of a course taught by the best teacher, sometimes as far back as ten years ago. You read and memorized the transcript, then took the exam.

During summer vacations we often visited my father's parents, who had moved from Capri to a hotel in Rapallo on the north Italian coast near Genoa. Belonging to an older generation, they had remained one hundred per cent American, unaffected by anything Italian. My grandfather even bought a tiny plot of land so that he could grow American corn. In Europe, corn is strictly for horses, but he loved corn on the cob, so he got the seed and grew it.

We happened to be visiting Rapallo when his first crop came in. Grandfather realized that Italians might not think too well of people eating corn, since it is not only animal food but messy besides. So he went to the trouble of getting those little spits that you stick in the ends of the cob to make eating it look more genteel. But still there was an uproar in the hotel dining room when we first ate our grandfather's corn. Disgusting, revolting manners!

We also vacationed at a seacoast town called Pollensa on the island of Majorca off the coast of Spain. A nice hotel room cost only a dollar a day. The town, a favorite with foreigners, is just a fringe along the beach on a large bay. One Brit had a sailboat that was a floating bar. Each morning at

11:30 he would set sail and go from house to house along the beach. His friends would come aboard, have a drink, and then he would go on to the next stop. By three he had to take a long nap.

One of my earliest jobs was as a bartender in Pollensa. Two friends who owned a bar decided to get divorced. Since they had to go to the mainland for this, they left me in charge for two months at the age of 17. This was a great educational opportunity in every sense of the word. I perfected my art of drinking. Although I already had considerable experience with beer and wine, I now had a broader opportunity. As bartender, mixing and pouring drinks for customers, I sampled everything, sometimes very generously. Next day I would lie on the beach and let the broiling sun burn it out of me. Then, back to work and back to sampling.

As a bartender, I also learned how to listen. There would be a dozen people at the bar, all talking. After a while you learn to listen to five or six conversations simultaneously. You can pick up a couple of words from a conversation and tell what the rest of the sentence is going to be. You can use your ears like radar to sweep the bar. I found this fascinating, because all the talk was local gossip.

When I was 18, teaching at the Ecole de Montcel and "studying" at the university, I took a quite illicit vacation with a girlfriend named Gladys. She was a very attractive British girl five or six years older than I. Her hair had copper tones, her pert face was lightly freckled, and her body was well shaped — everything a young man could ask for. It is amusing to consider what were then the proprieties. We were driving from Paris all the way to Biarritz, sharing the same hotel room and the same bed every night. But because she was going to visit relatives near Biarritz, it would have been highly improper for us to arrive in the same car. So we drove in two cars, her Model A Ford and my third-hand Fiat with one door that wouldn't open. That made it look right.

From Biarritz, we drove across Provence to the lovely town of St. Paul de Vence, home of the famed inn and restaurant, La Colombe d'Or. We could not afford La Colombe d'Or, but we stayed in a cheaper hotel right across the square. Can you imagine being 18 in St. Paul de Vence and living with a beautiful girl? What better future could the world possibly hold in store for you?

As a schoolteacher in Paris at age 19, I had possibly my best looking year.

I might have stayed in Europe forever except for the business of earning a living. My job as a schoolteacher was quite a good one because I got bed and board in addition to my pay, but I didn't have working papers. France has a very interesting and very French system. In order to get working papers, you have to have a job, and in order to get a job, you have to have working papers. They applied this strictly to foreigners, because at that time in the early 1930s, the unemployment in France was as terrible as it was in the U.S. They didn't want foreigners holding down precious jobs that could be filled by Frenchmen. The government kept sending me notices about not being legally employed, and I got around that for a while by sending them a change of address every few months. I hoped the French bureaucracy would get farther and farther behind and never catch up with me. But it did.

I finally accepted the fact that they didn't really want me in France. Since I was supposed to be an American, I thought it might be interesting to see my own country and go to college. So I applied to Harvard, the only place I'd heard of. I don't think I'd heard of Yale. I wrote Harvard that I was qualified to enter as a junior, which I thought I was after two years at the University of Paris, however slight the work was. Harvard answered, "No, sir, you come as a sophomore or you don't come at all." So I answered that I wouldn't come.

Not long after this exchange I found myself at a Paris cocktail party. In the middle of a crowd of people, one Frenchman seemed to know a lot about America. He was Georges Doriot, who would become a famous general in World War II. He was a professor at the Harvard Business School.

I began asking him a lot about the U.S. and ended up by saying, "Is it true that all Americans are businessmen and that the only thing they do in America is business?"

Doriot said, "Not quite, but it does help to know about business."

I said, "Well, I don't know anything about it. I don't know what business is. I don't even know the difference between a stock and a bond. What do I do about it?"

Doriot looked at me and said, "Don't worry. I'll send you some papers. You just fill them out."

I forgot all about it, but three weeks later I got a batch of questionnaires from something called the Harvard Graduate School of Business Administration. I filled them out rather casually, thinking no harm done, and mailed them off. In early August I got a notice to report to the Business School on September 11. So instead of going to Harvard College as a sophomore with three years of undergraduate work ahead of me, I was skipping college and going straight to graduate school.

Harvard was — and is — a mysterious institution.

LAND OF OPPORTUNITY

◇◇◇◇

I CAME TO THE UNITED STATES IN SEPTEMBER 1935, JUST A few days short of my 20th birthday. My first day in America was dismal.

My mother had come over with me to get me settled. Our liner docked in Hoboken, certainly an inauspicious beginning. We were met by her brother, Malcolm, who drove us across the George Washington Bridge and into New York City in a truck. A truck! I was acutely embarrassed and tried to scrunch down to hide myself so that other people couldn't see me. But it wasn't really a truck. It was one of the early station wagons with wooden panels on the sides. I had never seen one before.

My uncle drove us along 58th Street in his "truck." I had seen tall buildings in Europe, of course, but here I was surprised to see them all jammed together. Driving between them was like riding down a canyon. I saw one building at 58th and Seventh Avenue that was covered with gargoyles. I thought gargoyles were only on cathedrals.

We stayed at the Blackstone Hotel. Once again my mother and I were crammed into two small rooms, my mother in the bedroom and me sleeping on the couch in the living room, sharing the same bathroom. I felt we were right back where we started, a crowded hotel in a strange foreign country.

I knew nothing about my own country. I had studied the geography of Switzerland in two different school years, and I could name every canton, but I had never studied the geography of the United States. I didn't know how many states there were. European schools were quite indifferent to America.

A few days later when I showed up at the Harvard Business School in Cambridge, I was astounded by the luxury of the accommodations. I

21

couldn't believe it. My roommate and I shared a suite: two bedrooms, a bathroom and a big study. Compared to everything I had seen in European schools, this was fantastic.

My roommate was another matter. He was from Kentucky. He had straw hair and his eyes were crossed. In spite of his obviously defective vision, he kept a shotgun under his bed. Every night he prayed aloud for half an hour. Here I was, a Frenchman, and this was what they matched me with.

There were perhaps 400 in my class, all these strange characters, all so different from what I was used to. We were put to work on statistics, finance and other aspects of business, none of which made any sense to me. I wondered why I had come.

After I had been at the business school for a month, they divided the class into two groups. Two-thirds had to take remedial English writing. I was not among them, although I had never had an English lesson in my life. I had learned it all by ear from my mother. People now talk about the literacy problem and how nobody today knows how to read and write, as if it were something brand new. But in 1935 in Harvard graduate school it was exactly the same.

I didn't get to know anyone well. Again I was an outsider. Since I had no friends, it was a fairly rough adjustment, and I was very lonely. My sister Di, with whom I had spent my entire life, was far away in the south of France, starting her career as an artist. I occasionally went skiing with other students from the business school, but there were no anchors for me.

I did all right in my courses, I passed everything. School courses never came easily to me, but the results were always good. In fact, somebody at Harvard must have made a terrible mistake because I got one of the highest grades in my finance course, and I didn't even understand what the hell my own paper was about.

But I hated business school, and after one year I quit. I found business dull, uninteresting, grubby — which is sort of funny when you consider what I've done since. My mother was terribly disappointed by my decision. She had financed me through business school, but now I would have to earn my own living.

This was in 1936, still the heart of the Depression, with unemployment well over 20%. Former stockbrokers were still selling apples in the streets.

I had no contacts, no sponsors, and my irregular European background was not much of a recommendation. I thought I'd better look into areas where my knowledge of the world might be considered a plus. I managed to get an interview at Armstrong Cork, a worldwide manufacturer of house products, but they had no place for me. I also had an interview at the New York *Herald Tribune*. It had occurred to me that a big city newspaper might appreciate my special background, and besides, journalism seemed about as far from business as one could get.

To my delight and astonishment the *Tribune* actually hired me. I became the lowest city room reporter, covering the most trivial stories for $25 a week. I considered myself very lucky to have landed any job. My decision to go into journalism disappointed my mother even more than my quitting business school, but she never said a word to me at the time.

What I was aiming at was to become a foreign correspondent for the *Tribune*. I tried to edge my way toward it by asking to be made the reporter for shipping news. I pointed out that I spoke French, German and Italian. After all, I argued, the ships do bring in a lot of foreigners, and I'd be able to interview them. The editor turned me down, saying, "They should learn to speak English."

That was America's attitude back then. Most Americans were isolationists. We had not yet joined the world. It is difficult to remember how much World War II changed this country.

Twenty-five dollars a week didn't go very far. What helped me most were the nights I was assigned to the Waldorf-Astoria Hotel, when somebody was giving a speech. I did not have to write up the speech, which had already been received and typeset by the *Tribune*. I just had to make sure the guy actually delivered the speech and didn't drop dead on the platform. The great virtue of the assignment was that every night I got a plate of chicken. That became my main meal of the day.

The *Tribune* had a few famous reporters, notably Homer Bigart, but I never thought of them as famous. To me they were just upper grade men and I was a lower grade man. The strangest character of all was Ogden Reid, the owner and publisher. He had a serious problem with alcohol, but in spite of that he occasionally appeared in the *Tribune* building. To reach his office he had to weave his way the length of the city room, and he was seldom able to make it on his own. His assistant, a little man named Wilbur Forrest, would get his shoulder under Reid's armpit and guide him past all of us and into his office.

One of the good things about working for the *Tribune* instead of for the rich and stately *Times* was that we would get three assignments a day while the guy at the *Times* got only one. They were not big assignments. I spent one whole month in what were called "the shacks." The *Tribune* and the other papers shared shacks in Harlem, the Bronx, Brooklyn, Queens and Midtown. The main purpose of the shacks was to help us cover police activities. A shortwave radio in the shack transmitted police news, and when you heard a certain signal or command, you knew it was a story worth going after.

A shack was a single room with broken-down furniture in a cheap building, filled with stale cigar and cigarette smoke. We young reporters were sent to the shacks to be educated by the broken-down old reporters who worked there. They taught me the importance of geography in life. If a lady had her purse snatched at Park Avenue and 57th, that was a story. If three men got killed in Harlem, don't bother because it wasn't worth a spit.

I stayed at the *Tribune* less than a year. They told me that if I was really good and worked hard, in three years I could be making $40 a week. I did not find this enticing.

An older *Tribune* reporter named Bill McCleary told me about a friend of his named Wilson Hicks. Hicks, the picture editor of that new magazine called *Life*, was looking for a sort of glorified copyboy/pictureboy. Strictly a beginner's job, but was I interested? Yes, I was.

At my interview with Hicks I faced a stern, intimidating man almost totally lacking in human warmth. Although nervous in his chilly presence, I thought I was doing quite well, answering his questions honestly.

The last question was, "And what do you know about pictures?"

I quite honestly answered, "Nothing."

I did not get the job.

But I made some kind of impression on Hicks because a few weeks later I was invited back to *Life* by the number two man, assistant managing editor Dan Longwell, a bouncy, busy, jumpy little fellow. *Life* had had a science and medicine editor with all the right qualifications. He was the son of an

Egyptologist and he had studied all the right subjects at all the right schools, but he had zero sense of journalism. They had just got rid of him and decided they wanted somebody who could make science and medicine interesting to other people.

I went through the same Q and A with Longwell, but when we got to the last question, I answered it differently.

"What do you know about science and medicine?"

"Oh, a lot, sir!"

I got the job — and $40 a week. I was only 22, but I was already an editor. Not only that but an editor with two researchers and a secretary. I hadn't the faintest idea what a secretary was for or how to dictate to her. My other great problem was that while I did have a bit of outdated knowledge about science, I knew nothing about medicine.

This was May of 1937 and *Life* was only six months old. There was no Time Life Building then — that would come later with the giant success and expansion of *Life*. Our offices were in the Chrysler Building at 42nd and Lexington. The whole organization — *Time, Fortune* and the new *Life* — occupied less than two floors.

Learning to be a science and medicine editor was both difficult and easy. It was difficult because nobody quite knew how to show science and medicine in pictures — that had not been done before. At the same time it was easy because nobody had any standard by which to criticize my stories. Since they had never been done before, there was no basis for comparison. In those early years of *Life* it was all so new. Every picture was a revelation. People had *read* about surgical operations, but they had never *seen* them. My job was to show them.

Gradually I got the knack of it, thanks to the cooperation of the scientists and doctors whose work was the subject of my stories. I would think up a science story, get it assigned and photographed. But when I saw the pictures, I couldn't figure out what the story was about. I would have to go back to the scientist and get him to explain it to me, even help me lay out the pictures in story form.

On one occasion I was so rushed that I had to lay out a science story not only before I understood it (that happened all the time), but before I could check back with the subject, who was Harold Urey, the Nobel Prize chemist. I laid it out anyway and showed it to the managing editor, John Billings. "That's fine," he said. He didn't understand it any better than I did. Then I rushed up to Rochester to talk to Dr. Urey. He explained the pictures, which had to do with heavy water, and helped me rearrange them in sequence. Then I rushed back to New York and got the whole thing photostated all over again. Billings never noticed any difference.

When I arrived at *Life,* the staff was still small. It centered around John Shaw Billings, an extraordinarily capable, even-tempered man who used few words. A Harvard graduate and a former newspaperman from the Brooklyn *Eagle,* he was a hefty, well-organized fellow. He could go through a stack of 50 pictures so fast that you thought he wasn't even paying attention, but at the end he would announce, "That's worth three pages" and say which pictures he wanted.

Billings was absolutely sure of what he was doing and therefore saw no reason for late-night closings. He put the magazine together by five o'clock in the afternoon and went home, leaving the rest of us to handle the checking and fitting. He is the one and only managing editor I have ever known who took that attitude. All the others postponed decisions, ran up overtime, started the presses late and piled up the costs. Unlike Billings, they wanted to keep their choices open to the last available minute.

The assistant managing editor, Dan Longwell, was just the opposite kind of man. He was short and frenzied, the jack-in-the-box who dreamed up new ideas, new departments, new this and new that. His mind darted off in all directions, his moods went up and down, he chewed his fingernails. His pockets bulged with newspaper clippings — not really clippings but just scraps he had torn out of the papers. He would fish one out, stare at it for a moment to remind himself what it was and then hand it over, saying with great enthusiasm, "Here's a natural *Life* story. A natural! We've *got* to do this." He had many good ideas, many terrible ideas, and Billings managed to separate the bad ones from the good ones. Most of the good ones got in the magazine — and sometimes a bad one, too.

Longwell's counterpart was the picture editor Wilson Hicks, who was the cold, grumpy city editor type. A love-hate relationship existed between Hicks and his staff photographers. He was mean, tough, dictatorial, and he would not deign to argue with anybody. On the other hand he did know his stuff, he knew and loved pictures, and the photographers respected that, even though most of them didn't like him.

The dozen writer-editors were a strange lot. David Cort, the foreign editor, was a martinet who delighted in driving his researchers to tears. Noel Busch tried to act like an elegant British dilettante. Alexander King was absolutely crazy. He had a red mustache and wore a green tweed suit and a pink necktie every single day of the year. He ended up in various drug hospitals. I eventually brought over from the *Tribune* a brilliant but timid little fellow named Lincoln Barnett. He was put in his office, and after a week he came to me and said, "Doesn't anybody ever talk to you here?" He had been so quiet that nobody paid any attention to him.

The man who taught me how to write picture stories was a delightful, homely redheaded editor named Joe Kastner. He told me that Billings wanted the writer to "talk into the picture," to explain to the reader what he was looking at and from what viewpoint. The essential trick in writing picture stories was to keep it very clear, very simple — try to squeeze as much information as possible into it without creating complicated sentences. One *Life* writer remembers that when he was just starting to learn under Joe Kastner, he would work desperately to create the perfect lead sentence for a textblock, something catchy or poetic or provocative. And then Joe would invariably strike out this masterpiece and make the block begin with the writer's second sentence.

Even after I had been edited by Kastner, my story was not finished. The final hurdle was the managing editor himself. Billings always called you into his office and you'd stand in front of his desk. He started off by saying, "Fine story." Then, without even having to read it all the way through first, he would edit the story beyond belief. He rearranged words and sometimes rewrote practically the whole thing. At the end he would say, "Thank you, that was very good."

After all that it had to fit. The textblocks and captions not only had to have the right number of lines to fit the layout, but they also had to "square," the lines had to flush right and left. You would be driven crazy late at night trying to "green" your copy to make it fit. There is a difference between what appears to fit according to your photostat and what will actually fit when your words get to the typesetter. You used a green pencil to mark words or phrases that could be dropped or added if necessary.

The story I especially remember writing was the famous, scandalous, explosive "Birth of a Baby." It was not my story. I did not think it up or assign it, I just wrote the captions. The pictures, which all ran the same small size on four pages, were taken from a serious documentary film sponsored by various medical organizations. It told the story of one woman's pregnancy from beginning to end. The pictures were grainy, and many of them were very dull indeed, but they did show the moment of birth itself. This sounds innocuous today, but in 1938 it was sensational. *Life* took the precaution — which also happened to be good advance publicity — of sending a letter to all its subscribers, warning that the story was about to appear and suggesting that if parents thought it was too graphic for their children to see, the four pages of the center spread could be removed.

"Birth of a Baby" created national uproar and debate, with lots of praise mixed with the outrage. The issue was banned in a number of cities. It was all superb publicity for the young magazine, and my pedestrian little captions were probably read by more people that year than read Hemingway and Faulkner combined.

For me the great discovery at *Life* was the photographers. They were a marvelous bunch — bright, imaginative, irresponsible, wild, adventurous. They loved their work and the expense account, in that order. They were keen on what they were doing, determined to get their story — and determined to have you carry their camera equipment. But they were frustrated by the *Life* system. The photographer created the pictures, but the department editor showed them to the managing editor without the photographer present. He never had any say about which pictures were important and why they should run in the magazine.

All the photographers resented this, but *Life* was by far the best place for them, the first place in America where photojournalism was practiced. Photojournalism is quite different from photography. It consists of reporting and telling a story in a related series of pictures.

Nowadays who is remembered from the first decades of *Life?* Not the editors or writers, only the photographers.

I cottoned to the photographers more than I did to the editors, possibly because so many of them were foreigners, like me. I spent more time drinking with Robert Capa than with anybody else. He told vivid stories about his experiences, some of them almost surely true. He was a character who had built a character inside another character, so that you never knew who the real Capa was. I'm not sure that he knew either.

Bob Capa was Hungarian, and many of *Life's* other early photographers were European. That is probably because of the Leica, the 35 mm camera that made photojournalism possible. Before the Leica, photographers used large cameras and flashbulbs, so the subject knew he was being photographed. The Leica made it possible for the photographer to be in a room with 20 people who were hardly aware they were being photographed. The Leica and the photographers and photojournalism all came out of Europe together.

Alfred Eisenstaedt was the mousiest little man you've ever seen, but with a determination and talent the like of which you have also never seen. He emigrated from Germany in the '30s and fell into the hands of a "friend," an agent representing photographers. Eisie was immensely successful at *Life,* but after some years he complained about how poorly he was paid. He was getting a very good salary, but when he showed us his checks, it turned out that the "friend" was taking 50% off the top without Eisie realizing it.

The great science photographer, a man very valuable to my department, was Fritz Goro, a highly-opinionated German. He *made* himself into a great science photographer. He developed techniques and devices that enabled him to photograph things that had never been photographed before. The scientists themselves were so impressed by his pictures that they often invited him to their professional meetings, where he was addressed as "Dr. Goro."

Dmitri Kessel, who had been a Cossack in the Czar's army before fleeing the Russian Revolution, taught me all about vodka and how many different kinds there are. We spent a long evening in his apartment where he tested my capacity by making me sample the dozen different vodka bottles he had lined up on his table.

Maggie Bourke-White, who was every lovely inch an American, was the grande dame. She always got her way with people, subjects, men, everything. Unlike most of the others, she was uncomfortable with a Leica and preferred large cameras with elaborate flashbulb lighting. She took endless exposures of every picture. She was more than a perfectionist, she was an obsessionist.

The first story she did for me was on the manufacture of paper. I did not go to Canada with her, so the first I saw of the story was when a large stack of 11 × 14 prints arrived on my desk. How exciting! All these pictures by this great photographer! What a difficult but fascinating time I would have making my selections from several hundred pictures. But when I went through the stack, I discovered that she had done what I later learned she always did. She shot only a dozen different scenes, but she shot each one with different cameras, different lenses, different lighting, different angles, different filters and f-stops. Then she had ordered at least one print of each version. Since there were only a dozen pictures, it was not such a challenge to lay out her story.

On top of everybody — photographers, writers, editors — there was of course Harry Luce. He was not as awesome as he later became. A six-foot figure, already balding before he was 40, he had extremely bushy eyebrows and a driving, barking voice when he was asking questions, which he usually was. I was too lowly to have much to do with him. The first time I met him was when he decided he should have lunch with his new science and medicine editor.

Five of us assembled in the elegant Cloud Club, a businessman's club with private dining rooms at the top of the Chrysler Building. Just five of us: Luce, Billings, Longwell, myself and a fellow introduced as Eric Hodgins. They quizzed me all through lunch. I thought I did extremely well, practicing my fakery that I knew a lot about science and medicine, making up answers whenever necessary. Only later did I discover that Eric Hodgins was a graduate of M.I.T. and — worse yet — that he had taught there. He was kind enough not to expose me.

Luce had a bad stutter that he later overcame. Perry Prentice, the publisher of *Time,* had an even worse stutter, to the point of being incomprehensible. If you had to listen to Perry Prentice and Harry Luce talking to each other, it was sheer agony.

After successfully bluffing for several months and getting stories in the magazine every week, I sent a brash memo to Mary Fraser, the business manager in charge of salaries:

TO: Miss Fraser

FROM: Heiskell

This is to remind you I have been here three months. When I arrived I was told by Mr. Longwell that such a period would be the maximum time for apprenticeship. I believe I do enough work to satisfy the bosses, also the quantity seems to pass the mark. Hence believe it is time to put me on a regular salary basis. What about it? (It being a raise)

??????

Do not put in waste paper basket.

I should probably have been thrown out the door, but Miss Fraser wrote across the bottom of my memo, "I recommend raise to $60 — doing swell job."

This was a 50% raise, the largest percentage increase in my long career. As time went by, I did not have to fake anymore, because I knew what I was doing. I decided my new ambition was to make $10,000 a year. Not many people were making that much in those days.

Ambition feeds on success. Ambition and luck, they go together. If you try something and fail a few times, you are tempted to give up. When I started at *Life*, my only ambition was to survive my claim that I knew a lot about science and medicine. I also had to learn about pictures and about how to write for a picture magazine. But once I learned I could do these things, it gave me confidence to try for more. I'm not sure to what extent my ambition pushed me to do certain things and to what extent opportunities simply came my way and I grabbed them. I had always been competitive in school and wanted to be the best, thanks in large part to the expectations my mother set for me. I saw no reason not to compete in my new world of journalism.

I thought I could eventually become a managing editor or a publisher, the two highest jobs in the Time Inc. hierarchy. I was curious about publishing and asked a lot of questions. How do we sell advertising? How do we buy all this coated paper for the magazine, and how much do we pay for it? How do we increase circulation? How do we decide what to charge for a subscription? Most edit people didn't care about these things, but I did.

Perhaps because of my curiosity and all my questions, I became a candidate for a job on the business side. Roy Larsen, a close friend of Luce's, was *Life*'s publisher. His second in command was C. D. Jackson, the general manager. Because of *Life*'s phenomenal growth, C. D. needed an assistant general manager, and he approached me.

C. D. was an elegant man, almost as tall as I was. He had grown up abroad and spoke excellent French, which of course appealed to me. I liked him personally, and he made the job sound very interesting. He and Larsen dealt with every management aspect of the magazine: ad sales, circulation, promotion, printing, finance. So at age 24 I switched sides, from edit to publishing. This rarely happens at Time Inc. Because of the switch, I eventually became *Life*'s publisher and later chairman of the company. (But I still think I would have made a good managing editor!)

Having come from edit, I continued to work closely with the editors. Magazine promotion should be a collaborative effort between the editor and publisher. Most people won't agree, but that's my idea of good promotion. The person in charge of promotion should work with the managing editor on choosing covers and on what will be featured in the magazine, because that is what you are going to promote.

At first I did not have enough rank to attend cover conferences, but later I was always there with the managing editor, the art director and several other editors. The various cover candidates were tacked up on a cork wall, along with alternate versions of each subject, so we would be looking at long rows of pictures, each with the red *Life* logo and the red band across the bottom. Preferably the cover should come from a major story rather than a minor one. The picture should stand out so that it would catch the eye of the newsstand buyer. We discussed cover headlines and captions. I went away from that conference to figure whether or not to run a newspaper ad that week, and if so, how to play it. Obviously I needed to know what the editor was doing.

I made a point of learning all about the printing business and got to understand the technical aspects, right down to ink quality and engravings. I asked questions, I visited the printing plant in Chicago, I studied about printing in books. That is how I got to know Charles Stillman, the boss of production. He and I agreed we needed an experimental laboratory to explore paper and printing. Nothing new had been developed in printing for decades. As far as we could determine, the printers did very little research on their own.

So Charlie Stillman and I created our own research outfit in Springdale, Connecticut, and began to make some useful improvements. But the major impact of Springdale was that it drove our suppliers crazy to see *us* trying to show *them* how to run *their* business. In due course they all got into research and many improvements were found.

I spent two lively learning years on the publishing side before something happened that temporarily brought me back to edit. In April of 1940, when World War II was eight months old, our Paris bureau sent an urgent request. The German armies were overrunning the Low Countries and threatening France. A crisis was clearly at hand. The bureau needed somebody in Paris who could speak fluent French, knew his way around and especially knew how to deal with the French authorities. In those days it was un-American to admit that a foreign language might be useful. I was chosen to join the Paris bureau and to help Carl Mydans, the *Life* photographer there. I had already known Carl in New York, a cheerful, earnest, energetic man about half my height.

I flew to Lisbon on the Pan Am Clipper and made my way to Paris by train, arriving late at night. Since Paris was blacked out, I arrived in total darkness. But I was tremendously excited to be back in what I still considered my true home.

I helped Carl as best I could. The main thing I did was make use of the friendships I had with local publishers. I spent much of my time purloining or buying pictures from them. They had many photographers out covering the war, and they could get around far more easily than Carl because they were French and had all the necessary credentials. I got a lot of war pictures for *Life* from these sources.

The rumor factory was unbelievable. Nobody knew where the Germans were. Nobody knew what the French army was doing because censorship was total. Some people in France were actually pro-German, looking foreward to a German takeover, so you did not know whom to trust.

The *Life* office was on the Champs Elysées on the ninth floor. We could stand on our balcony and watch the German planes bombing the Renault factory across the river. Sometimes we went down into the bomb shelters, but this was so unpleasant that we didn't make a habit of it.

I was in Paris little more than a month before we realized that the French collapse was almost complete. Unless there was some kind of miracle, my country was going to fall to the Germans. We had to get out of Paris or risk being taken prisoner. I went shopping around for a car to escape in. Being a correspondent, I had the right to buy gasoline, unlike most people. The only decent car I found was a magnificent old maroon Auburn, with great big pipes coming out of the engine, probably weighing about five tons. I bought it and equipped it with two 40-gallon drums of gasoline that I carried in the back in case of emergency. (The photographers were not the only ones who knew how to use an expense account.)

Less than a week before the Germans arrived, we set off. Our caravan consisted of the whole bureau: the *Time* and *Life* people, their wives, the members of the photo lab — a whole string of cars. Del Paine, the Paris bureau chief, rode with me in the Auburn. We also had with us Max Corre, the editor of a French newspaper who had been drafted into the army and then assigned to us as a bodyguard. We were headed for the city of Tours, some 100 miles southwest of Paris, where somebody had lined up a house for us. But everybody else was also headed out of Paris, including portions of the army.

Imagine a narrow old French road clogged by thousands of refugees, plus tanks and military trucks, all trying to make their way south to Tours. It took us 16 hours to get there. At one point the traffic congestion so exasperated me that I swung the Auburn out into the opposite lane and hurtled past a line of clanking tanks. Del Paine, sitting in the front seat beside me, was both terrified and outraged. While I was carrying out this reckless maneuver with the threat of head-on collision, he kept shouting, "Heiskell! You're fired! Heiskell! You're fired!"

While we were in Tours, the city was bombed, the first time I had been really close to falling bombs. The sound of a bomb coming down is like the ripping of a sheet. If you hear that sound, you know it's going to be close, so you lie down fast. We did a lot of lying down, but none of us was hurt.

After several days in Tours, Carl Mydans and I had a completely loony idea. We would go back to Paris and photograph the Germans coming in. These would be historic pictures, surely a cover and a lead. We gave not the slightest thought, not the tiniest intelligent consideration, to how we would get our pictures out of Paris and back to New York. Nor did we think about what the Germans were likely to do to us, which would be either to shoot us or throw us in prison.

Carl, our bodyguard Max Corre and I took off in the Auburn, equipped with sleeping bags and our drums of gasoline, bound for Paris. Of course everything else was still streaming south, so it was slow going against the traffic. By nightfall we reached a village some dozen miles from Paris, and since we could not use headlights, we had to stop. We parked in an open field, unrolled our sleeping bags inside the Auburn and went to sleep.

In the middle of the night the sound of a barking dog woke me. When I stuck my head out the window to see what might be wrong, something hard poked me. It was a rifle. We had been discovered by members of the *Garde Civile* — World War I veterans patrolling the countryside. Apparently they had decided we were spies who had parachuted into their territory, though how you can parachute an Auburn is quite a question.

"Hands up! Get out of the car."

It is difficult to get out of a car with your hands up if the rest of you is inside a sleeping bag.

They marched us down to the village, where they locked us up in a dark room. I listened to them talking in the next room. Carl kept asking, "What are they saying? Translate! Translate!"

What they were discussing was whether to shoot us now or take us to some other place where somebody else could shoot us. I did not translate.

The discussion went on a long time, more than an hour, before the door finally opened. A man in uniform said, "Follow me."

Carl and Max and I looked at each other, and I said, "I guess we better."

He led us out of the house and back to the field where we had parked the Auburn. The man was a police officer, not a soldier. He made us collect all our belongings and carry them to the local police station.

The police inspected everything. They tested our flashlights, holding them against the wall before they pushed the buttons, just in case they were disguised weapons that would fire. We endured four or five endless hours of interrogation as well as inspection. I spent a lot of time screaming in my impeccable French, "I want to talk to my ambassador."

The most incriminating evidence against us was that our papers were in perfect order. By French reasoning, if your papers are in perfect order, they must be forgeries. We finally convinced them we were not German parachutists, and they let us go.

I asked the police, "Where are the Germans?"

"They are entering Paris right now."

That meant Carl and I were too late to get our historic pictures. Nothing to do but drive back to Tours. This time the trip took 24 hours, with me doing all the driving. By the time we reached Tours, my hands were double their normal size from gripping the wheel so hard.

The rest of our bureau people had already left, crossing the French border into Portugal and heading home through Lisbon. But since remnants of the army were still fighting, Carl and Max and I spent two more weeks in France, sleeping in the fields and photographing and reporting whatever we could.

One afternoon in June we stopped at a French army barracks to ask directions. There was the usual sentinel box out front, with the uniformed sentry standing at attention. As we drew closer, I saw that tears were flowing down his cheeks. He told us he had just heard the news.

France had surrendered.

MY FIRST WIVES

◇◇◇◇

WHEN I WAS LIVING IN PARIS AT AGE 18 AND 19, I HAD A number of girlfriends and thoroughly enjoyed myself. I found it easy to meet girls, to talk to them and to get along with them. But when I came to the U.S. in 1935 to go to business school, I didn't seem to meet any girls at all. There were girls all around, of course, but I didn't know what to say to them or how to make friends. Once again I was an outsider in a new country, a new society, trying to find my way. I was a frustrated and rather lonely young man.

It wasn't until I had been in America nine months and was working at the *Herald Tribune* that I finally did meet a real American girl, under plausible, natural circumstances. I had my mother to thank for this event.

A classmate of my mother at Vassar had married a wealthy businessman in Tarrytown, N.Y. When she learned that my mother was back in America, she invited her to Tarrytown for a weekend, and my mother asked if she could bring me along.

I was used to arriving at strange new places with my mother, so I was not at all nervous when we drove out from the Tarrytown train station — not until I saw the house. It was a huge stone mansion on top of a hill. I felt as though I were coming to visit a castle.

The house was dark inside, no better lighted than a castle. The walls were all dark paneling, and the heavy furniture was as dark as the walls. Mrs. Scott introduced my mother and me to her family. Her husband looked like an Irishman — athletic, ruddy, energetic. I paid no attention to the two sons, Harold and Brace, because there stood The Girl.

"And this is my daughter, Cornelia."

"Everybody calls me Nini."

We shook hands, as we had both been brought up to do. She had a friendly, outgoing smile. She was about my age, on the tall side, attractive, with brown hair. She was very lively, very American. She wore one of those checked skirts with an oversized safety pin, a sweater and saddle shoes. It was *the* costume, *the* uniform, of the day. To me she instantly represented American girlhood — all those girls I had so far managed not to meet. She could have posed for a *Life* cover on the wholesome American look.

During that weekend, while keeping my eyes on Nini, I was also meeting her whole family. It was my first real introduction to American family life. *Here is America! Here is an American family!* Nini's mother was gentle and maternal, and her brothers seemed nice enough, but her father turned out to be an irascible, intemperate, dogmatic character who knew with total conviction what was right and what was wrong — mostly that he was right.

He had inherited the presidency of a pharmaceutical company whose chief product was an anti-inflamatory medication called antiphlogistine. This was a sort of guck that you spread on your chest when you had flu or a cold. It reminded me of my days in Switzerland when the treatment for the same illnesses was called cupping. You held a lighted match under a little glass cup to create a vacuum, then clapped it quickly onto the patient's back, where the vacuum kept it in place. When you had put on two dozen of these, the patient was thoroughly cupped. If one had good back muscles, one could ripple the cups so that they tinkled against each other in a bizarre musical fashion. Whenever I think of antiphlogistine, I always think of cupping — perhaps because they were equally effective. As far as I know, neither is in use today in any civilized country.

But at that time antiphlogistine produced a lot of money for the Scotts. Enough money so that when Nini and I got engaged, as we did after a suitable courtship, she was able to decree a sumptuous wedding. Nini and I got married for all the normal reasons — love, lust, youth and whatever — but in my case there was an additional reason. I wanted to belong. I wanted to belong to a stable American life, with children, grandchildren, a large family, a real home — the whole American pie.

Years later my sister Di told me that our mother thought I was too young to be getting married, as indeed I was, and that she also felt guilty because she was responsible for bringing Nini and me together. However, my mother never tried to dissuade me, and even years afterward she never said she thought I had made a mistake. She was terrific at holding her tongue. I guess I was very lucky that I never had anybody telling me what to do at every step of my life.

The Scotts went all out on the wedding preparations. Nini lined up close to a dozen attendants, and much time was spent designing the bridesmaid dresses and bouquets. Nini had many friends and was always a part of things. Here was something she could really throw herself into.

My own performance was relatively shabby. Since I still had few friends in America, I scrambled to collect five young men to serve on my team. I got one colleague from the *Tribune*, and I drafted two former classmates from business school, practically at gunpoint. I don't know where the others came from — perhaps they were Nini's brothers. My sister Di was still living in France, so my mother was my only relative.

The wedding day was everything Nini could ask for — and everything her parents could buy. I cannot now remember Nini's wedding dress, but I remember my own. I wore my first cutaway and striped trousers. I had to be helped into my outfit to make sure everything was in the right place. Oddly enough, I was not nervous. I thought this was a great event and that I was going to have a very good time. I did.

We were married in a giant church ceremony conducted by the Scotts' own minister. The parade of the bridesmaids up and down the aisle was magnificent. This was followed by an even more giant reception at the stone mansion on the hill.

We stood in a receiving line at the entrance to the front hall, Nini and I, her parents and my mother. My mother had not been the least bit weepy all day, and she did not weep now, but she was quiet. The receiving line took a long time because the Scotts had invited everyone they knew, and it seemed to me that all of them came. Waiters brought us glasses of champagne while we shook hands and smiled and smiled and smiled.

With the receiving line finally over, we moved into the living room to withstand a series of champagne toasts, but at last the dancing began. I had a very good time, along with a number of glasses of champagne. The wedding banquet, the wedding cake — one can hardly imagine a more totally American wedding. Just what Nini and I both wanted. After this day, I certainly felt that I belonged.

We finally drove away in a car festooned with all the customary ribbons, confetti, gags and grafitti. If we left out a single American wedding tradition, I can't imagine what it was.

We spent our honeymoon at Pink Beach in Bermuda. I don't remember who paid for this, but it certainly was not the groom, with his still-minuscule salary. Since my mother's wedding present to me was a Ford (then about $500), I suppose the Scotts must have paid for the trip.

When our boat docked in Bermuda, at the port in Hamilton, we climbed into a horse and carriage piloted by a black driver. Back then, cars were not allowed on Bermuda. Clopping along the narrow road, we had a romantic journey of more than an hour to the resort of Pink Beach. Pink Beach was not pink, but the three or four small cottages were. A maid came in to clean and make the beds, but Nini did our own cooking. Today Pink Beach is a major resort with a huge hotel. I have had to explain to my grandson, who has stayed there, what it was like in the olden times.

After the honeymoon we settled in an apartment in Tarrytown. To me, after my cramped years in hotels and boarding schools, it seemed spacious and luxurious. A honeymoon in Bermuda, an apartment in Tarrytown, commuting to and from New York City, it was all the things that paint Americans as American. I had Americanized myself quite thoroughly.

Shortly after our marriage we drove with Nini's parents to a football game at Yale, where her father was an alumnus. On the way home, Nini and I were sitting in the jump seats of the crowded car. I don't know who was driving, probably one of her brothers, but I know her father was sitting in the back seat right behind me. We were not far from Tarrytown when he clutched his chest and said he had a terrible pain.

We stopped the car and all got out on the roadside. We stretched Mr. Scott out flat on the floor of the jump seat area, and someone ran off to call an ambulance. The ambulance finally came, and the attendants lifted him out of the car and into their vehicle for the drive to the hospital. He had suffered a heart attack and died less than a week later without ever coming home. I had certainly not been close to Nini's father, but since this was my first encounter with a death in the family, that scene remained vivid for me — Mr. Scott lying there on the floor of his car, mortally stricken, while the rest of us waited helplessly by the side of the road. Nini herself was shattered.

We lived in Tarrytown for three or four years. My daughter Diane, named after my sister Diana, was born there in 1940. She was a very difficult baby who screamed all night every night. This is not just the dazed memory of a first-time father. I have since had personal experience with my other children and grandchildren, and I still claim that Diane's nonstop screaming was unique.

I might have continued my Americanized life indefinitely if *Life* had not sent me to Paris to help the bureau, just when France was collapsing. Aside from the adventurous aspects of those two months, the psychological impact of going back to what had been my country from age 12 to 19 was enormous. What happens to you as a teenager really fixes you for life. This was my Europe, where I was created. Suddenly I was pulled back to all my roots. France was my home, and I saw it destroyed. A part of my life was being destroyed, and I witnessed it and felt it.

The experience affected me severely. When I returned to this country, I was once again an outsider, a European. I was once again a Frenchman, who had lost his true home. I realized that nobody over here wanted to get involved. This was especially true of my own new family, the Scotts, and most of their friends and neighbors in Tarrytown. They did not want to get involved in Europe — they did not even care.

I was stunned. Here I was, age 25, my world had vanished, and nobody gave a damn. They did not even want to talk about it. I thought about it constantly and brought it up all the time in conversation. I was quite impossible. I'm sure I was considered a terrible bore. People's eyes glazed when I started to tell them why Europe mattered so much. "What's wrong with Heiskell? What's the big deal?"

This rift of mine was not unique. Many other people thought the fate of Europe was vital to America, but they thought so intellectually or analytically. Few of them thought so for the gut reason I did: that's where I came from, that's what I was about, my whole youth, my whole upbringing.

That rift between my own feelings and the indifference of so many Americans did something serious to me. It also started to do something serious to my marriage. It wasn't Nini's fault. It was just me and America. I was an American Frenchman facing an America that did not care. The insensitivity of this nation was awful, terrible, for anybody who knew what was going on in the world. The total lack of interest appalled me. It had a profound effect on my marriage. It was as if Nini had stayed on one track, and I went off on a completely different track. There was never a blatant argument between us about Europe, but the effect was as harmful as if we had fought about it.

What I had joined — an American marriage, an American family, an American life — what I had wanted to be a part of, to belong to, I now didn't really approve of anymore. Probably I should not have been so emotional — but I was.

Of course, when America's own war started, everybody came over to my side. I no longer had that particular outsider problem, although the harm to my marriage had been done. For most Americans, the war began on December 7, 1941. But by the time of Pearl Harbor, the war for me was already more than two years old.

↩ An unusual event had taken place on my return flight from Lisbon to New York, after I had witnessed the fall of France in the summer of 1940. It would alter my life in a most major way, although not until half a dozen years later.

When I reached Lisbon from France, the city was chaotic, filled with refugees, all trying to escape from Europe and most of them wanting to go to America. Everybody remembers from the movie classic *Casablanca* that Lisbon was the place all the refugees were trying to get to. That is where Ilsa and Victor Laszlo are flying off to through the dense fog at the close of the movie. But if the Laszlos thought escaping from Casablanca was a problem, wait till they reached Lisbon!

Lisbon, as a neutral city, was a fascinating place crammed with fascinating people. There were spies from every country as well as the hordes of refugees, many of them Jews fleeing from the Nazis. One of my colleagues and friends there was Pierre Lazareff, the former editor of *France Soir*. I suggested to *Life* that he and I do a roundup story on what had happened in France. The New York office agreed, and we worked on it for a week. Then the question arose as to what I should pay Lazareff. He was, like many Jewish refugees, penniless. We found out what it would cost to send him and his wife to America on the Pan Am Clipper, and that is what I paid him.

However, I could not get him seats on the Clipper. That took more than money. That took clout and just the right credentials. I did arrange for Lazareff and his wife to go to Brazil by freighter. It took them three months to reach the U.S., where he went to work in Washington for the forerunner of Radio Free Europe. After the war they returned to France, where they both had brilliant careers in journalism. She was the founder of the very successful *Elle* magazine.

One of the most interesting people I met in Lisbon was Joseph Kessel, a well-known French-Russian writer who was also Jewish. He and I went out one evening at midnight to listen to *fado. Fado* is a Portuguese lament, terribly sad. For some reason, *fado* singing always starts late in the evening and continues into the early morning hours. It gets sadder and sadder as the night goes on and everybody gets smashed. All the people in the night-club are sitting there with tears in their eyes, moaning and sobbing along with the music. The first night Joseph Kessel and I went to hear *fado,* he got as smashed as everybody else, and at two in the morning he started to eat his drinking glass. He simply chewed up the glass and swallowed it. I was fascinated. I spent my remaining evenings in Lisbon watching Kessel eat glass.

Then it was time for me to fly home on the Clipper. Thanks to *Life,* I did have the necessary money, clout and credentials. The Clipper was the only quick, direct route to the U.S., so the demand for places was extraordinary.

Next to Lindbergh's *Spirit of St. Louis,* the Pan Am Clipper was the most glamorous plane ever to fly across the Atlantic. Unlike Lindbergh's plane, it could not cross the ocean in a single hop. It had to stop in the Azores to re-fuel and again in Bermuda before flying the final leg to New York. The whole trip took about 30 hours.

The Clipper was a really weird bird, partly a plane, partly a boat. It could take off and land only on the water. It had a V bottom with a step under-neath and a high wing across the top. The main cabin was right under the wing. When the plane started to take off, the bow dug down into the water under the thrust of engine power, just like a boat, and the waves came up and literally covered the cabin windows on both sides. It was terribly excit-ing because the water rushed right past you, not underneath you but right beside you. The Clipper strained and strained and strained until it got up

Madeleine Carroll, my wife for more than a decade, was the most glamorous movie actress of her time, starring in such famous films as The 39 Steps *and* The Prisoner of Zenda.

onto its step. Then at last you could feel the resistance falling away, and you finally became convinced that this thing *could* take off.

There were no rows of passenger seats like today. The main cabin was a single long living room. In each of the four corners was a table and set of chairs, and between the tables there was space to walk around, stand around and talk. Very luxurious.

Among the passengers on this most glamorous of planes was the most glamorous woman I have ever met. *Life,* with its cheerful sense of infallibility, pronounced Madeleine Carroll one of the four most beautiful movie actresses in the world. I cannot vouch for the other three, but there is no question in my mind about Madeleine.

For her trip home on the Clipper, she was wearing a blue hat, not very broad-brimmed, and a blue suit with a white blouse. She had soft blonde hair, large blue eyes and classic features. She was half Irish and half French, always a dangerous combination. She told me she was returning to Hollywood from her chateau south of Paris, which she had been forced to leave when France fell. At the time of our Clipper flight she was 35, ten years older than I, but there was an instantaneous flash of something between us.

Everybody on the plane knew everybody else within the first hour, and most of them were fairly significant people or they could not have got on that plane. But Madeleine and I had little time for anyone else. We spent the entire flight talking to each other, mostly in French, which she spoke as perfectly as she did English. We spoke with sadness about the France that we both loved. We ate all our meals together, served on the corner tables in the Clipper's "living room." We had our wine and champagne together.

Did anything else happen between us? Alas, for all its glamor, the Clipper fell short when it came to sleeping accommodations. Behind the main cabin in the long tail of the plane was a series of — well, to call them "bunks" would be to aggrandize them. They were halfway between hammocks and bunks, one above the other, and each passenger had his or her own assigned space in compartments that were only slightly separated from each other. Had the bunks been as comfortable and private as today's bunks might be, something might well have happened between Madeleine and me. I certainly thought of it, and I'm quite sure she did too.

As it was, when the flight ended in New York, we said goodby with expressions of pleasure about the time we had shared. Since the flight was only 30 hours long, there was no lasting impact. Or at least we didn't think so at the time. We would not see each other again for seven years.

When the U.S. finally entered the war, C. D. Jackson, *Life's* general manager, went into government service, and in 1942 I was promoted to his job of general manager. It had been exactly five years since I was the lowli-est cub reporter on the *Herald Tribune*. Now at 27 I had the second most important business job on the hottest magazine in the country.

Each time I moved up in my career, I left colleagues behind. I think that in my professional life I unconsciously kept a little distance from everybody in terms of friendship. I had no close personal friends except Roy Larsen, and he was more a father than a friend. I think I must have kept my rela-tionships in a kind of loose equilibrium, so that when I moved up to some new height, there would not be a lot of churning behind me. But perhaps it is just my nature that I never got very intimate with my colleagues. Women, yes, but not colleagues.

I have always liked women more than men, even as friends. Women have a better appreciation of money than men do, not because they like to col-lect it but because they think of it in terms of use. Men like to collect money so they can look at it. I get terribly bored when men wind up talking about money, as they always do. I certainly like to accumulate money, but I've never spent much time thinking about it, and even less time talking about it. I do have to think about it a bit more now, in old age, because I have things to settle, like wills and trusts and bequests. But mainly I think of money as something to use and enjoy. Clothes, houses, travel, good food and wine — I think money is great fun.

⤳ During the war years *Life* became even hotter, because it was *the* war magazine. We had the best pictures and reporting on both the warfronts and the homefront. Roy Larsen, still the publisher, was doing so much spe-cial work for Luce and for the company as a whole that he delegated to me much of the publishing responsibility.

Nini and I bought a house in Greenwich, and our son Peter was born there in 1944. Nini became the complete homebody. She had her house and children. She indulged in many sports — golfing, riding, swimming. As al-ways, she had many friends and was active in Greenwich social and com-munity life. The Greenwich world became her whole life — while the magazine became more and more *my* whole life. This was no sacrifice for me. I loved it.

I was terribly, terribly busy. In addition to all the problems of publishing under wartime restrictions and paper shortages and price controls, I was also in charge of our work for the Office of Naval Intelligence. ONI called on us for the manpower and talent to produce a special confidential Navy magazine called the *Recognition Journal*. We produced recognition charts of planes and ships and landing zones and targets. I spent a fair amount of time traveling to and from Washington on the jammed wartime trains. My office hours grew longer and longer. My career became my life. It is, I'm afraid, a rather common story in American corporations, but this was especially true at Time Inc. because of the frequent late hours, and especially true under the added pressures of wartime.

And I was a commuter — generally a bad thing for any marriage. What a horror! The Monday morning conversation on the train is nothing but golf. One guy is telling his story. The other guy isn't really listening, he is just waiting to tell his own story about what happened to him on the seventh hole. A dreadful way to begin the work week — unless you happen to be a golfer. I tried to avoid commuting by spending some nights in the city.

By the end of the war, in spite of home and children, my marriage had become a disappointment, a shell. We were both able to put up with the shortcomings, I suppose, although it seemed more difficult for me than for Nini, who had her homebody compensations in Greenwich life. I don't know how long this rather empty marriage might have continued — perhaps for years. But in 1947, for the first time in seven years, I ran into Madeleine Carroll again.

Considering how many vivid memories I have of Madeleine, it is strange that I cannot remember how or when we met for the second time or what she might have been wearing. Whatever the circumstances, we both felt that same "flash of something" we had felt on the Clipper. Bit by bit — glamor, beauty, background, our love of France and the French language — this became a very hot romance.

With the fire of the romance on one side, and the disappointment of my marriage on the other, I was badly torn. I don't recommend it to anyone. Madeleine was unmarried, living in both Los Angeles and New York, but she finally settled in New York. She was the one who changed my name to Andrew. Although christened Andrew Heiskell, I had never been called anything but Bob all my life, in my family, among friends and at work. But Madeleine preferred Andrew, and I was so charmed and so smitten that I thought this was a splendid idea. *All right, everybody, I'm no longer Bob, I'm Andrew.*

The resulting confusion went on for years, since a large number of people who had known me as Bob felt entitled to continue calling me Bob. It is difficult to change one's name without actually moving to a different country. A newspaper once printed my name as Andrew J. Heiskell. Other publications picked it up, and it took me ten years of protest and correction to get that *J.* out of circulation.

Nini was not the least interested in breaking up. She knew about Madeleine, but she was trying to hang on to the marriage — for the children, for pride, for her life in Greenwich, the whole way of life. After the birth of our son Peter several years earlier, she could not have another child for physical reasons, but now out of desperation she decided we should adopt one. Obviously I did not want to.

There were tears and arguments about everything, endless talking about what to do or what not to do. It was dreadful over a long period. Eventually we separated, and I moved to New York's Tudor City, a large apartment complex on the East River. Although I knew by this time that I wanted a divorce, Nini was unwilling.

Separating from my wife and children was not only an agony but something I am not proud of. What it did to Nini and to Diane and Peter was terrible. I can only say to myself, what would the alternative have been? What would my life have become if I had not left? Something totally different. But I am not pretending it was anything but terrible. And the repercussions were, as is so often the case, longlasting. When I left home, a campaign of vilification began, mostly against me but also against Madeleine. Some of the damage that grew out of my departure would not be fully repaired for almost 40 years.

In 1948 Madeleine accepted the lead in a play, *Goodby, My Fancy,* a comedy by Fay and Michael Kanin. During its out-of-town tryout period, I took the train down to Philadelphia after work each evening for an eleven o'clock after-theater rendezvous, then took the train back the next morning in time to go to work. It was far more exhausting than commuting to Greenwich, but with the difference that this time I wanted to commute. Luckily, I was still in my early thirties and in good health.

When *Goodby, My Fancy* moved to New York and opened at the Morosco Theater, I could stop commuting. Nobody knew about our affair except Madeleine's delightful agent and close friend, Robby Lantz. He was a roly-poly Berliner with great wit and charm, a successful agent in movies, plays and books. Robby found out about Madeleine and me only by accident.

One evening he dropped in unexpectedly at the theater and knocked on the door of Madeleine's dressing room. "It's me, Robby."

She did not answer his knock right away. When she finally told him to come in, she was seated at her dressing table. While Robby chatted, he noticed that she was behaving very peculiarly. He could see she was nervous, and he knew her well enough to know that she was never nervous.

He finally looked at her and said, "Madeleine, let me guess. There is somebody in your bathroom."

She laughed nervously and said yes.

Robby said, "Let me guess further. Since you are acting so strangely, it's a man."

She said yes.

"Well," Robby said, with smiling, old-world courtesy, "let the poor fellow come out."

Madeleine laughed and said, "Come on out."

I opened the bathroom door, behind which I had been hiding, and walked out. I knew who Robby Lantz was but didn't recognize him, and he didn't recognize me. Madeleine introduced us.

Then Robby said, "Oh yes, you're the publisher of *Life*." He had absolutely no difficulty figuring out that an affair was going on.

Madeleine told Robby we were madly in love and would like to enlist his help. "We'd like to go to the theater together, discreetly of course. And maybe go to a quiet restaurant now and then. Robby, would you reserve the tickets at the box office in your name? And would you make the restaurant reservations in your name? We have to keep this a total secret."

Robby was delighted to help in a secret affair of the heart. "Of course!"

He did help us with theater tickets and reservations, but we went only to matinees in obscure seats, and the restaurants were quiet and small. Madeleine moved into my big, high-ceiling apartment at the top of Tudor

City. Remarkably, astonishingly, our affair remained a secret. Nothing appeared in the gossip columns. Even my *Life* colleagues knew nothing about it.

This was impossible. Here was I, already a major New York figure in the most prominent publishing company, married, with children and a house in Greenwich. And here was Madeleine Carroll, one of the superstars of Hollywood, phenomenally famous, in a current Broadway show, while at the same time her movie, *Lady Windermere's Fan,* was opening at Radio City. Two more exposed people could not possibly be imagined.

This was the day of Walter Winchell, Leonard Lyons, Irving Hoffman — all those men with their columns. It was *the* time for gossip columns, much more so than today. And then out in Hollywood were the movie dragons Louella Parsons and Hedda Hopper, columnists who could make or break a star. Yet Madeleine and I, with the help and connivance of Robby Lantz, kept ourselves out of the news and out of the gossip columns completely.

Today Robby Lantz gives a very generous analysis of our achievement. "Never a word about them," he says. "This is technically impossible, but they did it. They were not only immensely tactful but also highly intelligent. In fact, today Andrew should take a week off, fly to London and explain to the Royal Family how these things are done."

But soon after Madeleine moved into my Tudor City apartment, our lives became enormously more complicated. She had had three previous marriages with no children, but within a few months of moving into Tudor City, at age 44, she became pregnant for the first time in her life. And I still did not have a divorce.

In those days that was a disastrous situation. To realize what would happen to us if anybody found out, we had only to look at the example of Madeleine's good friend, Ingrid Bergman. At the very same time that we were worrying about the possible discovery of Madeleine's pregnancy, Ingrid Bergman was being virtually stoned to death for her affair with the Italian movie director Roberto Rossellini. She was still married to a Dr. Lindstrom back in Sweden and was the mother of their daughter Pia.

When it became public knowledge that Ingrid was pregnant by Rossellini, the lid blew off. Stromboli, which was both the title and the location of the film they were making together in Italy, became a tabloid watchword. The "Stromboli Scandal" rocked not only the entertainment world but the rest of the world as well. It destroyed Bergman's career for years. It also destroyed her screen image as a beautiful, wholesome and upright star.

Madeleine had an identical screen image. As the star of *The 39 Steps,* as the princess in *The Prisoner of Zenda,* she was as beautiful, wholesome and upright as Ingrid. We were determined that what was happening to Ingrid Bergman would not happen to us. It seemed impossible that we could pull it off in secrecy, but we had to try. We never even considered getting an abortion. We both wanted the baby, and Madeleine felt that God had finally rewarded her.

The first thing we agreed on was that we had to find a place to hide. We wound up renting an old Victorian rattletrap house in Sneden's Landing, a quiet, elegant small town up the Hudson River from New York. Sneden's Landing is a turn-of-the-century suburb that lies partway down a steep hill between the highway and the river. Although we went for walks, we kept out of sight as much as possible and were never recognized. Madeleine's career went into hibernation, but this was easy for Robby to explain. She did not like Hollywood, neither the people nor the atmosphere, she was never there except when working, and she often turned down scripts.

We got a doctor and a gynecologist, but we excluded everyone else from our lives. We lived in Sneden's Landing quite happily — and nervously — for half a dozen months. I became a commuter again. I kept the Tudor City apartment because I needed a mailing address and a place to bring people for business discussions while I was actually hiding out in Sneden's Landing. My colleagues still had no idea what was happening.

Madeleine had a healthy pregnancy, but because she was 44 and having her first child, there was even more concern for her welfare than would have been true today. At last her time arrived. I drove her in from Sneden's Landing to our Upper East Side clinic, where only her doctor knew her identity. Our daughter was born without incident, and we named her Anne Madeleine.

Soon after the birth, while Madeleine and the baby were still in the clinic, one of the nurses looked at the new mother and said to someone else, "Isn't that Madeleine Carroll?"

51

Panic and consternation! But the doctor was up to the occasion. He and I sneaked Madeleine and the baby and a trustworthy nurse out of the clinic and into the doctor's own house in the East 70s. There is no better place to hide than right in the middle of New York City. Somehow the nurse's recognition of Madeleine at the clinic did not get out. The event never reached the gossip columns.

Finally my wife Nini did agree to a divorce and went to Reno. (She married again not too long afterward, and to my dismay she changed our son Peter's last name from Heiskell to Chapin, her new husband's name.)

Once Nini's divorce was granted, the problem was how were Madeleine and I to get married without its becoming a major news event. After a considerable amount of discreet inquiry, we located a small out-of-the-way church in Baltimore. We chartered a single-engine plane and flew there to get married — at last.

The news of our marriage did not get out right away, and when it finally did, nobody tumbled to the timing of the baby.

Now we did not have to hide in Sneden's Landing any longer. We decided we wanted to buy a house in the Darien, Connecticut, area. We knew we wanted it to be on or near the water, and we were willing to pay $40,000 to $50,000, a good price in those days. We put ourselves in the hands of a real estate lady and spent weekend after weekend driving around in her beat-up old car, looking at houses. She showed us everything there was, but we couldn't find anything we liked.

Finally the real estate lady said, "There's this one house. It's above your price range, and I'm not even sure the people want to sell. I don't want to waste my time on it, but I'll introduce you to the lady."

She did introduce us to the owner, and of course we fell in love with the house. It was a big white clapboard house with many windows, right on the water on a bluff overlooking Long Island Sound. It was on Long Neck Point Road, a lovely wide street with large trees and large houses.

The owners were a man and wife, but the wife did all the talking. She was sixtyish, a little heavyset, animated, pleasant, rather sure of herself. One of the things she was sure of was that she did not want to sell the house, although she was happy to walk us through it and show it off. She was also happy that the famous movie star Madeleine Carroll was interested in her house.

As she said goodby to us at the front door, she told us, "If I ever change my mind, I'll let you know."

Next weekend Madeleine and I came right back and brought with us a bottle of champagne. While her husband was upstairs, reading in the library, the woman sat with us in the first-floor living room. We poured the champagne down her gullet, and we put on the charm act to the nth degree. I am fairly good at this but nothing compared to Madeleine. While the lady drank her champagne, Madeleine smiled and chatted and secretly thought about how she would redecorate the living room. That is what all women always do.

At the end of the afternoon — and the end of the bottle — the woman finally said, "Okay, I'll sell it." Her husband was never allowed to participate. She sold the house right under his nose without ever telling him. The price was $75,000. Madeleine and I each put up one-third, and we borrowed the rest.

We moved in with two-month-old Anne Madeleine and a Scotch nanny. That week we got the damnedest hurricane I ever saw. The 100-mile-an-hour winds came screaming across the open Sound, aimed directly at our house, driving stupendous waves before it. The four-foot-thick stone seawall was sheared off at the base as though by a giant knife, and the big shattered stones were strewn across the beach like marbles. The electricity went out. We lost more than 100 window panes. When I dared go outdoors to assess damage, I had to bend forward almost down to the ground against the wind, like a ski-jumper taking off and leaning way out over the tips of his skis.

Madeleine behaved wonderfully, with no sign of panic. Scotch nannies, of course, do not panic under any circumstances, and the baby was too tiny to know what was going on. Personally, I was terrified. We all survived, but it cost us a third of the price of the house to repair all the damage.

The next time we saw the real estate lady, she was driving a shiny new green Oldsmobile. That made us quite cross. We had bought her a new car by taking a house she was not willing to waste her time on.

BOY PUBLISHER

◇◇◇◇

IN JANUARY 1946, FIVE MONTHS AFTER THE END OF THE WAR, I was named publisher of *Life*. I was only 30. It was great, very exciting, at that young age to be publisher of the country's leading magazine, the one all our ad salesmen proudly and arrogantly called "The Big Red." I became something of a celebrity. Everybody was saying, "Oh look, he's only 30 and he's the publisher of *Life*." My colleague Jim Linen, who would later be president of the company when I was chairman, had already been named publisher of *Time* a few months earlier, but he was an old man of 33.

I had performed many publishing duties for Roy Larsen during the war when I was general manager, but now the whole job flipped completely. During the war we had had severe paper restrictions, so we literally had to ration advertising pages, only so many to any one advertiser, and only so many ads to an issue. We also had to ration the number of copies we printed, with the result that almost every issue sold out on the newsstands. We constantly worried about whether or not we could get enough of the tiny wire staples that bound the magazine together. We kept experimenting with how few staples we could use without the magazine falling apart in the reader's hands.

Suddenly, with the end of the war, the lid was off. Circulation and advertising growth were so rapid that we ran into serious bottlenecks. By far the worst of these was what we called circulation fulfillment.

Each subscriber's name and address was embossed on a small aluminum card about the size of a credit card. The cards were all linked together on chains and then wound around big reels. Each time a new subscriber signed up, the chain had to be unlinked and the new card had to be inserted by hand in the proper place. Each time a subscription expired, the chain had to be unlinked and the old card had to be removed by hand. Card by card, this was not difficult to do, if one was careful and had skillful fingers. The women who worked in fulfillment became adept at it. However, with our postwar explosion in circulation, we might have to add 50,000 new subscribers in a single week, as well as remove all the expires. This took many, many fingers and an inordinate amount of time. We were never up to date or anywhere near it.

When the reels were as current as possible for that week's subscriber list, they were used to print out paper labels in large rolls. These rolls were trucked down to the printing plant so that a name-and-address label could be slapped on each copy as it came off the press.

We realized that our aluminum-card system belonged to the Middle Ages. It couldn't cope with the pent-up public demand for magazine subscriptions. It was nearly catastrophic. People complained — many, many people. They had signed up for a subscription, they had paid their money, and now they weren't getting what they paid for. We would receive tens of thousands of complaints every week about not getting the magazine, and there wasn't very much we could do about it. In fact, the complaints were so numerous that we couldn't even answer them. That doesn't make you very popular.

On behalf of *Time* and *Fortune* as well as *Life,* Roy Larsen kept badgering IBM to come up with a better system. "If you don't find some way to do this electronically," he told them, "we'll have so many employees we'll probably go bust." At one point we had 3,000 employees — or 30,000 fingers — working in Chicago fulfillment.

In the end what saved us was, of course, the computer. Computers were huge and primitive in those days, but they enabled us to type each new subscriber's name and address into the memory bank, delete the expired subscribers, and run off a complete fresh tape every week.

We got our printer, R. R. Donnelley, to build us a grand new plant in Chicago, just for *Life.* It was a long brick building housing giant new high-speed presses. We were in such a hurry to get into it that we started printing there before all the walls were closed in. The presses were grinding out the copies inside walls consisting of canvas tarpaulins. We were so impressed by it that we took advertisers to the plant to watch the copies come streaming off the presses. They, too, were invariably impressed.

We were scrambling for paper as well as printing capacity. Quality coated paper was in short supply because everybody wanted it. I arranged an urgent trip to Crown Zellerbach headquarters in Portland, Oregon, to negotiate a major long-term contract for paper. Charlie Stillman, who was in charge of production, and I made the transcontinental flight in one of our two company planes, a small twin-engine Electra.

All went well as far as Denver, where we overnighted. The next morning we took off to cross the Rockies. Since the cabin was not pressurized, there was a limit to how high we could fly before we ran short of oxygen. As we climbed toward the mountains, I noticed that the clouds were thickening. Charlie Stillman paid no attention to the weather. Always a serious fellow, he was hard at work on the proposal we would make next morning to Crown Zellerbach. He was filling page after page of a yellow pad with careful notes and figures. The clouds got so thick that I could not see ground anywhere below.

Then I noticed that the plane seemed to be zigzagging. I walked up to the cockpit to consult the pilot.

"Well, yes," the pilot told me. "The radio isn't working, Mr. Heiskell. We've lost radio contact."

In those days the radio was the *only* way of finding out where you were if you had lost visibility. What we were doing was flying over or through the Rockies at a height lower than some of the peaks. The pilot was flying as high as he dared. He couldn't fly any higher because we would run out of oxygen to breathe. I considered this a very unpleasant situation.

I decided to do the best thing possible under the circumstances. I went back to the cabin, opened the bar and mixed myself a martini.

Charlie looked up from his work. "You shouldn't drink here, at this altitude."

"Charlie," I said, "you shouldn't be working here. We don't even know where we are."

He went back to his work, and I went back to my martini.

The pilot lucked his way through the mountains, the skies cleared, and we landed safely. A telegram from the home office was waiting for me at the airport. It said, "Don't fly anymore. Pilot does not have a license." I thought of wiring back, "Pilot also doesn't have a radio."

Next day at our meeting with the high muckamucks of Crown Zellerbach in their corporate office, Charlie Stillman brought out his pad and,
in his dry, even voice, began to outline our intricate proposal. He started
off well, but as he went along I noticed that he seemed to be having trouble. I leaned over to glance at his pad. What had begun as clear writing
on the early pages had become simply a wobbly line on the last pages,
thanks to lack of oxygen. I came to the conclusion that in a crisis it is better to drink martinis than to work. We managed to sign the paper contract anyway.

⮌ During the war when I was general manager, I had had some experience selling advertising, but that was more a case of rationing and restrict-
ing than competitive selling. When I became publisher, it turned out to be
about half my job. That was because I liked it.

Selling ads is very much like fund-raising. If you get turned down, you
get discouraged, but if you succeed, it stirs you on to bigger and better efforts. When I was on a roll, I didn't hesitate to suggest to a big customer
that he should buy 50 pages a year, one every week. I went out on calls with
all our salesmen — to lunches, dinners, cocktails and office meetings, not
only in New York but in Chicago, Detroit and Los Angeles.

The salesman liked it because the publisher got him into top-level meetings he would otherwise not have. When the publisher was with him, instead of dealing with the account executive at an ad agency, he saw the head
of the agency and his top lieutenants. Instead of talking to the vice president for advertising at Sears Roebuck, he got to talk to the president. At
these meetings, the publisher talked more than the salesman did, but at
least the salesman was there in the room to smile, listen and say a few
words. After such a meeting, there was a substantial ruboff. If the troops,
either at the agency or at the corporation, knew that the salesman and his
publisher had had lunch with the big boss, the salesman's stock went up,
and his next phone call or visit was treated with more respect.

It wasn't all fun, because in the course of many sales calls, I did have the
privilege of meeting some dreadful people. I had lunch in Detroit with Bill
Bennett, the goon that Henry Ford had picked to run his company because
he knew Bennett would be ruthless about labor unions and Communists.

After lunch we moved over to a couch, and Bennett began to wriggle and squirm around in obvious discomfort. Finally he reached behind his back, pulled out his gun, laid it on a side table and went on talking.

Sam Bronfman of Seagram's and Charles Revson of Revlon were another pair of monsters. Both were impressed by their own power and eager to display it to the visiting *Life* publisher. These two men pulled identical stunts on me. Each man peremptorily summoned his president and proceeded to beat up on him in my presence, just to show me his power and absolute authority. Sam Bronfman did this in the Seagram's bar. Charles Revson did it in his fancy corporate dining room. It was extremely unpleasant to watch and listen to this kind of megalomania, but since both Seagram's and Revlon were big advertisers, I managed to endure it.

As the postwar ad pages poured in, weekly issues grew to more than 200 pages, and we began to have terrible problems positioning all the ads. Advertisers, especially the big ones who ordered a number of pages, thought they deserved special treatment. They had certain demands that were impossible for us to satisfy. Everybody wanted to be in the front of the magazine or on the back cover. Everybody wanted to face a full page of edit, on the theory that interest in the edit would attract more attention to the ad. Everybody wanted that page of edit to be something pleasant or amusing or beautiful, not something grisly or disgusting.

When success overcame us, we had to face off ads in the front of the magazine, putting one full-page ad opposite another full-page ad, and no advertiser liked that. Furthermore, every car or cigarette advertiser insisted on being widely separated from every other car or cigarette advertiser. Many advertisers started buying cheaper half pages instead of full pages or spreads. Because most picture stories don't display well when squeezed between a half-page ad and a full-page ad, this forced us to run more and more textpieces to fill our own edit half pages.

Our solution to all these demands was to try to rotate positions as fairly as possible. We would meet the advertiser's demands one week but then sort of ignore them for a while until his turn came around again. As Yale's football coach Herman Hickman once said about his troubles with the alumni, his policy was to keep them "sullen but not mutinous."

Since we managed to execute this policy with reasonable success, my worst personal problem with advertisers was not positioning but trying to explain away some of our stories that the advertisers found damaging or offensive. I spent a lot of my time putting my head on the chopping block when the editors did something awful. One of these was a full-page picture of a horrible car wreck, with a shattered Plymouth wrapped around a tree trunk. The name "Plymouth" was clearly visible above the twisted grill. The editors, in their wisdom and wanting to draw an interesting conclusion from this photograph of mayhem, tossed in the comment that the picture proved postwar cars were made of lower-quality steel.

This did not delight the Chrysler Corporation, the maker of Plymouth and a large advertiser, especially since the gratuitous comment about post-war steel quality turned out to be quite untrue. I had to go out to Detroit and let them beat up on me in a succession of meetings until they were sat-isfied that I had no more blood left in me to spill.

Campbell Soup, one of our treasured regular advertisers always insisted on a righthand page, and we always managed to give it to them. Once, how-ever, the result was disastrous. There on the righthand page was a color photograph of a steaming bowl of delicious, yummy soup. And there on the facing lefthand page, the editors elected to run a full-page picture of the gigantic rear end of a hippopotamus. The accidental juxtaposition was hi-larious. It amused everybody except the Campbell Soup executives. I spent a long dreary day at their Camden headquarters explaining that it was a dreadful accident, a most regrettable incident, a witless insult to a beloved advertiser, a moment of inexcusable carelessness on the part of our other-wise virtuous editors, and that it would never happen again — never, never, never!

Sometimes I got in trouble all by myself, without any help from the ed-itors. I was often asked to give my okay to a new ad. Advertisers were always coming up with some new gimmick or approach that might not meet our standards or might offend our family readers. One day Clay Buckout, my ad sales director, brought me a color spread ad and said, "Here's one I think you ought to look at."

I looked at it. It was a closeup portrait of a gorgeous, sexy blonde with long, wavy hair. The headline read, "Does she, or doesn't she?" It was, of course, the first ad in the famous Clairol campaign for hair coloring.

I hit the roof. "That," I said, "is disgusting. It is the worst kind of sniggering sexual innuendo. 'Does she, or doesn't she?' Everybody will know what that question *really* means. It's in bad taste. I won't run it."

"The agency is pretty high on it," Buckout said. "It's going to be a big campaign. Lots of pages."

"I don't care. That is not going to appear in our magazine. All our women readers will be offended. And a lot of men, too. Tell them no."

He told them no.

Both the ad agency and Clairol protested. I told them my decision was definite and irrevocable. We went back and forth in that vein for a while, until finally they said, "Can't we be rational about this? Why don't we ask a lot of women how they interpret this?"

So they conducted a large opinion survey, and it turned out that I was practically the only one who thought the headline was dirty. Most people thought it was catchy, interesting, intriguing. On our own, we conducted a private survey among Time Inc. women employees with the same result. It seemed that I was the only one with a dirty mind. I finally had to give in.

We ran not only that Clairol ad but many more. It became one of our best accounts. But I was a laughing stock in the advertising community because the story was all over town that Heiskell had tried to turn down the most successful ad of the year. For months afterward, whenever I met Bruce Gelb, the head of Clairol, he would smile, shake his head and say, "Poor old Heiskell."

Sometimes the pressure from advertisers took a political form. During the height of McCarthyism in the mid-1950s, a man who represented supermarket chains asked to see me. Since food advertising was a major category for us, I made an appointment with him. Into my office walked this burly fellow in his 50s, a smooth kind of rough diamond. As soon as he opened his mouth, I knew he was a real fascist.

"Mr. Heiskell, your magazine is plainly anti-McCarthy and pro-Communist. I've been reading it. You obviously have a lot of Communists on your staff, and I tell you to get rid of them. If you don't, the chains I represent will see that all food advertising is pulled out of *Life*."

This was at a time when the television networks were caving in to McCarthy pressure. They were pulling programs and pulling writers and actors who offended McCarthy's many fierce supporters. However, I was not going to join them. Besides, my visitor's arrogance made me very angry.

I told him, "All right, I've listened to you. Now you get out of here — out of my office and out of this building — and don't ever come back."

He never came back, and I never heard anything more about it. Often a firm response can eliminate a problem.

In spite of an occasional crisis caused by something the editors had done, my relations with them were generally excellent. During my long years as publisher, I dealt with three different managing editors, but in effect there was really only one. Dan Longwell, the lively fussbudget who had originally hired me as a spurious science and medicine expert, retired from the job the same year I became publisher. His successor, Joe Thorndike, had a short reign of less than three years. He was a trim, intelligent, good-looking man with a fine sense of organization. He knew how to delegate, which many editors do not. But he was an odd duck, terribly walled in, a rather cool, reserved, New Englandish type. I couldn't ever feel that I was talking to the real Joe Thorndike. He had a lot of technical competence, but I never got the feeling that any blood was flowing through his veins. I had no sense that he was in touch with the country.

My real partner at *Life* was Ed Thompson, who was managing editor from 1949 to 1961, a long tenure that embraced some of *Life*'s best years as well as years of increasing troubles. He was the opposite of Thorndike in almost every way. He had grown up in North Dakota, graduated from the state university and been picture editor of the *Milwaukee Journal* before coming to *Life*. A born leader, he was a bluff, pink-cheeked, confident, professional midwesterner. He did not actually have a speech impediment, like Harry Luce's stammer, but he had a tendency to mumble and to speak his thoughts and give his orders in elliptical, half-submerged phrases. Staff members would listen intently to these mysterious pronouncements and then immediately assemble outside his office to ask each other, "What did he say?" The staff, which adored him, affectionately referred to Ed as Mumbles.

I was in Ed Thompson's office at least two or three times a week and would be involved myself in everything that went on there editorially. We argued about anything and everything, ranging from the magazine to anything else.

There was little friction between us. What friction there was didn't have much to do with political or social issues but with what we should be doing with the magazine. I was constantly nagging him about it. Should it have more news? I thought we had worn the news angle a bit thin. Should *Life* have more big acts? Big acts are difficult to pull off, they're expensive, and they dominate an issue. If it's an act that doesn't appeal to very many people, then it's a problem no matter how good it is.

But we did choose to go in the direction of the big act: multi-part color series such as *The Picture History of Western Man, The World We Live In* and *The World's Great Religions.* Out of these series we were later able to create books that made handsome profits, leading eventually to the creation of the Time-Life Books Division.

I thought up one big act that saved us a great deal of money. The two most unprofitable issues of the year were the holiday weeks at Christmas and New Year's. All the advertisers had already made their big pitch for Christmas sales and holiday travel, so they dropped out of those two issues. We were spending the usual amount of editorial money and all the paper and printing and mailing costs to produce two issues that had virtually no advertising support.

It occurred to me that it would be much cheaper if we could publish only one holiday issue instead of two. But how could we justify that to our customers? I suggested to Ed Thompson that we put out a Yearend Special Double Issue on a single subject. We would have to throw in more edit pages than usual, but it would still save us a bucket.

It worked even better than I had hoped. The advertisers decided that a special double issue would have extra special appeal for the readers. Instead of avoiding the two regular holiday issues as they had in the past, they flocked into the single special issue and made it a fat profit center.

During the postwar years we became the magazine of record for the histories and memoirs of famous men: Winston Churchill's *The Second World War* and *A History of the English-Speaking Peoples,* the memoirs of Lord Montgomery, the Duke of Windsor, President Harry Truman, General Omar Bradley, General Douglas MacArthur. Some of these projects were hideously expensive (a million dollar fee in two cases), some were not. When, late in the day, Charles De Gaulle's memoirs were offered to us, Ed

Thompson and his articles editor Ralph Graves agreed that the work was purely for French citizens, not for American readers. At the same time they felt they could not insult the great De Gaulle by just saying no thanks. So they made a token offer of only $25,000, knowing that the property would wind up in some other magazine. Somewhat to their dismay, De Gaulle accepted. I suspect that Le Grand Charles simply wanted to appear in the same magazine that had published all the other great memoirs.

Lining up and negotiating with these famous authors gave me as publisher some unique personal experiences (*see following chapter*), but they served a far more significant purpose. They and the big picture act series helped to attract and to keep subscribers, and subscribers were now our foremost publishing goal.

During the war, newsstand sales had been our big bonanza. Newsstand sales are much more profitable than subscriptions, provided you don't get high returns. There are no expensive mailing costs, not only for the magazine itself but for all the letters you have to send inviting people to become subscribers and then for all the letters you have to send inviting those subscribers to renew.

Renewals are key. By far your best prospect for a subscriber is someone who has already signed up once. And if you can get him to renew three times, he is probably yours for the rest of his days, automatically and at minimum cost. He then becomes a highly profitable customer. We went to extravagant lengths to win those renewals. A sequence of nine letters went out, four during the weeks before the subscription expired, one on the week it expired, and four more after expiration date. These letters were called Pre-Drop 4, Pre-Drop 3, Pre-Drop 2, Pre-Drop 1 and then Drop. They were followed by the four Post-Drop letters, each one offering a "last chance" to return to the fold. Everybody got four last chances. Each of those nine letters required postage. Each one had to be created and then tested. An absurd and costly but necessary sequence.

Then you have to worry about whether or not anybody is going to bother to open your wonderful letter. Maybe it will just be thrown in the trash. You try to devise ways, tricks, to get the person to open it — offers, false offers, premiums, what have you. And then you have to test the effectiveness of the envelopes, as well as testing what's inside the envelope.

After the war, with the disappearance of the urgent human need to see what was happening in the war zones all over the world, *Life*'s newsstand sales dropped off. We had to distribute many more newsstand copies to get the same number of sales, and the profit dropped accordingly.

And there was a sociological factor that also hurt us at the newsstand. Many of our regular customers joined the great American exodus to the suburbs. At that time there weren't many newsstands in the suburbs because the suburban mall and supermarket did not yet exist. People who used to buy the magazine at their big-city newsstand were now busy driving cars everywhere and had no place to stop and shop for *Life*. To keep up our circulation we had to convert those people into subscribers.

But that is what our major competitors were also trying to do, and we had more direct competitors than most magazines. The *Saturday Evening Post* and *Collier's* were weekly, large-size, general interest magazines, like *Life*. *Look*, while a bi-weekly, was also a large-size, general interest magazine, and furthermore it specialized in pictures, as we did. All four of us were trying to get the same kind of people to open the same kind of envelope and read the same kind of letter that would induce them to accept the same kind of offer — and then to pay for it, once they had accepted. "Bad pay" was always a headache. Not only did we not receive the money promised to us by a new subscriber, but we had to spend more money writing letters and making phone calls to persuade the delinquent to cough up what he owed us.

While the subscriber did not care in the least who his fellow subscribers might be, the advertiser cared very much. And if the advertiser cared, so did I and so did all the rest of my publishing staff. The advertiser was impressed not only by the sheer mass of readers he could reach through our magazine but also by the quality of those readers. So we fought not just the tyranny of numbers but the tyranny of demographics.

What practically all the advertisers were looking for was the young, well-to-do family, preferably with a couple of children, who, in the phrase of the times, was "forming a household." Forming a household meant building or buying a home in one of the nice new suburbs and filling it with a refrigerator, a washing machine, a car (or better, two cars) and all the other objects, gadgets and products advertised in the pages of *Life*, including Clairol and

Campbell's Soup. Ideally, the parents smoked and drank, and with any decent luck the kids would grow up to do the same. Catch 'em early!

With *Life* leading the charge, the four big general interest magazines, plus the monthly *Reader's Digest,* chased those readers all across the country. We chased all other kinds of readers too, because sheer numbers also mattered enormously. None of us could afford a drop in circulation, because advertisers, who have a keen nose for other people's troubles, would interpret this as weakness and behave accordingly — namely, they would place their ads somewhere else.

To compete against each other, the magazines got into circulation price wars, with introductory trial subscription offers of "25 issues for only $2.25 — an astonishing 9 cents a week!" *Astonishing* was the right word. Every time such an offer was accepted, it cost the magazine money. The hope, of course, was that once these bargain-buyers had sampled the magazine, they could be induced to renew at a more profitable price. This did not always work. One woman told a *Life* editor, "Oh, I just *love* your magazine! I subscribe to it every time you have one of those nice trial offers."

All during the 50s, the circulation combat between the big magazines was fierce. During the 60s, it would become mortal. Besides — and this was the biggest "besides" in the history of magazine publishing — there was also television.

⤿ I was fortunate to be publisher of *Life* during its most successful years. But we never made as much profit as the huge revenues would lead you to expect. In 1956, our most profitable year, we had revenues from advertising and circulation of $300 million, but our profit was only $17 million. No self-respecting business would consider a profit margin of less than 6 percent acceptable.

This was not, I hasten to say, a question of indifference or even bad management. *Life* was a terribly expensive product in a number of ways. Because we always carried the latest news, we had to print it very fast, and the faster you have to print, the less efficient it is. The *Post* and *Collier's* could print their issues slowly over three weeks' time because they carried no breaking news. That meant they could make full use of their presses. We closed the magazine late Saturday night and had it on the newsstands

Monday and Tuesday. That meant high-speed press-runs for 48 hours, followed by a lot of inefficient downtime.

Life also had abnormally high paper costs. Not only did the big page size require many more tons, but because of our use of pictures, especially color, we had to buy high-quality coated paper for better reproduction. What you *don't* get with a bigger page size and better paper is a proportional increase in price for advertising. Our pages were twice as big as *Time's* and four times as big as the *Digest's*, but we couldn't get away with charging that much extra.

Since we were spending a lot of money to gather last-minute news and to print it fast, the subscriber had to receive the magazine promptly in order to appreciate what we were giving him. With five million subscribers scattered all over the country, we found that the U.S. Post Office could not possibly do the job without a great deal of help from us. We pre-sorted the magazine at the printing plant by address areas and shipped it by train and truck to the nation's post offices. All they had to do was stick the sorted bundles of magazines into the individual postman's bag. Minimum trouble for them. Maximum trouble and cost for us.

Editorial costs were higher than those of our competitors, but I didn't begrudge them. Edit costs were only a small percentage of the total budget, perhaps five percent. The only reason for begrudging them at all is that a publisher has to have some control of overall costs. If they go wild in one place, they will go wild in another. If we were too profligate editorially, we could trust Donnelley to hike their printing prices another 2 percent. Profligacy in ad sales is not visible. It's not very interesting, and nobody even talks about it. But everybody can see the editors — and especially the photographers — spending money, so you try to keep a modest lid on it.

For all these reasons, *Life* never delivered to the company the kind of profits such a huge and hugely successful enterprise should have produced. Over its entire 36-year lifespan, it probably did little better than break even. It lost money in the early years when its runaway success forced the company to spend a lot of catch-up money for paper and printing. In the war years, high corporate taxes took most of the profit. We had good years in the 50s and then some bad money-losing years in the late 60s. All in all, "the most successful magazine in the world" was about a wash.

But *Life* did contribute something else to Time Inc. *Life* had clout. What the salesmen called The Big Red was indeed the biggest magazine around, and everybody — ad agencies and clients — knew it. This stature rubbed off on our other magazines, to their benefit if not necessarily to their delight. For the other publishers and salesmen, it was easier to sell and promote and get special treatment if you belonged to the same company as The Big Red.

And then there is a measure that had nothing to do with money. No magazine was as beloved as *Life* at its height. It educated an entire generation of Americans. It was revelation because it was pictures. The first time I knew anything about India was through Margaret Bourke-White's picture essay on that country. That happened over and over and over again. Science, medicine, art, the world — Americans had never visually been to Africa, Asia or Australia until we took them there.

The first time *Life* went around, it was bound to be a success, and it was bound to have an enormous emotional impact on that generation that had never *seen* the world — or *seen* any of the other things they might have read about. Suddenly they saw it and — *Wow!*

So many people kept old copies of the magazine in their attics. Sensible people would never keep copies of *Time* in their attics. They kept what they had *seen* for the first time. They were the first generation that was allowed to *see* the world.

It distresses all the editors who were so proud of themselves, but I still think *Life's* success was primarily technological. The small camera, fast film, coated paper — those three things made *Life* possible. And then another technological invention, television, killed it.

But we had that window. And the whole country looked through it with us.

CAUTION: FAMOUS WRITERS AT WORK

◇◇◇◇

FAMOUS MEN ARE FAR BETTER STATESMEN AND GENERALS than they are writers. As *Life*'s publisher, I had to negotiate with a number of eminent men who were selling their memoirs to the magazine. They asked for a lot of money and they got it, but then a strange thing usually happened. Or rather, it didn't happen.

Once they had signed a contract with us and received an advance, they had a curious indifference to what was supposed to happen next —namely, they should now sit down and actually write the book we had paid for. Even when we assigned and paid for a ghost writer, they were much too busy being famous to get down to work. They seemed to think that a book would somehow spring into existence without their having to do anything. If they ignored it, maybe the problem would go away.

President Harry Truman, General Douglas MacArthur and very especially the Duke of Windsor were all masters of avoidance. But the one stunning exception was Winston Churchill. Unlike the others, he was a writer, an historian and a former journalist. He had published many previous books, and he actually enjoyed writing — or at least he enjoyed dictating, which is how he composed his books. But while Churchill did write, and wrote superbly, he had many other devious traits which I was to experience firsthand and at great expense.

Immediately after the end of World War II, Luce approached Churchill about writing his first-person history of the war for *Life*. Churchill had just been thrown out of office by the British electorate and said he did not feel like writing, but he would bear Luce's interest in mind. From what I later learned about the former prime minister, this may have been a negotiating tactic.

In any case, Luce and the rest of us treated him with unctuous respect and generosity, hoping that someday he would write his war memoirs for *Life*. The first week I was publisher, January 7, 1946, *Life* reproduced in color 16 of Churchill's paintings, a story for which we paid him $20,000. Within the next month we also published two of his hitherto secret wartime speeches to Parliament, for which we paid him $50,000. Luce thought the speeches were boring. "It was, of course, a pig in a poke," he wrote Managing Editor Dan Longwell. "And I believe *Life* has to buy some such pigs in order to keep a position in the meat market." (Luce *did* have a sense of humor, more often in memos than in conversation.) "Also, it can be worth the space plus the money if, in some sense, Churchill becomes 'our author.' "

And eventually he did. He signed a contract for his memoirs of *The Second World War* with his good friend Lord Camrose, the owner and editor of the *Daily Telegraph,* a highly respected London newspaper. He had begun work on volume one. So it was Camrose with whom we had to negotiate when he visited us in the fall of 1946. Despite *Life*'s loss-leader purchase of Churchill's paintings and secret speeches, Camrose said the memoirs would go to the highest bidder. The bid for first serial rights — the right to publish excerpts before the books appeared — would have to be at least a million dollars. That sounded to me like Churchill talking.

The *New York Times* was also interested in the war memoirs. Julius Adler, the *Times* general manager, came up with the suggestion that we buy Churchill together and publish him simultaneously. Julie Adler had a personal interest in the project. He had been a general in the First World War and still liked to be addressed as "General." His *Times* office was festooned with swords, guns, bayonets and other military memorabilia. His mouth watered over the prospect of publishing Churchill's war memoirs.

Life and the *Times* put together a bid of $1,150,000, a world record at the time. *Life* would pay $750,000 and the *Times* would pay $400,000 for this multi-volume work. Just how "multi" would become a source of hefty dispute. The loose understanding at the time was that Churchill would probably write five volumes.

A number of loose ends had to be resolved before the contract could be signed, so Julie Adler and I flew over to London to wrap it up. We met Lord

Camrose at the *Daily Telegraph*. His big desk was near a window at the far end of his long office, which was formally decorated in the Georgian style. Camrose was quite bald and quite heavy, with a round face, pink cheeks and somewhat of a belly. Although he was softspoken, he was the absolute boss at his paper, a total dictator. Lord Camrose was Lord Camrose and that was that. In his own expert opinion, the only person higher than Lord Camrose was his good friend Churchill. Nevertheless I liked him.

Julie Adler and I took comfortable armchairs in front of Camrose's desk. Behind us, perhaps 20 feet away, two men in their 30s sat side by side in straight-backed chairs. I wondered if they were some kind of bodyguards, but I learned later that they were Camrose's two sons. They never said a word, never opened their mouths. So British!

Negotiations began.

"One serious problem," Camrose said, "is that Churchill does not want to be pinned down as to the number of volumes."

"Fine," I agreed cheerfully. "Julie, okay with you? Whatever he writes, that's what we'll excerpt."

"I'm afraid you miss my point. If he writes five volumes, as we have been discussing, that works out to two hundred thirty thousand dollars per volume for first serial."

"Right."

"It's too early for him to be sure at this stage, but suppose he writes six?"

"Great. The more the better."

"I agree. But Winston feels that if he writes six volumes instead of five, you should pay him an additional two hundred thirty thousand. And if he should write seven —"

If this had not been such a proper British office, I would have leapt to my feet. "But we have a *deal*."

"Of course."

"It's for the most money ever."

Lord Camrose appealed to our sentimental sensibilities. "All the income from this project," he said solemnly, "is in trust for his heirs."

I did not feel the least bit sentimental, and neither did Adler. "That has *nothing* to do with the price."

Camrose looked sadly at the heartless Americans. "Oh yes, it does."

We went round and round on this point, with no one gaining any ground.

I decided to raise a different issue that had concerned all of us in New York. "I think we need protection in the contract, in case our author is unable to finish the history. He is, after all, seventy-three."

"He is in splendid health, I assure you."

"Just the same, at that age —"

"No, no, you don't have to worry about that."

"But we do worry about it."

"You will see for yourself when you go out for your visit."

A few days later Adler and I drove out to Churchill's country estate of Chartwell, 25 miles from London. Walter Graebner, our bureau chief who had dealt with Churchill on his paintings and secret speeches, was included. It was a beautiful day, perfect for a trip to the countryside. Churchill always made this drive with a secretary beside him in the back seat. He boasted to Graebner that he could usually dictate a thousand words between London and Chartwell — "and never less than eight hundred."

A driveway brought us to the long house with high gables and chimneys set between tall trees. Churchill, dressed in his famous pale blue jumpsuit with the zipper up the front, came to the door to greet us. He was in a great mood and full of cheer. After introducing us to his wife Clementine and his daughter Mary, he led us into the living room, where the cheer took the form of glasses of champagne before lunch. On the wall, in addition to his own landscape paintings, a huge artistic rendering of the Normandy landing hung over a couch. To give us a closer view of it, he climbed up on the couch to take it down. I felt sure he was going to fall over backward, putting an end to our project, but he managed it very nicely. I think he was deliberately showing us that he was in spry good health.

Lunch with the family was a parade of liquids: red wine, followed by port, followed by brandy. The legend that Churchill was a hearty drinker is true, but so are most of the upperclass Englishmen I have known. I enjoy drinks myself, but I could not do any afternoon work if I drank at lunch the way Englishmen do.

After lunch Churchill proudly took us on a vigorous tour of his 80-acre estate. His house stands on a hill, and behind the house the land slopes down to an expanse of rolling green fields and woods and ponds — a beautiful view of the Kent countryside. Churchill toddled along in his jumpsuit and slipper-like loafers, pointing out favorite features in a continuous stream of entertaining patter. He especially wanted to show off his "waterworks," a system of dams and channels that he had built himself by hand and trowel. He was a bricklayer — he even had a union card — and he had created all his little pools with waterfalls that poured over brick walls.

Suddenly he interrupted our tour and toddled off in the direction of a stand of bushes. Then he stopped, turned around and asked, "Would you gentlemen care to join me?"

After all our liquid refreshment, we certainly did. And so the statesman whom *Time* would soon proclaim "The Man of the Half-Century" shared a pee with me beside a bush in Chartwell. No long-lens *paparazzi* existed in those far-off golden days, so there is no record of this memorable moment.

When we returned to the house and it was time for us to leave, he walked us out to our car. He jabbed a finger at his own chest and said, "The body is sound, the body is sound." I.e., we were not to worry about his ability to finish the history. During the entire time we spent at Chartwell, money was never mentioned.

But back in London, it was. We negotiated again and again with Lord Camrose until the joke around London became, "Forget about Churchill's memoirs. Just read the contract, it will be more interesting." This was American law versus British law. British custom is that you sort of shake hands and trust to God. The American way is that you have to specify everything in writing.

Finally I came up with what I thought was a brilliant suggestion for settling the dispute over the number of volumes. We would pay $230,000 each for the first, second, third, fourth and last volume. If Churchill wanted to write three volumes in the middle, that was his problem. We could run only so much of it in *Life* and the *Times*. On the other hand, the book publisher, Houghton Mifflin in Boston, would probably be happy to get as many as ten volumes. Churchill finally accepted this approach, which is why I felt so brilliant.

But the sequel showed that Churchill could not be outwitted or outmaneuvered. With the contract signed at last, he began to have trouble with his writing, especially when winter arrived. He said he simply could not work. England was too cold, too miserable. He just could not do serious work under these conditions.

"Well," I asked London, "where *could* he work?"

The answer came back: Marrakesh in Morocco.

Great! Off to Marrakesh!

But Marrakesh presented a little problem. Under the stern Labour Party travel restrictions of that day, he could take only 20 pounds out of the country. I got the hint. I said, "Fine, we'll fly you to Marrakesh and take care of your expenses." Anything to encourage progress.

As I should have guessed, Churchill doesn't exactly travel alone. We had to buy a number of plane tickets for his party. But in the three months he spent there, he did lots and lots of writing. When he returned to England, the writing slowed down a bit, and then when the following winter approached, it screeched to a stop. Everything was again absolutely terrible.

Okay, back to Marrakesh.

But now, he said, he was too old to fly commercial. We got that hint too and shipped him and his entourage by a chartered plane. The amount of work he got done was again prodigious. At the end of the season, we sent another charter to pick him up and return him to England.

The third winter he insisted on a bigger plane, and since he wasn't quite sure what his plans might be, the charter plane better stay there in Marrakesh. It stayed there. He wrote like a factory, dictating to his battery of secretaries.

When it was all over, I asked somebody to add up the total expenses for the Marrakesh capers. They came to just about the cost of one extra volume, which is exactly what he wrote. And I bet he knew it.

In the end we published installments from all six of his volumes on *The Second World War.* Of all the personal accounts of that great conflict, Churchill's was the most important, and I am proud that *Life* published it. But I do think we paid the full freight.

I had another encounter with "our author" in 1953, when he was back in office as prime minister for the second time. We had had *very* slight preliminary negotiations on his next multi-volume project, *A History of the English-Speaking Peoples* — not your catchiest title. Actually for him this was a very old project. During the 1930s, his years in the political wilderness, he worked on it constantly. By September 1939 when the war began, he had written half a million words, but he put it aside — first for the war itself, then for his war memoirs.

When I was in London on a completely different matter, I suddenly got a message at my hotel to be at 10 Downing Street the next morning. I had never seen the prime minister's official residence and looked forward to my historic visit. Promptly at five minutes to ten I rang the doorbell. What happened next was very different from what happens at the White House.

The door opened and a dustman stood there. He wore a gray denim apron down to his knees and held a feather duster in his hand. I said, "I am Andrew Heiskell. I am supposed to see the prime minister at ten o'clock."

I did not have to show any identification. He invited me in. The ground floor was dark, empty, unbelievably depressing. He led me to a dingy little waiting room. "Somebody will come for you soon," he promised, and went back to his work.

Nobody came. Finally the dustman himself returned and said, "Follow me, sir." He led me to a small elevator, held the door open and told me, "Push Three."

At Three I walked out into a small office containing file cabinets and a nice, attractive young secretary. She said the prime minister would see me "in a few minutes," and then she disappeared.

When I am left alone in a strange room, I snoop. On top of one of the file cabinets was a piece of paper with the heading "P.M.'s Schedule." I've always been interested in who has lunch with whom, so I checked through the whole week. Churchill had only one lunch scheduled, on Thursday. I thought to myself, "Oh boy, wouldn't Truman or Eisenhower like to have that kind of schedule?"

The young secretary returned and led me to a door. She opened it, and there I was — in Winston Churchill's bedroom.

He was lying in a big brass bed. His legs were under the covers, and above the covers showed the top of his pale blue jumpsuit. Across his lap, a bed desk held a messy pile of papers. On the bedside table was a hideous green-and-red plastic telephone. He was smoking a cigar and had scattered ashes all over himself. His eyeglasses were way down at the tip of his nose, and he looked at me over the top of them, beaming a friendly greeting.

"Draw up a chair, young man."

I drew up a chair, and we began discussing his *History*. He said it was full of good stuff and was even more significant now than when he wrote it, because of the great cooperative triumph of the English-Speaking Peoples during World War II. We talked about when *Life* might publish excerpts, how many installments, what kind of illustrations, both historical and photographic.

From time to time he reached over to the bedside table to pick up a glass containing a yellow-brown liquid and took a sip. Plainly this was not medicine. After one such sip, he said, "Young man, you wouldn't tell on me, would you?"

"No, sir. Absolutely not." I suspect he did not want his beloved wife Clemmie to learn that he was imbibing at ten in the morning. She probably already knew.

We went on with our discussion, which he interrupted to ask, "Like a cigar, young man?"

I didn't smoke cigars, so I said, "No, sir, thank you."

More discussion. Then, "Would you like a little whiskey?"

Again I said, "No, sir, thank you."

But then I thought of my children and my grandchildren to come. How silly I would feel to have to tell them that I turned down the prime minister of England and The Man of the Half-Century in his very own bedroom at 10 Downing Street.

"Sir," I said, "can I change my mind?"

And so I had a cigar and a scotch. I hiccupped all the rest of the day, but it was worth it.

We did publish *The English-Speaking Peoples* with lavish and beautiful color illustrations, and it was good stuff indeed. Like this, on the death of Richard the Lion-Hearted: "He received the offices of the church with sincere and exemplary piety, and died in the forty-second year of his age on April 6, 1199, worthy, by the consent of all men, to sit with King Arthur and Roland and other heroes of martial romance at some Eternal Round Table, which we trust the Creator of the Universe in His comprehension will not have forgotten to provide." Or this, on Lee's long retreat from the lost battlefield of Gettysburg, through the rain and across the Potomac to Virginia: "He carried with him his wounded and his prisoners. He had lost only two guns, and the war."

The *History*'s success in *Life* was more one of esteem than of popularity, but again I was proud that we published it.

I never saw Churchill again, but that morning in his bedroom is a delightful last memory.

↝ As a writer, President Harry Truman was not only far worse but far more reluctant than Churchill. "I am not a writer!" he told everyone involved in his memoirs. And he wasn't.

Luce had enthusiastically made the original approach to Churchill, but he hated Truman for beating out Dewey in 1948, for firing MacArthur, for being a Democrat and for a dozen other reasons. So it was *Life* Managing Editor Ed Thompson and I who went down to Washington while Truman was still in office.

One is supposed to be profoundly impressed by his first visit to the Oval Office, but I was not, perhaps because Truman himself was so businesslike and so ordinary in appearance and manner. Thompson and I took seats in front of his desk. He was perfectly friendly until we got to the subject of length.

Unlike Churchill, Truman raised no problem over money. *Life* bought world rights for $600,000, and Truman got a favorable tax ruling from IRS that the income could be spread over five years. Truman's problem was length.

"I won't guarantee," Truman said with that flat firmness for which he was famous, "more than a hundred thousand words."

Since we would be selling off the book rights, this meant trouble. *Life* would only run excerpts, but the book publisher would want something far more substantial. The word for it in book publishing is "heft."

"Mr. President," I said, "that's just not enough. The book publisher will want much more."

"No, no," Truman said, "I can't do that. I will not do more than a hundred thousand words."

Even though he was not a writer, Truman was an ardent reader of history. He should have known that 100,000 words, the length of an average novel, was feeble for a man who had inherited the presidency under desperate conditions and had made the decisions to drop the atom bomb, to go to war in Korea, to fire General Douglas MacArthur and to launch the Marshall Plan. He should have known, but he didn't.

"No," Truman said, "I won't promise any more than that. Maybe it will run longer, but I don't want to be held to it."

In the end, after time and persuasion and a second trip to Washington, we settled for 300,000 words. In the end, after three years of work, he delivered a manuscript of 500,000 words, many of them not very interesting.

Thompson and I had our picture taken with the president. I read in David McCullough's wonderful biography *Truman* that when he was photographed with two people, the President liked to stand in the center with his arms crossed in front of his chest, clasping hands with the man on each side with the opposite hand. I looked up our picture: sure enough.

Truman went home to Kansas City and set to work — sort of. We gave him a dictating machine, and he reluctantly talked into it, answering questions put to him by a series of scholars and assistants. These long dull monologues were duly transcribed, but even Truman was unimpressed. "Good God, what crap!" he wrote on one transcript.

The principal approach, by him and his assistants, was to pull out bits and pieces of papers and documents, which by themselves would have added up to 200,000 words. But he was reluctant to create the connections between the pieces of paper. He was not about to do any real work. It was not because he was lazy — nobody ever accused him of that — but writing was not his thing.

When Ed Thompson visited Kansas City after two years to see how our author was getting along, only 35 manuscript pages existed, along with piles and piles of undigested documents and transcripts. One after another, outside writers were brought in to help, but Truman and his staff proved difficult colleagues. Delay and drudgery were the order of the day.

When we were finally able to publish our *Life* excerpts in 1955–1956, Harry Luce pulled off two of his worst stunts. He read in advance the excerpt that contained Truman's thoughts about China, the editor in chief's special hobbyhorse. Luce's arrogant memo said: "My angle is that the one

Harry Truman bestows his patented crossed-arms handshake on me and Life managing editor Ed Thompson. I have similar pictures of me with other U.S. Presidents, but this is easily the best handshake.

thing Truman must never do is to 'think.' The man of no doubts, no thoughts — that is the strength, charm and outrageousness of Harry S Truman." He ordered up a *Life* editorial reminding readers that in 1948, "We called Mr. Truman's China policy one of 'disastrous neglect half-hidden by irrelevant sermonizing.' It still reads that way in his *Memoirs.*" This editorial ran along with the Truman excerpt on China, so we wound up attacking our own author in the very same issue.

Luce was even worse when Truman explained how and why he had relieved MacArthur of command in Korea. Luce, a great admirer of the general, invited him to respond to Truman, again in the very same issue. MacArthur did so with relish, attacking Truman's "petty instincts based upon spite and vindictiveness."

Harry Truman didn't know how to handle writing a book, but he did know how to handle critics. He had endured worse than Harry Luce and Douglas MacArthur. He never said a word of complaint to us about either the editorial or the general's reply. He just ignored them.

↪ MacArthur became another of our non-writers for *Life*, once while I was publisher and once when I was chairman of Time Inc. In both cases the go-between was MacArthur's longtime aide and sycophant, Major General Courtney Whitney. This snivelling, third-rate mini-general sold us his own story, titled *MacArthur's Rendezvous with History*. I fear that I am on record in the Time Inc. company history as having proudly announced that it would be "MacArthur who speaks, even though the byline is Major General Whitney." Actually, the writing was so frightful that it turned out to be neither MacArthur nor Whitney who spoke but a *Life* editor named A.B.C. Whipple. Cal Whipple rewrote Whitney's manuscript. He did not get a byline, but he deserved one, as his memo to Ed Thompson relates:

> I have retaken the Philippines. By the grace of God Almighty, and despite superior enemy forces, I have accomplished the impossible in what without a semblance of a doubt is the greatest rewrite operation in the history of the last 48 hours. I am now preparing to effectuate plans, as audacious as they are daring, to occupy Japan and fight the Communists in Korea with my Army, my Navy and my Air Force while at the same time overcoming the obstacles thrown in my path by Washington with no other resources than those of Courtney Whitney.

Once around with MacArthur and Whitney should surely have been enough for any one magazine, but we had a second encounter with them in 1963. This one was entirely Luce's baby. He personally contracted with the 84-year-old general to publish what would be called MacArthur's *Reminiscences*. As Luce told *Life*'s managing editor, "He wants precisely what we paid Churchill — a million dollars." Actually, *Life* had paid Churchill only $750,000 for its share of *The Second World War*, so the old megalomaniac got more than Churchill — and for much, much less.

Luce's remarks at a press conference announcement were even more fatuous than mine had been nine years earlier. "Never in my forty years as an editor," claimed Luce, "has there been anything to exceed in importance this publishing event." *Reminiscences* will "rank with the greatest historical writings of any age."

Fat chance, with Courtney Whitney once again involved. MacArthur assigned $100,000 of his million dollar fee to Whitney for all his work on the book. How much of *Reminiscences* was MacArthur talking and how much was Whitney is unknown, but the project was a disaster. Because MacArthur died, *Life* got away with publishing only seven installments instead of the nine that Luce had promised.

↬ The Duke of Windsor was no great shakes as a British monarch, but he was a world class non-writer. The unhappy collaborator on his memoirs, *A King's Story,* was Charles J. V. Murphy, a *Fortune* writer borrowed for the occasion by *Life.* Charlie Murphy was an imposing man — imposing to others and to himself, tall, handsome, silver-haired. His great expertise was military affairs rather than royalty, but he was a very good writer, and in the long run good writing triumphs over lack of knowledge.

Murphy had to move his office to wherever the Duke and Duchess happened to be, Paris or Cap d'Antibes on the Riviera or Monte Carlo. The Duke turned out to have a poor memory and an extreme distaste for work. Murphy spent more time trying to get the duke to work than actually working with the Duke. They had a firm schedule — two hours in the morning and two hours in the late afternoon. The Duke occasionally made the morning session, if the Duchess had not kept him out at a party or at a casino all night, but he rarely kept the afternoon appointment. If the Duchess said, "Come on, David, we're leaving," the Duke left, even if he was in the middle of a sentence. Murphy estimated that even without the endless interruptions from the Duchess, the Duke's effective attention span was about two minutes.

What should have been a stint of six months to a year dragged on for three-and-a-half years, and as the time went by, Charlie Murphy gradually became the Duke of Windsor. He adopted his voice, his tone and his manner. He had always been on the pompous side, but now he became British pompous rather than American pompous. We all kidded him and called him Your Grace.

When Madeleine and I arrived in Paris shortly after our marriage, Charlie called me at the Ritz. "Andrew," said our staff Duke, "the Duchess is giving a dinner party for you and Madeleine on Thursday."

I said, "Thanks very much, Your Grace, but we didn't bring any evening clothes." Since the Duchess *always* gave black-tie dinners, I assumed that was the end of it.

Not at all. Messages went back and forth with Charlie as the relay point, and after 24 hours the Duchess decreed, through Charlie, that she would make an exception for Madeleine and me. The dinner would *not* be black tie.

The Windsors had moved from their Ritz apartment (the largest in the hotel) to a grand house on the elegant rue de la Faisanderie, a few blocks from the Bois de Boulogne. Our dinner party was a preposterous performance. Perhaps 20 guests, none of whom we knew, had been invited to meet us, and the Duchess made sure we met each one.

We walked into a rather immense living room with guests seated around the edges, all of them dressed in black. Charlie Murphy, being a mere hired hand, was not among them.

The center of the room was empty space — except for the Duchess herself. She was very drawn, skinny, a dried-out looking woman in black. Her black hair was in curls tight to her head. She was loaded with jewelry, although perhaps less loaded than if this had been a proper black-tie dinner.

Her hostess style was highly organized, almost military, and without much charm. The Duke was present but barely a presence. As soon as I had a glass of champagne in my hand, she said, "Now, Mr. Heiskell, I want you to come meet so-and-so."

I was introduced, sat down beside the lady and tried to find an area of conversation. Just as we seemed to have found one, the Duchess reappeared at my side.

"Now, Mr. Heiskell, come with me and meet so-and-so."

This went on six or seven times during the champagne hour, up and down, up and down, back and forth across the room. Madeleine was being put through the same rotation with a series of male guests. Neither of us managed a single coherent conversation with anyone. It was frustrating in the extreme, but the Duchess was indifferent. Not until we sat down to dinner did I have a real chance to talk to anyone.

The dining room right off the living room was equally spacious. Our dinner for 20 was a small one, the room could have seated 40. Silver candelabra were everywhere — on the table, on the sideboards. No electric light in the room. Madeleine and I did not dine next to either the Duke or the Duchess. Although the dinner was supposed to be for us, we left feeling that we were only a pretext for the dinner.

Charlie Murphy survived his collaboration with the Duke, whose story did finally appear in *Life,* much to everyone's amazement. But Charlie had not made his final escape from the Windsors. Four years later the Duchess undertook her own autobiography, *The Heart Has Its Reasons,* with Charlie as her ghost. Her story ran in *McCall's,* not in *Life,* but Charlie liked to tell a story about his collaboration with the Duchess.

One day while he was interviewing her, with the Duke listening, she mentioned that during her affair with the King that led to his abdication and their marriage, she had exchanged detailed letters about it with her former husband, Ernest Simpson.

"For security reasons," said the Duchess, "we always referred to him as Peter Pan."

"Peter Pan!" Charlie said, his eyes gleaming with a reporter's zeal. "Did you, by any chance, keep any of those letters?"

"Oh yes," the Duchess said. "All of them. They're right upstairs." She turned to her husband. "David, they're in that gray jewel box in my dressing room. Run get them."

Over his years of collaboration, Charlie Murphy had heard the Duchess give the Duke a thousand orders, so he knew this one would be obeyed like all the rest. The Duke got to his feet and left the room to go upstairs. He was gone a very long time. The Duchess and Charlie went on with their conversation, but all Charlie could think about was what a juicy treasure those Peter Pan letters would be.

Finally the Duke reappeared. He carried a large gray jewel box and wore his customary bland, slightly baffled expression. He opened the jewel box and showed it to the Duchess and Charlie. "There aren't any letters," he said.

"No letters!" exclaimed the Duchess. "That can't be!"

Telling this story, Charlie Murphy would pause and then lean forward to deliver his punch line. "You know what I think? I think Peter Pan flushed those letters down the toilet."

꘎ The last writer I want to tell about is me. After I switched from edit to publishing, I covered only one story during the rest of my career, and that came by total accident. However, it was a beauty: the sinking of the Italian passenger liner *Andrea Doria* on the night of July 16, 1956.

I was just starting a luxury vacation on the *Ile de France*. My wife Madeleine, our daughter and my mother-in-law left New York that afternoon. After dinner we all went to bed early in our beautiful suite of cabins. I slept soundly — until a change in the ship's motion woke me up. I pulled aside the curtain and looked out the porthole into the dark night.

There in the ocean in front of me a brightly-lighted little toy ship lay on its side in the water. I could see three bright blue, lighted swimming pools. It looked so artificial. How very strange, I thought. And then I realized it was not a toy ship but a real one. Oh my God, I thought, it's a shipwreck.

I had been publisher of *Life* for six years, but instantly all my editorial instincts returned, and the juices began to flow. While I quickly threw on some clothes, I remembered there was a *Life* photographer on board named Loomis Dean, who was transferring to the Paris bureau. I had to find him and put him to work, but I didn't know his cabin number. The purser's office! I tried to telephone, but no answer. I could hear feet pounding up and down the corridor outside our suite.

I hurried to the purser's office, brushing past stewards and crew members who also were in a great hurry. An excited steward told me that one liner had run into another liner in the fog off Nantucket and that the *Ile de France*, as the nearest ship in the vicinity, had received a radio summons to come to the rescue of the *Andrea Doria*. The other liner in the collision, the *Stockholm*, was banged up but in no danger of sinking.

I found the purser's office. Nobody there, but the door was unlocked, an open invitation to an old *Life* reporter. I walked in and ransacked the desk until I found the passenger list. Yes, there was Loomis Dean.

I raced to his cabin and pounded on the door. Sure enough, he was still sound asleep. I yelled through the door, "Loomis, there's been a wreck. Get up! Get up! Get your cameras!"

I waited with the greatest impatience for him to dress. Another passing steward told me that lifeboats were now coming over from the wreck. They would soon be arriving at a big cargo door on the starboard side.

I yelled again at Loomis. "Hurry up! We'll miss the pictures!"

At last he emerged, festooned with 35 mm cameras around his neck, each with a different lens. He said he would go up on deck to shoot overalls of the scene — one of which eventually made the cover.

I hurried through the corridors and down the stairways to reach the big, wide-open doorway in the side of the ship. Floodlights illuminated the ocean below, which fortunately was fairly calm. Cargo nets and rope ladders hung down the side of the ship so that survivors from the *Andrea Doria* could climb aboard.

I saw another man taking pictures. I knew that on a news story you try to corner every roll of film in sight.

"Who are you?" I asked him.

"Oh," he said, still snapping away, "I'm a *Life* photographer."

I knew at once that he must be a phony. People were always claiming to be *Life* photographers, either to get better access or just to make themselves look important. But this one really *was* a St. Louis stringer for *Life,* so now I had two men shooting for the magazine. Things were looking good.

As the 800 *Andrea Doria* survivors began coming aboard through the doorway, I kept asking them if anybody came off the boat carrying a camera. Some were Italian, some were German, some were French, so all my old languages came in handy. Finally I found a man who said he had overheard a teenage boy say that he had seen someone on the *Andrea Doria* taking pictures. He described the boy — about 16, medium height, either Austrian or German. It took me 20 minutes moving through the crowd of refugees before I found him.

"Yes," he said, "that's right. I saw a man taking pictures."

"Where is he? Can you find him for me?"

The boy shrugged. He did not seem very interested.

I pulled out my wallet. "Fifty dollars," I said.

This did not impress him.

"A hundred dollars," I said.

He became very interested and went off to find the man he had seen. Finally he came back with an immensely ordinary middle-aged Austrian wearing a belted jacket. He said his name was Heinrich Schneider. He had no camera in sight, so I thought the boy must have made a mistake. Then Schneider pulled aside his jacket and there was his camera, tied to his belt. He said he had shot perhaps a dozen pictures, and the roll of film was still in the camera. He knew he had something of value. We haggled, and I finally bought his film, sight unseen, for $2,500. He trusted me that *Life* would pay him and handed over his camera.

The *Ile de France* returned to New York to unload the refugees, and I turned over Schneider's camera to a *Life* messenger. Then we set sail for France for the second time in two days.

I learned later that when the *Life* Photo Lab technicians developed the film I had bought from Schneider, they thought at first that it was blank because it was so dark. But when they looked more closely at the negatives through a magnifying glass, they saw images.

The story ran in *Life*'s August 6 issue with a cover and a 15-page lead. Schneider's exclusive pictures opened the story.

MY NEW EMPIRE

◇◇◇◇

BY 1959 I WAS EAGER TO DO SOMETHING DIFFERENT. I HAD
been publisher of *Life* for 13 years and thought I had lived through every
possible variation — good years, medium years, poor years. I was publisher during the best year in *Life*'s history, 1956, when we ran over 4,600
pages of advertising and made a profit of $17 million — 70% of the entire
company earnings. Of every dollar spent on all general magazine advertising throughout the U.S. that year, *Life* got 17 cents. But only three years
later in 1959, because of a severe recession and the intense competition of
television, *Life*'s profits vanished, along with 1,000 ad pages. Over my long
period as publisher, I had seen the best, and I thought I had seen the
worst — although much worse would come in the next decade.

At any rate I was restless. My wife Madeleine was tired of New York life
and especially tired of New York business life. She was now 54. As a world-
famous beauty and movie star, she did not like the idea of growing old in
America, where every accent is on youth. She wanted to live in Paris, which
she had always loved. Besides, the French had the highest respect and re-
gard for former film stars or, for that matter, former stars in any field of entertainment. The French view is that if you were once popular and beloved
and excellent, you stay that way all your life.

Since I still thought of Paris as my true emotional home, the city where I
grew up, this seemed like an interesting idea. I suggested to Roy Larsen, Time
Inc.'s president, that I leave *Life* and move to Paris, where I would become the
company's senior European representative. My suggestion was partly personal preference, but I also thought that Time Inc., an all-too-American
company, should expand into the world. And finally I just wanted to do something different. Roy said he would think about it — which usually meant no.

By coincidence, Jim Linen felt much as I did. He had been publisher of *Time* as many years as I had been publisher of *Life,* and he too thought he had dealt with every problem a publisher could face, some of them many times over. He too was restless, but he had no thought of moving to Europe. Jim was thinking of quitting the company to run for either governor or senator in Connecticut. This was no fantasy. He knew everybody, he had wonderful contacts, he would have no trouble raising campaign funds, and he was as gregarious and energetic as anyone I've ever known. A super salesman of magazine advertising, he would probably be just as good at selling himself to the voters. He was 47, a stocky man of average height, with rimless glasses, a hairline that was beginning to recede, and a jaunty, boundless cheerfulness. A friend said of Jim that he had "an adrenal gland as big as a baseball."

I had known Jim since 1940 when he was *Life's* ad sales manager just before the war. I've never seen anybody so completely charged up, selling every minute of the day and night. Half the time he was selling himself, which is what a good salesman does. Incredible energy. I was very impressed by him. He drank a lot, and sometimes he got a little maudlin, but that happens to everybody. He was very fit, playing 27 holes of golf a day, traveling fast and furiously.

Now he was as restless as I was. Neither of us was using the threat of departure as a lever. We simply believed that nothing interesting lay ahead for us at Time Inc. All the battlements on top of the castle were fully manned, and the heights looked impregnable. Harry Luce was still in place as proprietor and editor and always would be. Roy Larsen, even after 20 years in office, was still president and always would be. Even Luce's brother-in-law, Maurice ("Tex") Moore was still in place as chairman of the board.

It was time for Jim and me to move on — especially me. Although I was personally close to Roy Larsen, who was practically a father to me, Jim was closer to Harry Luce, and he was more a businessman than I was. If somebody up there on the battlements dropped dead, leaving room for one of us to get promoted, it was likely to be Harry's favorite, not Roy's.

During the summer of 1959 and the spring of 1960, management turned out to be less impregnable than Jim and I had thought. Knowing that they might be about to lose us, Luce and Larsen suddenly made drastic changes in the way the company was run.

The first major move was that Luce named Hedley Donovan editorial director, a clear signal that this was his successor. Donovan had never worked on either *Time* or *Life,* our two most important and successful magazines. Instead, he had been a *Fortune* writer and editor and, for the past six years, its managing editor.

Less than a year after Luce made Donovan his deputy, Roy Larsen sat me down for a talk. Considering that this was the most important talk of my entire professional career, I am embarrassed to say that I cannot remember where it took place. Perhaps I was so bowled over that I forgot all about the setting. But I certainly remember what he said.

"Andrew, Harry and I have decided that it's time to make some changes. I've been president long enough, so I'm going to step down and become chairman of the executive committee. Harry and I and Tex have decided that Tex has been chairman long enough, so he's going to step down too."

Roy looked at me with his charming, bird-like smile. "That creates two openings. We thought you and Jim might like to fill them. You as chairman, Jim as president."

I was absolutely thrilled. I thought it was terrific. But at the same time, right there while Roy was telling me this wonderful news, in the back of my mind I thought to myself, *This sharpens the Madeleine problem. How am I going to handle the home front now?*

While Roy was telling me the stupendous news, Harry was telling Jim Linen. I also don't remember where and when and how Jim and I celebrated, but we were both elated. I was as thrilled to become chairman at 45 as to become publisher of *Life* at 30. I have always been lucky, and I have always enjoyed every promotion I ever got. This was the biggest of my life.

Next day I had the first of several sessions with my predecessor, Tex Moore. I *do* remember where that took place. It was in Tex's spectacular 60th floor corner office at the law firm of Cravath, Swaine and Moore.

Tex was a curious figure in company history. Since he had married Harry's sister Beth, he was part of the family, and since he was both intelligent and genial, he could have had any job in the company except Harry's and Roy's. But Tex was neither a journalist nor a businessman. He was a lawyer, the senior partner of New York's most prestigious firm. Cravath was counsel for Time Inc., and Tex was Harry's personal lawyer. He was con-

This is the formal company portrait of Jim Linen and me when he was named president and I was named chairman of Time Inc.

servative about management, about getting involved in new projects, and about the company's financial position. Harry had confidence in Tex, recognizing that he was terribly conservative but liking to have him around, just to play safe, just to make sure we didn't do something foolhardy.

With his responsibilities as senior partner of a major law firm, Tex could not have given much time to being chairman of Time Inc., even if he had wanted to. And he didn't want to. He was a very part-time chairman. While he technically presided over the board of directors, everybody knew that everything was really up to Harry, and if Harry happened to be traveling, then everything was up to Roy. Tex was a courtly gentleman and expert on all matters of law, but he was more a counselor and adviser than an active chairman. I would not have wanted to be a chairman à la Tex.

Nevertheless Tex undertook to educate me on my role, my duties and my responsibilities. In those days no business school courses taught you how to be a chairman or president. You couldn't sit down and read a textbook. Besides, nobody can teach people to be leaders. You can train them to be bullies, but you can't train them to be leaders.

Tex lectured me. He liked to lecture everybody, even Harry and Roy. He was a handsome man with a well-kept figure and well-kept silvery hair, but what was most well-kept was his voice. His Texas accent had vanished long ago (if it hadn't, he could never have become senior partner of Cravath), but he had developed a slow, stately speaking style. Very slow and very stately.

"Now, young man . . ." he would begin, and then launch into a lengthy, abstract, legalistic discourse on some arcane aspect of chairmanship. By the time he got to the point — if indeed he ever reached it — I had forgotten where he was headed. I liked him, but he was quite tiresome, just talking and talking without ever saying much. Of all the lessons Tex tried to teach me, I remember only one: "When you pick somebody to be on your board of directors, be very, very careful, because he is going to be yours forever. You can divorce your wife, you can disinherit your children, you can fire all your employees, but you can never get rid of a director."

Even before Jim's and my appointments were announced, I made a radical decision. I told Harry and Roy that I intended to go abroad right away for an extended period of time, to look around, to see where Time Inc.

might expand. I would make Paris my base. For some reason they did not faint or vomit or renege on my promotion.

My decision was part rationalization, at which I have always been very good. While I was delighted to be chairman, Madeleine was not. If she was already tired of corporate life in New York City when I was *Life* publisher, she knew it would be worse when I was chairman. She made it clear that she would spend a lot of time in Europe. Since we were still very happy with each other, I had to figure out an excuse for the new chairman to join her.

But it wasn't all rationalization. I also thought, somewhat seriously, that since Jim was going to be more or less the chief operating officer, and since the whole company couldn't report constantly to two people, it would simplify matters, at least at the start, if I were not around to confuse people. I was taking a wild chance. Harry and Roy might well have looked at each other and said, let's get somebody else to be chairman. But they didn't.

Neither in the official announcement nor in any of our talks with Harry and Roy were Jim's and my roles ever defined. Jim was sort of supposed to worry about operations, and I was sort of supposed to be concerned about long-range planning and strategy, but nobody spelled it out. Jim and I never defined it either. From the company's point of view, the lack of explicit definition may have been the best way to hang on to both of us. If they had put one of us clearly in charge, the other might have left.

The empire Jim and I inherited in 1960 was almost 40 years old and was still primarily a publishing business. With revenues of $300 million we ranked 177th on the *Fortune* 500 list of the biggest industrial companies, and we were by far the biggest magazine publisher.

The brightest new star in the empire was our book division, for which I immodestly but accurately claim a major share of credit. In 1950 during my early years as *Life* publisher, we produced our first book, *Life's Picture History of World War II*. It was a fantastic success, selling more than 600,000 copies, mostly by mail order to our subscribers, and making a profit of $1.5 million. We had found a large pot of gold.

When we followed this by other successful books based on multi-part series in the magazine — *History of Western Man, The World We Live In, Great Religions* — everybody said, "This is so terrific, why don't you go into the book business?" Everybody badgered me, especially Roy Larsen. But I knew that going into the book business would force us to create books, not just publish one-shot volumes based on what had run in the magazine. A real book business would require a steady, regular flow of books, not just occasional mountain peaks. I told everybody that I would not go into the book business until I could find somebody who knew all about books and all about selling by direct mail.

As it turned out, the right person was already looking at us, sniffing around Time Inc. to see if we could go into business together. He was Jerry Hardy, a 41-year-old vice-president of Doubleday. When we learned that we were looking for each other, I invited him to lunch. He was a most engaging fellow, full of charm and wit and knowledge. His most striking features were bright eyes and a large, bulbous nose. He understood direct mail because he had supervised all the Doubleday book clubs, a direct mail operation.

We needed only a few exploratory conversations. In October 1959, during my last six months at *Life,* I hired him. He was one of the few senior Time Inc. executives ever hired from the outside. When I set Jerry Hardy up in business, I was more organized and specific than usual. I wrote out a short prescription: "I expect you in five years to do $25 million volume, to make a $5 million profit, and to make us feel proud." Jerry remembered that I also warned him, "Don't do anything to embarrass us."

In hiring Jerry Hardy I created one of the few enemies I can clearly identify in my 43 years at Time Inc. Robert Elson, a former assistant managing editor, was now *Life*'s general manager. Because he had overseen the publication of several of our one-shot blockbusters, he thought he had earned the right to be head of our new book division. He was a good journalist and a good manager, but he did not know either the book business or direct mail. I believe that a person must be chosen for an important job not because he "deserves it" or because he has "earned it," but because he is the right person for the job. Elson never forgave me, but in later years he wrote the first two volumes of the Time Inc. history, widely praised for accuracy, fairness and frankness. I have repeatedly consulted Elson's volumes for this book, and I must say that, enemy or not, he treated me as fairly as any character in his history.

We gave Jerry a *Life* editor named Norman Ross, and I told them, "If it doesn't work, one or both of you will have to leave." However, it worked beautifully.

In April 1960, the month I officially became chairman, Hardy and Ross sent out their first test mailing, a brochure for a series of books to be called the *Life World Library.* Jerry decided from the start that he wanted to publish serial books, 15 or 20 or 30 related volumes on the same subject. Each volume in the *World Library* would deal with a different country, beginning with Russia. Each would sell for the remarkably low price of $2.95. People would sign up as "subscribers" and pay for each volume as it came out. The volumes would all be the same size and format, so that if a subscriber kept on buying them, he would eventually wind up with a handsome "library" of books — and we would wind up with a handsome pile of money.

The test brochure was crucial. If the brochure drew a good response, we would proceed. If not, we would abandon that idea and try something else. The brochure for the *World Library,* as for all the other series we would publish, was a masterpiece of deception. The potential subscriber received through the mail a large, fat envelope containing a glorious four-color foldout prospectus printed on glossy coated paper. A large color photograph showed a stack of books, and on the spines one could read *France, Italy, England, China* and so on. The initial book on Russia lay open to a "random" spread containing color photographs, captions and running text. The brochure was so large and so handsomely printed that one could actually read both the captions and the text. The subscriber might well think — and was meant to think — that this book and all these other wonderful books had actually been created and were ready for mailing. Actually, the "random" spread of *Russia* was the only spread that had been laid out, written and typeset so that it could be photographed for the brochure. Everything else was window dressing. None of the books existed, except for that solitary spread on Russia. Why go to all the expense of creating an entire book until you are sure somebody is going to buy it?

A 2% subscriber acceptance would have been enough. But the response to our glamorous brochure was fantastic: almost 8%, an unheard-of figure. Obviously Hardy and Ross should proceed at once to turn those mythical books into real ones.

The *World Library* was the first of a series of mammoth successes, to be followed by *Science, Nature, Art, Foods of the World, The Old West, World War II*, etc., etc. Traditional book publishers, understandably jealous, could not believe we could publish such handsome volumes with such a large page size, such good paper and so many color photographs at such a low price. The secret was in selling by direct mail instead of through bookstores, which take 40% of your money. The enormous volume of sales also helped us keep the price down. I was free to go off to Paris with not a single worry about my new book division.

⌐ Madeleine and I and our 11-year-old daughter made our home in a small luxury hotel near *L'Etoile*, also patronized by General Charles De Gaulle during his visits to the capital. Anne Madeleine was sent to a convent boarding school north of Paris, coming home to the hotel every other weekend and for vacations. She was a very pretty brunette, tall and mature for her age. She had a natural self-discipline even before the nuns got to work on her. Their strict convent schooling would eventually become a source of dispute between Madeleine and me. Anne Madeleine's rebellion, when it finally came, would lead to the greatest tragedy of my life.

But for the present, Madeleine and I were glad to be back in Paris, speaking French, eating in French restaurants and drinking French wines. Madeleine was able to enjoy Paris more than I did, because I was often on the road. I took my self-imposed assignment seriously, trying to figure out how Time Inc. could expand into the world outside the U.S. I talked to editors, publishers, television broadcasters and politicians, not only in Paris but all over Europe.

During this period I had to deal with a special problem that my many years of experience in France enabled me to solve. We were trying to build a new Time-Life Building on the Avenue Matignon. We owned the land, and we had received the necessary government permit to excavate for a foundation. We had, in fact, dug the hole — a great big hole some 30 feet deep. But despite every effort our people had been unable to get the many other permits that the French bureaucracy requires. A foundation permit, an electrical wiring permit, a plumbing permit, an elevator permit — the list went on and on, as it tends to do in France. The situation was complicated by the fact that we were not only an American company but one with a strong journalistic presence, freely critical of French policy and politicians. No bureaucrat was willing to run the risk of granting us approval. My colleagues were desperate because they could not thread their way through the maze of permits and regulations.

As anyone who grew up in France knows, the system was never designed to be solved, at least not in what might be considered a practical American fashion. There *is* no path through the maze. You can go round and round in it forever and never emerge. That's what the maze is there for.

After listening to my colleagues' woes, I said, "Here is what we will do. We will give a cocktail party — a great big marvelous irresistible Time-Life cocktail party. We'll rent the bank offices right next door to our excavation, and we'll have an elegant cornerstone-laying ceremony. We'll invite the head of every department that has the right to grant us a permit."

We sent out engraved invitations. I knew that if the department heads came, it would mean everything was basically all right — French style. If they didn't come, then we had a serious problem and would have to think of some other way to deal with it.

But of course they came. Everybody came. I made a flowery welcoming speech — in French, of course. I said how proud and happy we were to be erecting this beautiful building here on this beautiful avenue in the heart of this most beautiful of all cities. And so on and so on, for quite a bit. We planted a ceremonial tree beside the excavation hole, and then we all trooped into the bank building for champagne, cocktails and elaborate hors d'oeuvres. Our *Life* photographers took many pictures of the happy guests. If any of the bureaucrats later claimed they had not attended our party, we could prove them wrong.

After the party finally ended, I told my colleagues, "All right, that's that. Go ahead with the building."

We proceeded to construct our Paris headquarters. We never did get all the required permits, but then we didn't need to.

During my jaunts to European countries, Madeleine stayed in Paris, but when I made a final round-the-world tour before returning to New York, she came with me.

I won't pretend this trip was all work, but everywhere we went I was looking into business possibilities for Time Inc. I set up our itinerary in advance with all our correspondents and stringers so they could make appointments for me with businessmen and politicians. Charlie Mohr in New Delhi said he might be able to arrange a meeting with the Dalai Lama, who had been expelled from Tibet by the Chinese. I told him go ahead. Our Tokyo bureau said it might be possible to arrange an appointment with Emperor Hirohito, and if Madeleine came along, they might be able to get the Empress as well. I said fine, set it up. It was fun being chairman.

The young Dalai Lama was living in northernmost India under what amounted to house arrest. The Chinese did not want him sneaking back into Tibet to foment religious uprisings. Since the Indian government wanted no trouble with the Chinese, they didn't want him sneaking back either. Charlie Mohr and I flew to the far-north Indian city of Pathankot, up in the mountains near the Pakistan border. Madeleine stayed behind in New Delhi because Mohr had warned that it would be a rough trip.

From Pathankot we drove three hours to the tiny town of Dharmsala at an altitude of 5,000 feet. The road was paved but only single lane. Each time we met another car, both vehicles had to move onto the shoulder, creating clouds of dust. At Dharmsala we were told that the Dalai Lama's "residence" was up a steep hill. Our driver found the narrow road and started up, a twisting and almost vertical climb. After half an hour we reached a U-turn that could not be negotiated by our car. Only a jeep could make it. Our driver backed merrily down the road at a frightening clip.

When we phoned the Dalai Lama's secretary to report our problem, he said their jeep happened to be in Dharmsala and would give us a ride. The Tibetan driver indeed gave us a ride, one of the scariest of my life. He drove up that hill as fast as he could, twisting and turning, spinning around the sharp curves. We held on, not knowing whether we would be bounced out of the jeep or whether the jeep would simply go over the mountainside.

Finally we reached the God-forsaken, broken-down hut where the Indian government allowed the Dalai Lama and a few of his followers to stay. The secretary sat in a small, cold little cubicle, his one miserable electric heater giving off a few waves of warmth if you stood within a yard of it. He gave us white scarves and told us we must present these to the Dalai Lama as a traditional "gift."

A door opened and there he stood, a young man of 17 who shook hands with us. He was about five-ten with a crew cut and horn-rimmed glasses. He wore a reddish-maroon robe with a heavy stole of the same color wrapped around his shoulders. He wore a yellow-and-red silk scarf. His boots had cleated rubber soles, and above his boots I could see bright yellow wool socks. His gestures were delicate, his manner restrained except for a small, nervous laugh, halfway between a giggle and a chuckle. His living room was bare except for two heavy couches, two armchairs and a round table, all in the German modern style of 25 years ago.

(Please don't think my memory is good enough to recall these details. I wrote a report on our visit, which I still have.)

He spoke at length of the famine that was bringing death to Tibet. According to recent refugees, rations were negligible. People were eating grass and tuber plants. Apparently the Chinese Communists were using starvation as a method of genocide.

When we asked how he spent his time, he said he meditated some seven hours a day. The balance went to correspondence and studying English and the sciences. He said he had much to learn because he was still young and had had very little experience.

Tea was brought in. I asked him if he would consider writing for *Life*. He said yes, although it was clear he had not yet written anything. (So what? He was not far behind another of *Life's* authors, the Duke of Windsor.)

He asked, "You mean if I wrote my full story, you would print excerpts?"

"Yes," I said, "just like Churchill."

He nodded that he understood our techniques, as well he should. Every week we sent him a special courtesy copy of *Life* by airmail.

Finally when we rose to leave, he handed back the white scarves we had given him, which we in turn handed back to his secretary on our way out. Obviously the system was able to get along on very few white scarves.

When we got back in the jeep, Charlie Mohr was feeling so good about our interview that he decided to be nice to the driver. As we started down the mountain, he said, "You are certainly a fine chauffeur."

These kind words were too much for the driver. He slammed his foot on the accelerator, and we hurtled all the way down the mountain at a horrifying speed.

↜ Getting to see Hirohito required less driving but more ritual. Madeleine and I went to call on him at his palace, where we were met by five chamberlains in striped pants and swallowtail coats. These men were there to prevent the Emperor from having any real contact with the outside world. Conversation with these characters was as stilted as one could possibly imagine, but we had to endure ten minutes of talk before we were ushered into the audience room, a small, surprisingly unimpressive salon.

The seating arrangement was standardized. One of the chamberlains explained that the Emperor would sit there in that armchair with his interpreter to his left. I would sit on that smaller armchair. Madeleine would sit on that couch to the Emperor's right, and the Empress would sit next to her, with her lady-in-waiting interpreter.

The doors opened and the Emperor and Empress appeared. He was a short, gray-haired, bespectacled little man in a dark European business suit, 60 years old and supreme ruler for the past 35 years. Until the American occupation after the defeat of Japan in World War II, he had also been god. Legend has it that on an earlier visit Harry Luce asked Hirohito, "How does it feel not to be god anymore?" There is no record of the Emperor's reply, if any. The Empress, in Japanese dress, was quite a poppet — gay and light-hearted. It was obvious that Madeleine was going to have a better time than I.

I bowed, Madeleine curtsied, and the royal couple came forward to shake hands. We all took our seats.

Conversation was arduous. Knowing that Hirohito was interested in biology and Darwin, I had brought a specially-bound copy of a *Life* book, *The Wonders of Life on Earth*. I had been told that if it was wrapped, the Emperor could not possibly open it in the presence of the donor. Since I hoped it would be a conversation piece, I told him that in view of his avid interest, I had brought this book, thinking he might want to glance at it. He glanced — and that was about all.

I asked him about the conflict between the younger and older generations in Japan. "Will this problem be of short duration, or might it last for several generations?"

He squinted, twitched a bit as he did throughout our meeting, and then answered, "I am sure that you who have traveled so extensively would be able to answer this question better than I can." This was as close to dialogue as we came.

After half an hour of this sparkling conversation, the Emperor turned to Madeleine and I switched to the Empress. I found this much easier, although more platitudinous. Finally the audience was terminated, to the relief of all. I could imagine the Emperor saying to the Empress as the doors closed behind them, "When I was god, I didn't have to do this."

 ᔕ It is amazing how much effort Jim Linen and I put into expanding into the world — and how little of it worked. Our adventures abroad in the '60s were a litany of disaster, one after another. Everything we touched turned to ashes, either right away or after a few years. The only truly successful and lasting foreign operation we ever had was the international editions of *Time,* and it is a stretch to call that foreign. Some years *Time* International made a bigger profit than *Time* U.S.

The outside world did not work for us. The minute we set up a business abroad, we had to cede control. We no longer had final say. Somebody else, often the foreign government itself, had the last word. We were trying to deal with chauvinistic nations who were proud of their own language and history and hated us, the filthy-rich Americans. They wanted our money, but they didn't want us.

Two examples, one in magazines and one in television, illustrate the familiar pattern.

We decided that the best way to cash in on our magazine skills was to create joint ventures with a distinguished foreign publisher. We would publish a magazine together. We chose the title *Panorama* because the word could be used in many different countries. We envisioned an entire family of *Panorama*s blossoming on newsstands all over the world. We started with Italy and Argentina — and never got any farther.

In Italy our partner was Mondadori, the country's biggest publisher, and in Argentina our partner was Editorial Abril, publisher of nine magazines. Our concept for *Panorama* was simple and persuasive, not only to us but to our partners. The magazine would be a *Time*-size monthly. It would have 100 editorial pages and as many ad pages as we could sell. Three-quarters of the stories would be from Time Inc. magazines, although some would have to be cut or adapted to suit local interests. The other quarter of the stories would be supplied by the local publisher, who would also be responsible for picking the right Time Inc. stories, translating them and then putting the magazine together each month.

The launch issue of *Panorama* Italy in October 1962 was a smash hit. All 280,000 copies, filled to the brim with ads, immediately sold out on the newsstands. The launch issue of *Panorama* Argentina, similarly festooned with ads, sold out 130,000 copies in two days. *Whee!* Another pot of gold — in fact, many pots of gold because there would soon be *Panoramas* in a dozen countries. Jim Linen and I thought we had our first giant success.

Not so. The sellout in Italy stemmed from heavy promotion and reader curiosity. Curiosity was soon satisfied. Four months later we got this report: "Italian *Panorama* has run into heavy weather, mainly due to the failure of the magazine editorially to meet the needs and wants of the Italian market. Circulation has dropped by almost one-half since the first issue . . . Advertising is running 50% below budget."

Much of the problem was language. We were trying to convert American stories and ideas and concepts into something that would appeal to Italians. Once stories were converted, they often had a quite different tone and impact. Despite desperate changes in editors and content and concept, nothing worked. Within three years we sold our stake to Mondadori at an after-tax loss of $400,000 — not a great deal of money but very discouraging.

The Argentine *Panorama* was more successful, but when it began taking a strong anti-American stance editorially, we were both annoyed and embarrassed. We eventually got out, and there were no more *Panoramas*.

In our effort to create foreign television stations, Brazil was a typical example. We chose as our partner Roberto Marinho, a major newspaper publisher and active politician. Since Brazilian law required that all stations be owned by citizens, Marinho had to be the owner, while we were only investors.

Like many Latin American countries, Brazil has laws and regulations covering both sides of practically every issue. One law says what you are doing is legal, another law says it is illegal. The question is, which law will apply in your case? It costs a lot in legal fees and aggravation to get the answer. When Marinho's political opponents challenged the legality of Time Inc.'s investment, two different government commissions went round and round and round on the subject. Our lawyers appeared time and again before both commissions. Meantime a currency devaluation turned one year's profit into next year's lost. The political uncertainty of our position dragged on and on until finally we had had it. We sold our share to Marinho, recovering our full investment.

For various reasons we also bailed out of television investments in Argentina, Beirut, Peru, Venezuela, Panama and Germany. Since we got part of our money back, we only lost $4–$5 million, plus a great deal of confidence. Only one foreign station, Hong Kong, ever made a real profit.

After my initial trip abroad, I was back in New York full time. Jim and I kept each other fully informed on what the other was doing. We both took part in all serious discussions and decisions, but some projects were more clearly mine and some were more clearly Jim's. He had worse luck than I did because his biggest projects were MGM movies and General Learning.

Encouraged by his friend Edgar Bronfman, the head of Seagram's, a huge advertiser and a fellow movie buff, Jim persuaded our board to buy 300,000 shares of Metro-Goldwyn-Mayer for $18 million. That gave us 5% of the stock and a couple of seats on the board. Unfortunately MGM proceeded to go through cataclysmic management upheavals, the stock price fell and we lost more than $10 million before we could escape.

General Learning was born in the bar of a country club in Greenwich, Connecticut, where Jim Linen was drinking martinis after a round of golf. John Lockton, the treasurer of General Electric, joined him. By the time they finished drinking, whenever that was, they decided that GE, the electronics giant, and Time Inc., the communications giant, should create a joint-venture company that would revolutionize American education by bringing computers into the schoolroom. The two companies promptly formed the General Learning Corporation, named officers and hired staff. On Roy Larsen's recommendation we chose a brilliant educator named Frank Keppel as chairman. He had been dean of the Harvard Graduate School of Education and was then assistant secretary of Health, Education and Welfare. Fortunately for us, he knew everything about education and educators.

GE and Time Inc. made the epic decision to invest $100 million to put computers into the nation's schools. Both boards of directors approved the step. We knew that IBM and Xerox and other companies also saw the potential of marrying schools and computers. This was one boat we were determined not to miss.

I got closely involved because the Book Division that I had recently created would obviously be a major supplier of materials for the forthcoming revolution.

I got a phone call from Frank Keppel: "Andrew, I have to see you. It's important."

I told him to come right over.

A tall, scholarly figure with horn-rimmed glasses, he came to the point as soon as he walked in. "Andrew," he said, "I suspect that you don't have much experience with the U.S. school system."

"Right," I said. "In fact, none."

"Well, there is one thing I think you should know. *Nothing* changes more slowly than a school system. Teachers, principals, school boards, they don't *like* change, and they are terribly slow to accept anything new. Anything new at all, but especially anything the least bit radical."

"You mean, like computers?"

He nodded. "Just like computers."

"You mean our hundred million might go down the drain?"

"Have you got twenty years to make it work? Otherwise . . ."

So I pulled the plug. It was not difficult to persuade General Electric, because nobody over there knew anything about schools either.

Not only did Frank Keppel's advice save both companies a great deal of money, but he turned out to be a good prophet about timing. It would be two decades before the computer made its way into U.S. schools in any serious way. Our idea was right but our timing was awful. The same was true for IBM and Xerox and all the other companies that tried to start the revolution too early. All of us were right — but 20 years too early. Time Inc. got out with a loss of about $10 million.

↬ Reading this record of non-achievement, both abroad and at home, one might well ask: why didn't Time Inc. fire both Heiskell and Linen?

Participants at the opening of the new Time & Life Building in Chicago were Harry Luce, my great mentor Roy Larsen, myself and Jim Linen.

A fair question.

Here is a fair answer:

- Our failures did not happen all at once but were spread out through the years.
- Most of them weren't expensive. The investments were usually not large to begin with, and when we bailed out or sold out, we often got our money back, or most of it, or at least some of it.
- Our failures, though many and varied, were on the whole rather obscure. Unlike the major public fiasco of Time Inc.'s magazine launch of *TV Cable Week* in 1983, the small failure of *Panorama* did not matter much to our directors, our stockholders or the press.
- While we were failing in new ventures, especially abroad, many other

parts of the company were doing very well. *Time*, both U.S. and International, was a success. Time-Life Books was a stunning success, its profits zooming to over $6 million in a few short years. *Sports Illustrated* finally became profitable, switching from an expensive drain to a major contributor. Our American TV stations made money, and Eastex, our pulp and paper mill, made a lot of money.

So in spite of our failures the balance sheet looked good. During the '60s Time Inc. did not slip backward on the *Fortune* 500 list, which is a good measure of how a company is doing compared to everybody else.

So Jim and I did not get fired for our relatively minor escapades. However, at the end of the decade two far more important events took place:

- Jim Linen did have to be removed for other reasons.
- *Life*, the heart of my personal and professional involvement, entered its death throes.

LIFE WITH MADELEINE — AND WITHOUT

◇◇◇◇

MADELEINE CARROLL AND I HAD TEN WONDERFUL YEARS together, two so-so years together, three peaceful years apart — and then finally a single night so appalling that I have never forgotten it.

When we fell in love, she was a world-famous, world-beautiful actress. After the birth of our daughter Anne Madeleine, she devoted herself more and more to being wife, mother, hostess and homemaker. She never appeared in another movie, never again appeared on stage. However, she never lost interest in the fact that she was an actress.

At her request her agent Robby Lantz continued to send her scripts and plays and screenplays. She read them with care, sometimes with excitement. She loved to discuss them. How would she be in this role? Was it really right for her? It was shop talk — a way of keeping her hand in without having to work.

Madeleine was easy for people to get along with because she always made that effort. She had no great sense of humor, she was not much of a storyteller, but all my friends and colleagues liked her. She always "presented" herself in the best possible way. This presentation is what an actress learns to do. Just the right tone of voice, the lovely smile, the friendly, graceful gesture, the display of keen interest in what the other person is saying. It wasn't phony, it was real. She made it real, as a good actress is able to do.

But in private with me, when we were alone at our house in Darien or in our apartment at Tudor City, she didn't put on that show. Her face was more relaxed, there was less motion, fewer gestures. She did not even move in the same way. When she was at home alone with me, she would walk from the living room to the kitchen in a different way from the way she walked when guests were present. Actresses learn to walk in a certain way.

I suppose it becomes ingrained. I don't think they say to themselves, "Now I'm going to walk in a certain way." They just do it.

But some things actresses learn do become permanent. Posture, for instance. The rest of us can slouch around, put our feet up on a desk or a coffee table, put our hands behind our head. Actresses don't. Their bodies simply assume a certain posture. Standing, sitting or walking, the posture is always there. Only when they lie down in bed does that posture disappear.

Madeleine was not extravagant except in one area. She never spent much money on clothes, and she was not preoccupied with jewelry. She did love hats, especially broad-brimmed ones, and she enjoyed going to Tatiana, the famous milliner at Saks Fifth Avenue, to try on hats and occasionally to buy one. But she only had half a dozen hats, not a hundred. She did not have 50 dresses or 20 suits. She was always properly dressed because that was part of her presentation. At dinner, even in the country or on vacation, she often wore a long dress or a long skirt, and she liked me to wear a jacket. But I think I actually liked clothes more than she did.

Her one whopping extravagance was real estate, and the home-decorating that followed in its wake. She had grown up poor in London, the daughter of an Irish schoolteacher. To her, real estate was a symbol of success, a showcase. She loved real estate, not because of its value as an investment but because it represented a way of life.

Before World War II, long before we were together, she bought a chateau 50 miles south of Paris, halfway between Paris and the chateau district of the Loire. It was really a huge villa, an elegant century-old country house, but Madeleine preferred to call it a chateau. Perhaps it was in good condition when she bought it, although I doubt that, but during the six years of the war it was not maintained at all.

When I saw it for the first time, I was both impressed and shocked. From the outside it was quite beautiful, even though the grounds and gardens were unkempt. The building itself was gray stone and must have been 80 yards long. The peaked slate roof seemed to stretch for miles. Wide, heavy steps led up to the ground floor, which had a series of tall French doors. But inside, there was only one functioning bedroom, a living room and a dining room. The rest of the chateau, 20 large rooms, was empty and bare. No furniture, no curtains, nothing. Madeleine and I did not have to be architects to see that the huge slate roof was in horrible shape. Already it leaked, and slates were falling off. We knew that if we did not repair it, it would simply fall in some day — a day not too terribly distant in time. But we also knew that if we did repair it, the cost would be ghastly.

We eventually put the chateau on the market, but it took several years to sell, even at a miserable price. Madeleine got back very little of the money she spent for it, but at least we sold it before the roof fell in.

Madeleine was solely responsible for a quite extraordinary event in my life. One day in Paris, where we were staying at the Ritz, she said, "Your father lives in Paris, doesn't he?"

I said, somewhat surprised because I had not thought of him at all, "Come to think of it, yes."

Madeleine said, "It's so strange. You haven't seen him for practically all your life, have you?"

"No, that's right."

"Well, do you think you might like to?"

I thought about that. It had been such a very long time, some 35 years. Like many outsiders confronted by what might turn out to be an emotional problem, I had played it safe and just pulled the plug. I had grown totally accustomed to not having a father and to never even thinking about him. But now Madeleine's question intrigued me. Finally I said, "Yes, that's a good idea."

I looked in the Paris phone book and sure enough, there he was. Yes, he was in Paris, and yes, he was listed. I could actually call him up. I could call up my father. I suddenly became quite excited. I picked up the phone and called. A man's voice answered.

"Is this Morgan Heiskell?"

"Yes."

I took a deep breath and said, "This is your son Andrew Heiskell."

Now this is what is so extraordinary. His voice sounded as if I had been talking to him every day. He didn't sound amazed or surprised. Instead he was quite blasé about his long-lost son being on the other end of the phone. No doubt he had pulled the plug, too. "Well," he said after only a few seconds pause, "come to dinner."

I said we'd love to.

"All right, come tomorrow night."

His apartment was on the Left Bank near the Invalides, a nice apartment on a quiet street. When we walked in, we shook hands, and then he immediately offered me a martini. Madeleine had champagne. He was short compared to me — six-foot-two or so. His wife was German, very much a *Hausfrau,* not glamorous or intellectual like my mother, but she obviously ran a good house, and she cooked us a good dinner.

The apartment was filled with beautiful old, dark furniture, 16th and 17th Century pieces, a wonderful aura of dark wood. My father explained that he had been among the last American civilians to leave Paris after the fall of France. He carefully placed all his property, including this furniture, in the name of a Swiss friend, whose neutrality would prevent the Germans from seizing it. He was one of the first civilians to return to Paris, coming back in with an advance American Army unit. All his belongings were still right here.

Our dinner together was easy, the most comfortable thing in the world. Maybe his tone of voice was right, as if we had seen each other last week instead of 35 years ago. Madeleine and I went away saying what a nice man he was.

A year or so later he retired from his managerial job at the Commercial Cable Company, the forerunner of ITT. He moved to the Swiss city of Lugano. He said he chose it because if was "the perfect combination," with all the efficiency and neatness and cleanliness of Switzerland, but since it was right on the Italian border, he got all the best of Italy too, including cheap Italian servants. I visited him in Lugano several times before his death. He always had a martini ready for me.

I called him Morgan. I did not call him Dad. It was a bit late for that.

↩ Madeleine's main real estate interest in Europe, soon to become mine as well, was her Spanish property. Before I came along, she bought 20 waterfront acres near the coastal town of Palamos, 60 miles north of Barcelona. The land was gorgeous. It rose up from two-thirds of a mile of beautiful beaches and bays and rocky promontories. Pines and eucalyptus and oleander covered the land, and their perfume was intoxicating. I was

This is how my father Morgan looked when I saw him in Paris after a hiatus of 35 years.

totally smitten: beauty and peace at a seeming endless distance from the rest of the world.

Madeleine had bought the place illegally because at that time foreigners were not allowed to own property in Spain. A Russian emigré named Voivotsky, who had lived in Catalonia for many years, showed her how a middleman could buy the property, then surreptitiously transfer it to her. Voivotsky himself had a 500-acre estate not far from Madeleine's. His house was way up on top of a hill. It took 15 minutes to walk down to his beach and twice that long to climb back up. When he gave a picnic lunch on the beach, his servants carried everything all the way down to the water, and then when lunch was over, they carried everything all the way back. I was terribly impressed.

On her own property Madeleine had started building a *castillo*, the Spanish equivalent of a chateau. The walls were massive dark stone, the roof was red tile. The U-shaped building had a huge patio in the center where we always ate lunch. When I first arrived, the *castillo* was three-quarters finished, but much remained to be done, including all the furnishing. We also had to build a half-mile-long driveway and do all the landscaping. Luckily for us, the dollar was strong, so Spain was cheap.

Madeleine's unlivable French chateau was accessible since it was only an hour from Paris. But her delightful Spanish property was highly inaccessible. First a 12-hour flight to Lisbon, then another three hours to Barcelona. Once there, we had to rent a car and driver and go another 60 miles to reach home. That, of course, is no distance — unless you lived in Catalonia in the 1950s. The roads were unbelievable, a mass of bumps and lumps and potholes. It took three hours of careful driving to get from Barcelona to Palamos. The cars were old, 15 or 20 years old. Everything in Catalonia was old. There was nothing to buy — no furniture and no manufactured goods.

Fortunately we could buy wonderful food — meat, fruit, vegetables. The land around us was fertile and well-farmed. Because no stores or markets existed, we bought direct from the farmers and at very low prices.

The true culinary treat came from the sea. The boats went out at dawn —we would hear the *thump-thump* or their one-cylinder engines — and return in the late afternoon. All the fish and lobster and shrimp and octopus were unloaded in large flats. The townspeople and buyers from as far away as Barcelona drifted down to the Palamos harbor for the auction. Actually it was a reverse auction. The auctioneer started at the top, calling out a high price for a flat of 50 or 100 pounds of fish. Naturally no one was dumb enough to buy at that price. Then the auctioneer began calling out prices in descending order. At a certain point one could feel the tension rising in the crowd until at last a voice cried out in Spanish, "Bought!" The throng relaxed until the next round. It was dramatic because there was only a single bid with no second chance.

Finishing the *castillo* and decorating it was a challenge. We could buy nothing in Catalonia in those days, but there were great artisans. When we needed a chair or a candelabra, we went to the artisan and designed the object together. Except for a few antiques, all our furniture and all our mattresses and cushions and pillows were created individually. All this was inexpensive but time-consuming. On one trip we would design and order a piece. On the next trip we saw it in a half-finished stage when it was still possible to make changes. On the third trip, God willing, the finished piece was delivered to the *castillo*.

Madeleine's special dream was an iron chandelier to hang in the Great Hall. This hall, the center of the U-shaped building, was indeed great: 70 feet long and 35 feet deep with a lofty ceiling supported by wooden beams. Somewhere Madeleine had found an old refectory table made out of a single 12-foot slab of wood. We tried to surround this with furniture of appropriately grand dimension. A big chandelier would be just the thing for this spacious room.

We consulted a famous ironmonger in a nearby town. We made endless sketches, and he then made a small wooden mockup. Fine, we said, that's it. At the end of a year we saw, in his workshop, an imposing mass of iron work. Our sketch had turned into a one-ton monster that required supporting metal rods in the ceiling beams before we could hang it up. Without the rods the chandelier would have torn right through the beams.

The beams were not too solid anyway because we had hungry termites. Lying in bed at night, we could hear them chewing away at the beams above our heads. It was a soft, steady little gnawing sound. When we spotted their holes in the beams, we squirted a mysterious liquid into the openings, supposedly killing the termites or at least discouraging them. In any case, no beams fell on our heads.

We managed to vacation at the *castillo* twice a year, usually in the spring and then again in September after the tourists had left. During the summer months we rented our place, several times to Robert Ruark. He wrote a lot of his bestselling novel *Uhuru* in our house. One fall we came back to find a copy of *Uhuru* in every room.

From my very first days at *Life* I had managed to get away with taking six weeks vacation. It started in the fall of 1937 when I asked for two weeks off to get married. Then the next summer I took my regular four weeks. When no one objected or questioned me about this pattern, I just continued the rhythm of two weeks and four weeks.

Life in Spain was so inexpensive that Madeleine and I decided to build a small second house in a pine-covered point right above the water. All we needed was a pencil, a piece of paper and our builder Señor Roig (pronounced *wretch*). We decided this house should be brick instead of stone, and for a very good reason. Not only were bricks cheap, but you can change your mind as you go along. "This window isn't big enough." No problem. Roig knocked out a couple of rows of bricks, and the window was now the right size. "This doorway is too large." Roig added a couple of rows of bricks, and then it looked fine. Every change we made cost about $50. If you did that with an American architect and builder, you could never afford to finish the house.

↬ Our idyllic, self-indulgent life in Catalonia was in sharp contrast to our normal existence in the U.S. Since the publisher of *Life* has many evening engagements — parties, dinners, professional functions — it was important to have a base in Manhattan. Also Madeleine enjoyed coming in from Darien for theater and restaurants.

Our base was a penthouse apartment in Tudor City. It was spectacular but totally impractical. The dramatic living room was 30 feet high with windows all around. It was so high that one had to erect a scaffolding to clean the drapes. The architect had put a kitchenette on the landing with a tiny stove and tiny sink. Although she did little cooking herself, Madeleine naturally wanted a proper kitchen. The only place to build one was on the top floor. Any dish cooked in the new kitchen had to be carried down a winding stairway to the dining room table on the ground floor. We turned the former kitchenette into a tiny bedroom for our daughter.

The terrace on top, looking westward into the city, was even bigger than the living room. People forget how dirty New York was in those days. If we wanted to take guests to the terrace, we had to go out an hour ahead of time, hose the whole place down and wipe off the furniture. Then for about three hours it would be clean. But next morning if you sat down, you would have dirt all over your clothes.

Although we were in Tudor City once or twice a week, Madeleine preferred to live in Darien, so I commuted. Many commuters in the publishing business are late getting home at night, but unless I had to stay in for a professional function, I was not. My working style was disciplined. I had learned to budget my time, to know what had to be done right now and what could be put off. Problems did not scare me, so I did not try to avoid them. While internally disciplined, I always tried to appear relaxed and good-humored. Since I knew that I personally did not have all the answers, I needed to involve my colleagues so that they would forge answers to problems. The more they felt they were contributing, the better off they would be. I worked hard and with clear purpose, but I never believed that long hours were the answer. I was always home for dinner.

Given this work ethic, I did not believe in working on weekends, or even getting telephone calls during the weekend. I made sure that everybody who worked for me knew there was virtually nothing in the world that could not wait until Monday morning for me to hear about it. I know many managers spend their weekends at the desk or on the phone, trying to convince themselves and others how important and indispensable they are. Since I found this totally unnecessary, I was able to spend many more pleasant hours with my family.

We had a Scottish nanny for Anne Madeleine, and Madeleine brought over a French couple who had worked for her in the chateau. When Anne Madeleine was five, we enrolled her in the Plumfield School just down the road from our house. She was a delightful, well-behaved child who inherited her mother's charm at an early age. She looked a lot like Madeleine but had a rounder face, a childish chubbiness.

Madeleine spent an enormous amount of time with our daughter — too much, in my view. Since this was her only child, born when she was past 40 and had given up hope for children, Anne Madeleine was tremendously important to her. Madeleine hovered over her all the time to make sure that nothing went wrong, that everything was just so. Perfect manners, perfect dress, shoes must never be messy. This attention and devotion were welcome when Anne Madeleine was young, but in the years ahead it would become too much and she would rebel. Of course, Madeleine did it all out of love and pride. She wanted our daughter to be perfect, but you can't do that. Children need space to grow. Anne Madeleine and I got along just fine, in part because I was less demanding than her mother.

My biggest personal challenge in these years was to recapture Diane and Peter, my children from my first marriage. At the time of the divorce their mother for all practical purposes kidnapped them. I was eliminated from their lives. She legally changed Peter's name from Heiskell to Chapin, her new husband's name. She wanted to change Diane's name too, but Diane was four years older and refused. I considered fighting the whole affair in court, but given the circumstances I could foresee nothing but blazing headlines about Madeleine and me, resulting in near fatal damage to the children and my new family. I had to accept a settlement that granted me no visitation rights. I saw Diane and Peter for only two weeks once a year when they were allowed to visit Madeleine and me.

Their first visit to Darien was all stress and little joy. Peter, who was only four when we separated and was now seven, had been brought up to believe that I was an ogre and that Madeleine was something worse. Diane was more independent but not at all friendly. Both kids were more sullen than rude.

Madeleine did not protest or hold these visits against me. She never said, how could you do this to me? But each annual visit was a strain for her — for both of us. It took so long, year after year, to break it down. You just have to live it out. It took Peter years to become reconciled to me, but time and patience finally won.

Our household was enlarged by the arrival of Madeleine's mother Helene, recently widowed. A simple French lady, she took the apartment over our garage. Madeleine's father had been extremely demanding, and Helene had spent most of her married life trying to fulfill those demands. Now, with no responsibilities, she was in seventh heaven. She was living with her beloved daughter and granddaughter. She even loved me, her son-in-law who spoke fluent French. As a fervent Catholic she was delighted that right next door to us was the Convent of the Sacred Heart. Whenever we came home to find Helene missing, we had only to look next door where she would be visiting the nuns.

✍ I do not know what happened to Madeleine and me. I do know when it happened. I also have some ideas about why, but I cannot guarantee that they are right.

In my last two years as publisher of *Life,* in the late 1950s, Madeleine began suggesting that we enjoy spending much more time in Europe. She had come from Europe and longed to return. Since I too had come from Europe, I could understand her dream, but at first I did not fathom its intensity.

When Jim Linen and I were named president and chairman of Time Inc., I instantly saw that it had a big shadow. The shadow was Madeleine.

Madeleine did not like my promotion. She repeated that she wanted to live in Europe. She did not like my becoming more and more entangled in corporate matters, while her own star was fading. She was 55 now, and she did not want to grow old in a country that celebrates youth.

From being a very loving couple for 12 years, we now became a couple staring at somewhat separate futures. I don't think she was running around with anyone else. I know I wasn't. We had no dispute except about where to live. We weren't tired of each other. I had thought I was blissfully happy, and then it all began to fall apart. I was very puzzled. One possibility is that, strange as it sounds, I may never have really understood her. She had had a number of lives before me, and she was a rather complex character, although it did not show in her behavior. I never found myself baffled by anything she did. She always seemed very logical. I suppose it could have been in Madeleine's mind all along that eventually I would revert to being a European and that we would then return to Paris together. I did not hear or sense that during our first eight or ten years — maybe I should have. In any case our goals were now incompatible.

I tried to build a bridge by spending my first months as chairman working out of Paris, but that could only be temporary. If I was going to be chairman, I had to be in New York. And Madeleine decided she really must live in Paris.

There was no single incident, no event. We had just gradually slipped away from each other. We discussed Paris many, many times but without ever having an explosive argument about it. Finally she said she would get her own apartment in Paris. I could let her go, or I could quit my job as chairman and go with her. I made my choice.

We agreed we would stay married and see each other from time to time. To my great sorrow and hers, Anne Madeleine, now 11, must go with her mother. Madeleine also took her own mother, who was in tears because she had at last found true happiness, living with us and the nuns in Darien. Madeleine rented an apartment in Neuilly beyond the Arc de Triomphe and enrolled Anne Madeleine in a strict convent boarding school that she quickly learned to hate.

Our occasional reunions took place either in Madeleine's Paris apartment or at the *castillo*. I missed Anne Madeleine and she missed me. She resented the discipline imposed by both the convent nuns and her mother. It would ultimately turn into rebellion and then self-destruction.

In the meantime, here I was alone in New York. I was 45, very tall, very healthy and said to be more than passably attractive. I had the biggest, most prized position in a glamorous, exciting company. For all practical purposes I was now a bachelor. There were not too many men around with that list of qualifications.

I took full advantage of the situation and for the better part of three years found it great fun. I have always enjoyed women, and now I found myself enjoying quite a number of them. I was traveling all over the world. I had girlfriends in Brazil, girlfriends in Lebanon, many girlfriends in New York. A great life — at least for a while.

Quite a few ladies were looking me over as a serious prospect. The movie actress Joan Fontaine told me we were clearly suited to each other because she had checked me out with Dun & Bradstreet. I wasn't quite sure whether she meant we should get married or that our finances should take the vows. I was fully protected against any sudden, hasty marriage by the fact that Madeleine and I were not divorced.

I did keep one thought firmly in mind. I told myself, "Andrew, I know you are going to get married again sooner or later, but for Christ's sake don't go marrying a twenty-five-year-old." I was not going to marry some young thing and wind up looking as silly as all the other men who make that mistake.

My life changed when, in April 1963, I attended a huge cocktail party given by the *New York Times* for the American Society of Newspaper Editors. The publisher of the *Times* hosted this party every year and invited several thousand people. I thought the chairman of Time Inc. should make an appearance, so I always went. One year the party took place on the Westchester estate of the Sulzbergers, the family that owns the *Times*. We were all startled when a helicopter clattered out of the sky to land on the lawn. Painted on the side were the words "World's Greatest Newspaper." Out stepped Colonel McCormick, owner and publisher of the *Chicago Tribune*. Since the Sulzbergers thought *they* owned the World's Greatest Newspaper, this was a particularly brash arrival.

The 1963 party was held on the 14th floor of the *Times* building on West 43rd Street. This floor has the publisher's office, the board room and a lot of open space. The publisher Orvil Dryfoos was in the hospital, dying of a heart condition, although no one knew at the time how ill he was. His wife Marian Sulzberger Dryfoos served as hostess. I had known her and Orvil before, but only slightly. I was better acquainted with her father Arthur Sulzberger, who had been the *Times* publisher for many years before Orvil took over.

As the *Times* party came to an end and most of the guests had left, I saw Marian sitting alone on a bench. She sat all by herself, looking quite lonely. That's what struck me: here is the wife of the publisher of the great *New York Times* looking so lonely at her own party. She wore a pinkish dress, very simple. She was very well coifed, very pretty. Her hair was gray as it had been since her early 20s. Since she looked as attractive as she did lonely, I went up to talk to her. That was our beginning.

Marian now says she was not so much lonely as exhausted. As official hostess she had had to shake hands with each arriving guest, answer questions about how her husband Orvil was doing, and then shake hands all over again when the guests departed.

I said, "You look very sad. I know you've been invited to *Time* Magazine's anniversary dinner. If Orvil's not out of the hospital, would you like me to escort you?"

Marian said, "That's very kind. I'll ask my husband."

We talked for a while and then I gave her a ride home.

When she asked Orvil at the hospital, he said, "The minute I'm down and out, look what you do!" Then he smiled and told her, "Sure, go ahead." Neither of them knew that he had only a very short time left to live.

Time's 40th anniversary dinner on May 6, 1963, was a stupendous black-tie affair in the ballroom of the Waldorf Astoria. Our guests were 284 men and women who had appeared on the cover. I escorted Joan Fontaine, a cover subject for one of her movies, and Marian, whose husband had appeared on the cover when he became publisher of the *Times*.

When I arrived at Marian's apartment, I asked for a safety pin. I gave her no explanation, just said I had to have one. Marian had three children and a nursemaid, so the apartment should have been full of safety pins, but she looked all over without finding one. At last she uncovered a little sewing packet from a trip to Japan, and inside was a tiny safety pin.

"Will this do?"

"We'll see."

I helped her into her coat and took her downstairs to the limo, where Joan Fontaine was waiting for the safety pin. She had broken her brassiere strap and needed the pin to hold herself together for the party. Joan always said later that Marian had managed to capture me by giving her such a lousy little safety pin.

At the dinner I had to sit on the dais. Every one of those 284 cover subjects had to be introduced. Harry Luce did some, C. D. Jackson did some and our master of ceremonies Bob Hope did some. Each introduction was only about ten seconds long. The party was a grand success except for one thing. Luce was furious that President John Kennedy sent a telegram instead of coming in person.

 ⤳ When Orvil Dryfoos died a few weeks later, I went to Marian's apartment to offer my sympathy and pay my respects. A few months later I asked if she would like to go out with me. After she recovered from

Orvil's death, Marian became an extremely popular widow. She was 44, very attractive and a member of one of New York's leading families. Her younger brother Arthur (Punch) Sulzberger took her husband's place as publisher, and Marian was a member of the board of directors. She went out with what she calls "a wonderful collection of characters," but in spite of all this competition, Marian and I got to be quite close in a relatively short time.

At that point I was beginning to weary of my bachelor life, enjoyable though it had been. Clearly it was not the answer to a lifetime. It was no more than three or four months before I knew that Marian was what I wanted, although I did not tell her so then.

I finagled with the *Times* to appoint Marian the paper's representative to IAPA, the Inter-American Press Association, of which I had been chairman. This gave us a chance to attend the IAPA spring conference together in Santo Domingo, where we had a marvelous time. At the conference in Miami in the fall, we again had a marvelous time.

At the end of this conference I said to Marian, "I've made up my mind."
She asked, "To what?"
"I've made up my mind to marry you."
"Then you'll have to propose."
"I can't propose. I'm still married."
"Then I guess you'll have to do something about that."

I was sure I would have no problem with Madeleine. After all, we had been living apart for three whole years, completely separate lives, and besides, she had always been a reasonable woman. I was prepared to settle the financial side generously, and to make every provision for our daughter. At first I even thought of writing her a letter, explaining that I now wanted a divorce, but I decided that was not the polite thing to do after a long and mostly happy marriage. I told myself, you can't write your wife about something like this. You have to tell her in person.

Since I was already scheduled to visit her and Anne Madeleine in Spain for Christmas, I decided I would tell her then. That was probably not the most felicitous thought I ever had. I should have said to myself that Christmas was not exactly the right time to announce my need for a divorce, but then I didn't think it was going to be that big an issue.

Because of the winter season Madeleine and Anne Madeleine were staying in the little house overlooking the water rather than in the big drafty *castillo*. I saved my speech until the second evening before dinner. We had always worn casual clothes in Spain, but because Madeleine believed in dressing for dinner, she had on a long gown, not fancy but floor-length, and I wore a jacket. It was evening, the lights were on. We sat in armchairs in the modest living room overlooking the sea. We were having a friendly glass of wine together. Anne Madeleine was out of sight in another room.

Now that the moment had come, I felt nervous. I realized this was going to be a little more difficult than I had thought, but I decided I had better get on with it.

"Madeleine, I have something important to tell you. We've been separated now for quite a long time — three years, in fact. I've been content to leave things the way they are, but now — well, I'd like to get married. To Marian Dryfoos, as a matter of fact. So I hope that you'll be willing to —"

I got no farther than that. She began to shriek, loud shrieks. In 15 years I had never heard her shriek before. She did not work herself up to a peak for half an hour and then finally burst into tears. It was as if the stage manager had said, "You're on now." She erupted into instant tears and screams. It was high theater, the big scene from Act Three.

In all our years together she had never pulled a scene on me. She was the most balanced person I could possibly have known. And yet this scene was utterly convincing. It went on and on, shouts and screams and tears and insults. I had never endured anything like it.

And then when she seemed to be finished, or at least slowing down, she yelled out, "Anne Madeleine! Anne Madeleine! Come in here!"

And after a few minutes when our alarmed daughter appeared in the doorway, Madeleine played the scene all over again from the top. *Daddy doesn't love us anymore! Daddy wants to leave us! Daddy hates us! He hates us! He wants to go away forever! He is going to abandon us!*

Anything I tried to say was like pouring gasoline on the fire. Anne Madeleine began to cry. Both of them were weeping, while Madeleine continued to hurl accusations at me. I was a heartless monster.

It was great drama played to the hilt by a fine actress. If the effect on me was so shattering, I can't imagine what it did to Anne Madeleine.

The performance convinced me that there was not the slightest point in my staying around to try to smooth things over. I can't remember one single thing about the rest of that evening. I can't remember what I ate or drank — if anything — or where I slept. The curtain had come down.

Next morning I got the hell out. I telephoned to Palamos for a car and driver and fled back to America.

At the Barcelona airport I sent Marian a brief cable: "BATTERED AND BRUISED, I'M RETURNING."

⌒ When I got back to New York and reported in full, Marian was not very enthusiastic. But she finally said, "Okay, I'll stick it out for 18 months." I thought that seemed generous.

Madeleine hired a high-powered divorce lawyer. I asked Tex Moore, the head of Cravath, my predecessor as chairman, a gentleman and Mr. Time Inc. himself, to represent me. Normally Tex would never touch a divorce, but he had handled my first divorce from Nini, and he was willing to do it again for me. He *loved* it. Instead of his usual dry, intricate law practice he had the refreshing change of a lively divorce suit. He enjoyed telling me how much Madeleine's lawyer was asking for and how tough he was to deal with. Tex was never short-winded, so I heard it all.

Tex and I managed to meet Marian's deadline. My scene with Madeleine took place Christmas week of 1963, and the divorce was settled during the fall of 1964. Marian had the pleasure of telling her father Arthur Sulzberger, "Daddy, I'm going to marry the husband of your former girlfriend."

Any man who gets divorced thinks the terms of the settlement were punitive, but in retrospect mine was not too awful. I gave Madeleine $250,000 of Time stock, half of what I owned, and I bought out her share of the Darien house for the same $25,000 she had put into it. Keeping that house was a great plus for Marian and me. We go there practically every weekend and often for longer visits. Madeleine took whatever furniture she wanted out of both Darien and Tudor City, leaving behind a giant decorating job for my new wife. Madeleine immediately sold the Time Inc. stock at $50 a share, just before it started its climb to $100. Fortunately I held on to my half of the stock.

Madeleine's theatrics were never repeated. In fact, it was just the opposite. In the years following the divorce, she and Marian and I got along fine. She always stayed with us in our New York apartment at United Nations Plaza. She sold the *castillo* and moved to Marabella. It always shocked me that she, who was so much a lady, would choose a place filled with spoiled rich people. Marian and I took a vacation drive around Spain in 1968, and at the end of our trip we wound up in Madeleine's house, much to everyone's surprise. Madeleine once told a mutual friend, "I'm so glad Andrew married Marian. She will take good care of him."

Since everything was so friendly between the three of us right up until Madeleine's death in 1987, how does one account for Madeleine's appalling, shocking behavior that night I told her I wanted a divorce? Many years later when he heard the story, Madeleine's agent Robby Lantz had a simple explanation: "Of course she exploded. She was an actress. An actress must always have her scene."

RUNNING THE WHOLE SHOW

◇◇◇◇

MY 20 YEARS AS CHAIRMAN DIVIDED INTO THREE PHASES: In the early 1960s Jim Linen and I were "feeling our way around" by putting our toes in the water in many different places — without much success. But since the company as a whole was doing all right, so did we.

The second phase was the late 1960s to the early 1970s, a period that featured the death throes of *Life* (see next chapter) and a depression that hurt all our magazines. Every depression hurts magazine advertising pages. This depression was worse than most because television was now stealing ad pages away from all magazines, especially from the mass magazines like *Life* and *Look* and the *Saturday Evening Post*. The general view in the business world at that time was that all magazines were going to die.

The third phase, from the death of *Life* in 1972 until my retirement in 1980, was a period of great activity, great action, great expansion and great success.

Three revolutionary changes in management took place in the '60s. The '60s were, of course, the decade of revolution in all fields — political, social and sexual. However, the '60s revolution at Time Inc. was only by coincidence.

In 1964 Harry Luce, who had been "the Proprietor" for four decades, appointed Hedley Donovan to succeed him as editor in chief. Luce took the title of editorial chairman, he remained on the board, and he was still the company's largest stockholder. But he spent more and more time at his winter home in Phoenix, and Hedley Donovan was now clearly in charge of all editorial affairs.

In 1969 Jim Linen, who had been drinking more and more heavily, suffered a slight stroke. That was sufficient cause for Hedley Donovan and me, with the wise support of Roy Larsen, to remove Linen as president and replace him with James Shepley. Larsen gave up his own title as chairman of the executive committee so that Linen could have it.

That same year the board, which had never been comfortable with Linen's and my undefined dual roles, named me CEO, the first in Time Inc. history. Shepley as president reported to me. The chain of command was at last clear — except, of course, for the unique independence of the editor in chief. That still bothered many board members but never bothered Hedley and me.

It was no surprise when Luce appointed Donovan editor in chief because he had publicly annointed him five years earlier. In February 1958 Luce suffered a serious heart attack at his home in Phoenix. None of us knew anything about it until several years later. Luce passed it off as "a bout of pneumonia," but it obviously made him think about who would be his successor if the next heart attack should be fatal. A year later he invited Donovan to a private dinner in his apartment and said, as Hedley reported to his wife later that night, "he wants me to be him." In September 1959 Hedley became editorial director, a title that had been vacant since John Shaw Billings' retirement.

Hedley Donovan was a large, handsome rock of a man, only one inch shorter than I, built and made in Minnesota. Very, very intelligent. Very, very good judgment. He was sparing in his words and opinions, but whatever he said made solid good sense. He had been an outstanding managing editor of *Fortune.* By sheer presence he exercised enormous authority, and he was respected by all the editors and writers. Respected, not adored. He was not the kind of man who could lead a charge uphill with all the troops cheering wildly behind him. The word most often invoked about him was *integrity.*

He had strong views, but they were not all of a certain shape, the way Luce's were. Once Hedley made up his mind, it was almost impossible to change it, unless you could produce a quantity of fresh new evidence. He did finally change his mind on Vietnam, but usually he held convictions that his editors considered unshakable. He was indeed stubborn. His silences were sometimes more effective than anything he said. He had a way of implying, by a very long silence, that you had just said something pretty dumb.

He had no visible weakness except martinis, and in those days they were not a weakness. He could drink them without any visible effect. Although he had two martinis at lunch every day, I never once saw him blink in the afternoon. Toward the end of his life martinis were less kind to him.

He and I enjoyed an absolutely splendid relationship for 18 years. He was my closest professional colleague in all my years at Time Inc. Roy Larsen and I were closer personally, but that was more of a paternal-filial relationship. Hedley and I were working partners. Any problems or disputes between church (edit) and state (publishing) were settled by us on the 34th floor with a minimum of fuss. We did not necessarily agree on everything, but we always agreed on what was important, what was less important, and what was unimportant. He was far, far easier and pleasanter to work with than Harry Luce.

Our offices were 20 yards apart, and we were in each other's office every day. I was more often in Hedley's office because I have always believed in just dropping in on people with no particular agenda in mind, just to hear what's going on. I've always learned more from listening to my colleagues than from reading reports and memos. Hedley was not like that. If he appeared in my office, he had something substantive to discuss. He was never a casual visitor. In fact, he rarely visited the offices of his editors but always summoned them upstairs to his own office. Every managing editor was accustomed to hear Hedley's secretary say over the phone, "Can you come up to see Mr. Donovan?" Perhaps he thought this style was more suitable to the dignity of his office. He had been a lieutenant commander in the Navy in World War II, and now he was the Admiral.

What surprised all of us, including Hedley, was that when Luce surrendered the title of editor in chief, he surrendered his authority as well. This required tremendous discipline on Luce's part. After all, he had been running the entire operation for 40 years. I was amazed that he could let go of it. He still had suggestions and criticisms, but he made them after publication, not before.

Harry always wanted to get his way by dint of reason and argument rather than by giving orders. He knew he could not hire and keep the best people, the best talent, if he was as dictatorial as William Randolph Hearst or Colonel McCormick. So he spent an incredible amount of time writing memos, trying to win his points without giving direct orders. Books make Luce out to be all-powerful, but he was not a dictator and did not want to be. He kept trying to *persuade* his editors, even after he turned the job over to Hedley. Both men enjoyed the competition of intellectual argument. Harry once told Hedley that he was satisfied to win one out of two arguments. Hedley said he felt more comfortable winning two out of three. (Both men were lying. They both wanted to win them all.)

In a sense, Harry died at exactly the right time, in 1967. His country and his company had been through a period of great growth. The drug scene had not yet overwhelmed us, and Vietnam had not yet become the albatross around the country's neck. All our troubles were lying in wait, but Harry died just before they took over.

Jim Linen, whom we replaced as president in 1969, was a sad story. Always a great salesman, he traveled around the world, showing the company flag, launching new editions of *Time*. But somewhere in the mid-'60s he moved from the business world of international corporations to the more glamorous world of kings and princes and presidents. He became infatuated with the important "friends" he made: the Shah of Iran, President Sukarno of Indonesia, Ferdinand and Imelda Marcos of the Philippines, the King of Thailand. That would have done no great harm if he had seen them when they visited New York, but instead he took to visiting them in their own countries. He probably thought he was accomplishing important things, establishing valuable relationships, but he was the only one who thought so. He was gone so much that people began to resent his freewheeling absences from his real job.

He was also drinking heavily and gaining weight. I kept telling him, "Jim, you can't go on this way because one day this is going to knock you down."

"I don't care, I'd just as soon go like that," he said, with a snap of his fingers.

I told him, "It's nice to think you can go like that, but you're more likely to get felled and be an invalid."

"Oh, no, no. Not me."

His drinking began to show a lot. Incident after incident took place at company dinners and even at public events. He was becoming an embarrassment to Time Inc.

When he had a small stroke, not at all incapacitating, Hedley and I faced up to the problem. We talked to several members of the board and consulted Roy Larsen, a very kindly and considerate man who was much older than Jim and better able to talk to him. We finally forced Jim to resign as president but let him stay on as chairman of the executive committee, with every privilege except responsibility.

Later a second stroke put him in a wheelchair for the rest of his life. Jim was determined that even this would not stop him. He continued to fly around the world, visiting his important friends, accompanied by a male nurse-servant-valet who wheeled him everywhere.

Jim's successor as president was James Shepley. He had had broad experience in both edit and business, a rarity in our company. He had been chief of *Time's* Washington Bureau, chief of correspondents for the *Time-Life* News Service, then publisher of both *Fortune* and *Time*. He was brilliant, irascible and explosive. When he exploded, the entire building shook. But he was very, very capable. When Hedley and I proposed to the board that he be made president and chief operating officer, we did so with some fear of what might happen. When he got *more* power and exploded, the explosion would be even louder.

But it worked out well. It was a good thing he had a boss, more as a brake than anything else. He took great interest in some of the new areas we were getting into: cable, pay cable, forest products. He did a good job and allowed me great freedom.

The final revolutionary change was my becoming CEO. I hated the term and still hate it. It's such a *noisy* title, very undemocratic. It sounds like you're beating your chest. I prefer the title chairman, which is clearly number one. You don't have to embellish it.

I did not like having a lot of people report to me, so I just had them report to Shepley. But everybody had a clear understanding up and down the line that I would wander around anywhere and talk with anybody, not to give orders but to keep well informed. I was probably the most visible executive that Time Inc. ever had because I was forever poking around the

During one of Time's *famous News Tours I enjoyed a tented desert picnic in Saudi Arabia with a quartet of Saudis and a borrowed sword.*

corners and asking questions and picking up ideas. Then I had my visions and desires executed through Shepley.

The '70s were years of many visions, and a lot of them worked out. Although we lost *Life,* we started three other magazines. *Money* had a slow start but eventual success. *Discover,* launched just before I retired, was unsuccessful and had to be sold. *People,* on the other hand, was the most successful magazine ever invented. We brought back *Life* as a monthly, which was more heartwarming than profitable. In the book field we had already acquired the esteemed trade publisher Little, Brown in 1968 and a decade later the equally esteemed Book-of-the-Month Club.

But publishing ventures were only part of the story. In 1973, only two months after closing down *Life,* we astonished Wall Street, all our employees and pretty much the entire civilized world by merging with Temple Industries. Nobody outside the forest products business had ever heard of Temple, a family-owned company that produced lumber, plywood and pulp, with headquarters in, of all places, Diboll, Texas (population 3,557).

What was Time Inc., the publishing company, thinking of? I can explain this today, but it's the same explanation I gave in 1973, which nobody could understand. It is both curious and, to me, fascinating, but it may still be beyond comprehension.

Back in 1941 Treasurer Charlie Stillman had begun investing in what later became Eastex, a pulp and paper business in, as you might guess, East Texas. Eastex made no magazine-quality paper, but the cheap paper it did make was an excellent hedge against the prices we had to pay for our magazine paper. Paper prices are highly cyclical. If — to our dismay — magazine paper prices rose, so — to our delight — did the prices Eastex got for its product.

Although few of our employees even knew that Eastex existed, it was extremely valuable. We owned almost 600,000 acres of timberland, and in years when our magazines did poorly, Eastex provided one-third of Time Inc.'s profits. The Temple acreage was almost as large as ours.

One thinks of forest lands as being one huge plot — say, 20 or 50 unbroken square miles of timber. Forest lands are *not* like that, at least not in East Texas. They are assembled in parcels, a bunch of acres here, another bunch there. They are really little squares, contiguous with other little squares owned by other companies. The Eastex acres and the Temple acres were closely intermingled, and over the years we had been doing convenient business together. We bought wood chips from Temple, which we needed for our paper mill, and they bought trees from us for their lumber and plywood. A nice, neat arrangement for both parties.

Then we heard that Temple was thinking of selling out to Champion, a rival paper company. If Champion bought Temple, it would build a paper mill and start using the Temple wood chips we needed for our mill. We would then have to go farther afield and pay much higher prices for chips, including the high cost of transporting them back to our mill. It seemed more intelligent for us to merge with Temple, paying for it with Time Inc. stock. We probably paid too much, especially since the housing industry was about to go into a prolonged slump, but that is why we did it.

After the acquisition, the Temple family was Time Inc.'s biggest stockholder. Arthur Temple, the president, became vice chairman of our company. This was a mixed blessing.

Arthur was personally delightful. He was a big, burly, Texan, almost totally bald. He usually had a fat cigar in his mouth — he didn't smoke it, he just twirled it and chewed it. He spoke in a Texas drawl, with a folksy sense of humor and a gift for down-home country imagery. When he attended executive lunches in our 47th floor private dining room, his comments were so vivid that Joan Manley, head of the Book Division, and Ralph Graves proposed to take notes and publish a little red book called *The Sayings of Vice Chairman Temple,* modeled after *The Sayings of Chairman Mao.* Alas, like many other publishing projects, this never came to pass. Only two of Vice Chairman Temple's sayings survive in memory. About a project that Arthur thought sounded very unpromising: "That looks to me like the rear end of a billy goat going uphill." And of a project that appeared to be doomed, but with the cost of failure as yet unknown: "We better pull that snake out on the road and see how long it is before we try to kill it."

Other sayings of Arthur's were more public and less welcome, especially to editorial staff members who were already distressed to have a Texas lumberman as vice-chairman. Down in Diboll, Texas, Arthur was used to speaking his mind on any subject without fear of repurcussions. But in an interview with two journalists from *Texas Monthly* and *Village Voice* he was asked, as a joke, if he planned to move Time Inc. to Texas. No, Arthur said, parts of Time Inc. had to be in New York, but then he added in his jovial style that other parts could probably do fine in Oshkosh or Atlanta. The *Village Voice* published a solemn story quoting Arthur as wondering "why *Fortune* couldn't be in Boston or Atlanta, *People* in Los Angeles and *Sports Illustrated* in St. Louis." Although that was not what he actually said, the uproar taught Arthur not to indulge in playful speculation with the media.

As vice chairman and major stockholder and eloquent persuader, Arthur talked the management and the board into buying the Inland Container Corporation for $272 million because it was "the best in the business." Well, it was the best, but the business it was best in was making corrugated cardboard boxes. If you wanted to ship anything anywhere in a cardboard box — a refrigerator, a case of wine, a carton of canned tomato soup — Inland Container was a good bet. In some ways Inland Container was an even more unlikely acquisition than Temple. With Temple, we could explain to anybody who would listen that it was all tangled up with our previously owned company, Eastex. Inland Container was harder to account

The Time Inc. board of directors was headed by editor in chief Hedley Donovan and me.
President Jim Shepley is to the left of Hedley, Vice Chairman Arthur Temple is in the last row
on the left, Roy Larsen is behind and between Hedley and me.

for, but the stock analysts and the Time Inc. staff and the general public all let it slip by without too much fuss. After all, if we had already committed the folly of buying a forest products company, what difference did it make it we added a company that made cardboard boxes?

Temple and Inland remained part of Time Inc. until after my retirement, when the new management spun off forest products as a separate company. I always felt good about Temple and Inland, even though few others did. In the end we probably broke even on the investment. The only damage we sustained came from Wall Street and investor confusion about what kind of company we were. That confusion undoubtedly held down the price of our stock during what was otherwise a major period of growth.

In the '70s we finally struck oil in an area that we had been involved in for years. We lumped it all together under the name of "video," but it was a multitude of different things. We had tried movies, we had tried to bring computers into the schools before the schools were ready. We had bought five U.S. television stations, the limit any company was allowed to own, but thanks to Luce's opposition we were too late for the major markets and wound up in places like Bakersfield, California, and Grand Rapids, Michigan. Even so, they were profitable, and when we finally decided to get out of TV ownership, we sold them for a delightful $90 million. I explained to the board that the reason for selling was that the stations had peaked in value, which turned out to be totally wrong. Okay, the board said, what are you going to do with all that money? I said airily, "Oh, we'll spend it in the video world." Fortunately nobody asked the obvious second question, "Like what?" I wouldn't have had the faintest idea what to answer.

We had also invested in foreign television stations, where we failed repeatedly — with the single exception of Hong Kong, which we sold at such a glorious price that it paid for all the others. *Rule of Thumb for Management:* one or two big successes, like the Hong Kong TV station or *People* Magazine or Home Box Office, can more than make up for quite a large list of small failures.

Home Box Office: who would ever have thought in its early days that this primitive pay-cable operation would turn out to be a success. In fact, based on our own experience in the early days of cable television, who would have thought that our cable investments would be a success? And yet the growth of cable and pay cable, along with *People,* would become our biggest triumphs of the '70s.

Home Box Office was not our idea. It was invented by a cable entrepreneur named Chuck Dolan, who hired a 33-year-old lawyer named Gerald Levin to help get HBO started. He also persuaded Time Inc. to invest. The service, for which subscribers paid a few dollars a month, started in Wilkes-Barre, Pennsylvania, and then tiptoed slowly and expensively across Pennsylvania and New York, delivering not very good movies and sports events to a handful of subscribers. The HBO signal could be delivered to cable systems only by a succession of microwave towers that had to be erected before new cable systems could be connected. Our investment grew and grew until finally we bought out Chuck Dolan. But we kept his young lawyer Gerry Levin to run HBO, because he was the only one who understood it.

I liked the idea of HBO, but I wasn't sure we could ever make it work as a business. When it was first brought to me, we talked about microwave towers as the transmission process, but we never thought about how we were going to get to the midwest, much less to California, in order to become a national business. If we had thought about how impossible it would be, we would never have started it. If I had finished Harvard Business School, I might have known enough never to start HBO at all. But now it was obvious to me that the step-by-step microwave tower process was hopelessly expensive.

Jim Shepley and Gerry Levin thought so too. One day they came to my office with a proposal: the hell with microwave towers, let's distribute HBO by the RCA satellite. We can reach the whole country all at once.

"How much will that cost?"

Shepley looked at Levin, who said, "Seven-and-a-half million dollars."

I said, "Seven-and-a-half million!" That was more than HBO's entire volume of business.

But that is what we decided to do, and it was the right decision. The stock market and the cable system operators thought so too. In April 1975 when HBO announced that it would deliver its signal by satellite to two cable systems in Florida and one in Mississippi, the price of Time Inc. stock went up 20% in five days. From then on, HBO was in the big time. Our satellite decision affected the entire video and cable and pay-cable industry. I wish I could say that I knew at the time how important the decision was, but I didn't. You never realize at the time that anything is important. You only realize that it is horribly expensive.

With HBO's success, we had both feet in the video business. We signed big contracts to buy exclusive rights to films. In fact, Hollywood considered HBO the greatest menace it had ever seen and feared it would take over the movie industry, which of course did not. But once we were in the movie business, we ran into all the mores of movie life, with its pay scales, its limousines, its company jets and its glamor. It took us a long time to figure out how to run it and how to separate it from the rest of the company's normal way of life.

In addition to HBO, which was pay cable, we had a convoluted experience in basic cable, following the emotional and financial ups and downs of that infant industry. At first we were very excited and invested in eight cable systems and several franchises that we expected to build later. They were scattered all over the country from New Jersey to California with no particular plan or rationale. We did not want to be left behind, the way we had been on owning major TV stations.

There were two compelling reasons for a customer to sign up for cable. Small towns and even middle-sized towns and suburbs were often served by only one or two TV stations. If a customer wanted more stations, he had to subscribe to cable. In the big cities that already had all three networks as well as a couple of independent stations, reception was often poor because the signals were blocked by tall buildings, Manhattan being the most stunning example. If a customer wanted good reception for all those stations, he had to subscribe to cable. And in both small towns and big cities, if you wanted to subscribe to HBO or any of the other emerging pay systems, you first had to subscribe to basic cable because that was the only provider. The whole situation sounded like a bonanza to early investors in cable — but we were wrong.

Laying cable was a huge capital investment. It cost around $10,000 a mile in areas where it was possible to hook on to existing telephone poles, but $100,000 to $300,000 a mile in big cities where you had to go underground. Again Manhattan was the most stunning example — and we owned it. As capital costs went up and up, we got cold feet and sold our systems to American Television and Communications (ATC), a large, well-managed cable company. ATC bought all our systems but one. They refused to take Manhattan. They wouldn't pay one dollar for it because it was so difficult and expensive to dig through Manhattan underground, and because they were afraid of all the local politics involved in every franchise decision.

I kept saying, "But you're crazy! If you control Manhattan, you sort of control the U.S." This was just repeating the experience of over-the-air television, where all three networks had their headquarters and originating stations in New York. But ATC would not budge, so we were stuck with Manhattan. The happy ending is that when we finally built the system, it started making $20–$25 million a year. Today it makes much more.

The stimulation of being in New York is very important. More ideas are floating around in New York than anywhere else. Washington is full of ideas, but they are all political. New York offers everything. Harry Luce kept trying to move us out of New York, one of his worst obsessions. We even bought some buildable land in Westchester, and as part of the exploration process a group of editors went out to Pleasantville to have lunch with some *Reader's Digest* editors. Near the end of the lunch one of our editors asked, "When do you get the *New York Times?*" The *Digest* men looked blank, and then one of them said, "I don't know, but if something important happens, somebody will tell us." That absolutely horrified our colleagues, who read all of the *Times* before they arrived at the office.

As part of our deal with ATC, we received about 10% of ATC stock. In only a few years the cable business began to look better and better, so we increased our holding to 20%. Finally, when our success with HBO and Manhattan Cable gave us a really powerful cable position, we went whole hog and acquired all of ATC for about $150 million. The acquisition made us a fortune, we became the second biggest cable company in America. Today cable is the most profitable part of Time Warner. Does that mean we were dumb in 1973 when we sold our cable systems to ATC, but smart four years later when we acquired ATC? Possibly.

But there is no question in my mind that we were dumb when we bought the *Washington Star*. It was a bad mistake, even more punishing to the company's ego than to its bottom line. Although I was briefly a newspaperman myself at the New York *Herald Tribune,* I got over it. Many newspapermen never recover. It's a lifelong disease, like leprosy.

The two former newspapermen who were major instigators for acquiring the *Star* were our president Jim Shepley and our editor in chief Hedley Donovan. Both had been Washington newspaper reporters, Jim for United Press and Hedley for the *Washington Post.* Jim had also been *Time's* Washington bureau chief for nine years, and Hedley had spent his war years in Washington in Naval Intelligence. Both knew and loved the city and had lived there for years. Besides, the *Star* had once been a great Washington newspaper until the *Post* eclipsed it. Maybe it could become great again. Shepley got a bright young financial expert named Nick Nicholas to work up numbers showing how profitable the *Washington Star* could be, and he presented them to the board with great enthusiasm. Putting all those factors together, I suppose they constitute the best excuse for a bad decision.

Because the *Star* was losing money, we spent only $20 million to buy it, but we spent another $65 million trying to fix it. The year after my retirement we gave up. We could not even sell it, we just had to fold it.

I think the one chance for the *Star* to work would have been for Jim Shepley to leave the presidency, move to Washington, become the publisher-editor and take on Kay Graham and the *Post* head to head. I kept sort of offering that to him, but he never said yes. In any case, it probably would not have saved the *Star*.

As our company grew bigger and bigger, it grew harder and harder for many executives to know what was going on in other parts of the corporation. Jim Shepley and Hedley Donovan and I all had a good grasp of the total picture. So did an absolutely invaluable man named Charley Bear. Short, full of energy, cheerful and brilliant, he had been the managing director of Time-Life International and was a company vice president. When Shepley became president, we persuaded him that he needed somebody who could keep track of everything and make certain that no ball ever got dropped. He wisely chose Charley Bear. Charley's title was Assistant to the President, but that does not begin to describe his role. Any department that we didn't quite know what to do with, we gave to Charley. As a group vice-president he was in charge of the personnel department, the legal department, the medical department and the Time-Life buildings and real estate all over the world. He was also Secretary to the Corporation and a member of the board, so Charley knew what was going on. But how were Hedley and Jim and I to inform the other top executives?

My answer was what came to be known as the Lunch Bunch, so christened by Charley's secretary. We met each Wednesday in a private dining room on the 47th floor. At first the group was only half a dozen, but as the company expanded, so did the Lunch Bunch. It consisted of people who had wide responsibility. It never went down to the level of publisher and managing editor, people who were responsible only for a single magazine.

I always had a fairly good notion, an agenda, of what we wanted to deal with each Wednesday. The most important thing for me was to get each of them to know what the other guy was doing and react to it. Once we ordered lunch, I went around the table, asking each one to report, usually on a topic that I had warned them about in advance. After each report, questions and comments were welcome, then on to the next. When they left that lunch, they shared everybody else's concerns. They were no longer outsiders who could say, "Oh, so-and-so is impossible, he doesn't know what he's doing."

Certain amenities went with the lunch. Before we sat down, there was half an hour of a stand-up cocktail or wine. This gave a chance for private conversations between two or three people who wanted to discuss some problem. If you did not have a problem, you could talk and drink for pleasure.

When we sat down to order, I often had littleneck clams for my first course because they were fresh and excellent. However, they were small and there were only six clams. One day I asked the waitress, "Could I have nine instead of six?" The waitress, who served us every week, said, "You're the chairman, you can have any portion you want." Everybody laughed, and from that day on, a frequent order around the table was, "I'd like the chairman's portion of littlenecks."

A far greater amenity than the littlenecks came during the period when Joan Manley, group vice president of books, was making business trips to Iran. The Shah of Iran had decided that he was going to drag his country into the modern world and that he would do this, in part, by importing better books. Since the Shah had all the money in the world to spend, Joan personally did the negotiating to get the various Time-Life Books series into Iran's schools and libraries. Whenever she returned from one of these trips, she brought huge tins of the finest Iranian caviar and donated them to the Lunch Bunch, served on big beds of ice with all the fixings.

These lunches were not all clams and caviar. I remember one lunch that went on until five o'clock because we were discussing how to do belt-tightening. I thought it important that they be part of the judgment process instead of having it imposed on them.

I did not myself learn much from the Lunch Bunch. If I was doing my job properly, I knew ahead of time pretty much what everyone would report. But the other members learned a great deal, and they all looked forward to the event. I still consider it a great management device. I recommend it highly — provided one can achieve the right atmosphere of give and take, of honest reporting, of full discussion coupled with humor. It cannot work if people are afraid, or if the chairman is a dictator. Those two conditions usually go hand in hand.

THE END OF *LIFE*

◇◇◇◇

IN 1959, THE LAST YEAR I WAS PUBLISHER OF *LIFE*, MY
magazine lost money. It was *Life*'s first loss since way back in 1938, when we
were trying to cope with the magazine's runaway success. Alas, 1959 had
different causes. We had an economic recession, which always hurts magazine ad pages. We faced the intense competition of television, especially
threatening to a magazine that featured news and pictures. And we were
burdened with the enormous cost of maintaining our huge circulation.

Just before Christmas, Harry Luce sent me one of his worry-wart
memos. This one was more prophetic than most. We had planned to increase our circulation to 6.8 million. With good reason, Harry now wondered about that goal:

> How *strong* is our circulation (not how big)? Maybe we can tell better in
> the spring. But I certainly don't want to go after 6,800,000 with the feel-
> ing that 20% of it is forced. *That* way is surely trouble.

Trouble for sure — but not new trouble. Our circulation had been
"forced" for years, just like all the other mass magazines. Forced circulation
was the name of the game. Spend, spend, spend to get more readers so you
can charge more for advertising. During 1959 we had actually *lowered* our
already-low subscription price from $6.95 a year to $5.95. We had *lowered*
our 32-week trial offer to $2.98 or barely over nine cents a copy, less than it
cost us to print the magazine. And in a desperate effort to increase newsstand sales we had *lowered* our newsstand price from 25 cents to a ridicu-
lous 19 cents. All this in order to get more circulation, in order to stay ahead
of the other mass magazines, in order to have even bigger numbers of read-

ers to peddle to our advertisers and ad agencies, all of whom were capti-
vated by the magic growing numbers of television.

In the year now beginning, 1960, *Life* would send out 82 million pieces
of mail, to attract new subscribers and to persuade old ones to renew and
then to pay their bills if they did renew. That number is worth a moment's
pause, in awe and horror: *82 million pieces of mail.* That same year in the
close presidential election between Kennedy and Nixon, the largest free
vote in history took place: *69 million.*

I responded to Luce in a memo that was my last major act as publisher
before becoming chairman. The document ran seven single-spaced pages
followed by 29 pages of statistics. Harry knew perfectly well that acquiring
and maintaining subscribers cost a lot of money and effort. Nobody
walked in the door begging to buy a year's subscription to *Life* at the full
rate. Since all our circulation was, in that sense, forced, the only real question was how much money were we spending to "force" each one. I made a
publisher's estimate that our "true" circulation — that is, the subs we obtained at a somewhat reasonable cost — was 5 million. All the rest, at an
unreasonable cost, was "forced."

As a for instance, I said we could look at the percentage return on our
circulation mailings. "Without trying to be facetious," I wrote, "I'd suggest
as another definition that when the public responds at 2.5% on a 32-week
for $2.98 offer, we're not 'forcing,' but that at 1.5% we are."

Remember: that trial offer was just over nine cents an issue. And also remember: when *Life* was launched in 1936, one of the names Luce considered for it was *Dime,* because that was all it cost. The 32-week trial
subscriber in 1959 was paying less per issue than he did 23 years ago at the
newsstand. That cannot be called progress.

Near the end of my memo to Luce, I proposed that we invest the money
to add four black-and-white edit pages to each issue and that we use those
pages — and all our other edit pages — to run big pictures — full page or
more. "I believe that the acceptance of *Life* could be improved immensely
by giving *Life* greater *pictorial* wallop." I didn't want more stories per issue,
just bigger and better pictures. This, I argued, would help us compete with
television.

"TV," I wrote, "has hurt us by providing the public with a lot of picture stories (westerns, plays, news and information). TV by virtue of providing motion, can do better than we can in presenting a *series* of images that tell or seem to tell a story visually. They are doing today what made us famous in 1937."

"But," I said, "they can *never* present the *great* picture. Even when TV has one, it cannot hold it long enough. Our good big pictures are unharmed by TV. Our small pictures have been made rather insignificant. Another reason for considering this course is that while we've been putting more and more money into edit, these dollars have not been translated into more value quantitatively for the reader. I'm sure the reader appreciates quality to a degree, but what he would like more than anything is the feel of more editorial bang for his 19 cents."

At the same time I was writing my memo to Luce, the new editorial director Hedley Donovan was also writing Luce a memo about *Life,* but his was much shorter. He concluded that *Life*'s circulation couldn't grow forever but should probably stabilize at 7 million. "Let *Life* be passed by whoever thinks they can stand the gaff." (A decade later Hedley was enthusiastic when *Life* raised its circulation to 8.5 million, but as he said ruefully after the collapse, "I had been wiser when I was younger.")

Although I did not say so in my memo to Luce, part of *Life*'s problem was that Ed Thompson was well into his 11th year as managing editor. He had been a great managing editor, perhaps the greatest, but he had run out of ideas and energy in that particular job. He was surrounded by the same old familiar faces and was unwilling to make changes.

Only three men in Time Inc. history were managing editors of one magazine for ten years or more — Ed Thompson at *Life,* Del Paine at *Fortune,* Andre Laguerre at *Sports Illustrated.* All three stayed too long at the fair. Eight years, the same as two presidential terms, was about the maximum time in office. The job is so demanding, especially on a weekly, that creative juices dry up. Not only does the editor do things by habit, but the people under him do things by habit. Some of them may be burned out or become alcoholic, but the editor does not want to take action against his longtime friends and colleagues — let the next man deal with that awkward problem. Everybody who worked for Ed was grandfathered. In the last years he had one important high-ranking editor whom the staff learned to consult only between 11:00, when he at last showed up for work, and 12:30 when he went out for a long, incapacitating lunch.

Luce finally replaced Ed Thompson in July 1961. He neglected to tell Thompson that he was replacing him with Ed's righthand man, George Hunt. Hunt, to his own great embarrassment, wound up giving Thompson the news. Luce had an ingrained cowardice about firing people and always managed to get someone else to do it. Actually, Thompson was not fired. He was named editor of *Life,* a higher position on the masthead but lower in every other way than managing editor.

During my first 12 years as chairman of Time Inc., I spent one-third of my professional time — and one-half my emotional commitment — trying to save *Life.* This is more time than I should have spent, and from a pure business view we should probably have given up sooner than we did. I've often wondered how many things I might have achieved in my first decade as chairman if I hadn't spent so much time trying to figure out what the answer was to *Life.* In retrospect, obviously, there was no answer. But you don't let anything that big and important go down the drain without making every last possible effort. I don't begrudge it.

I was well aware that *Life* had a very serious problem that was not going to be solved by a better circulation letter or a better sales force. That was not the nature of the problem. You are left with asking about edit.

A magazine exists because of its editorial content. Everything else is important but subservient. We had been tinkering with the magazine before 1960, but we were determined to find an editorial solution because that was the only thing that might pull us out of the hole. I wasn't mad at Ed Thompson, but his magazine was not working.

A magazine must fill a void, and to do that it must have a clear sense of purpose. Then of course you have to implement it properly and hope to God that the readers will (a) be numerous and (b) be well enough off financially to attract advertising. Only a few successful magazines have survived without advertising. Even *Reader's Digest,* with its clear-cut purpose and inexpensive page size and paper, eventually took ads. Even *National Geographic,* with its clear-cut purpose and extraordinary status as a tax-free institution, allowing it to have lower mailing costs than anybody else and to keep all profits, eventually took ads.

I am towering over two of the greatest and shortest Life *photographers, Alfred Eisenstaedt and Carl Mydans. Eisie and Carl were two of the original five* Life *photographers.*

In the normal magazine market you depend on the advertiser, and in one way or another you have to create an audience that is of value to him. To do this, you have to be very clear about what you are. The names Time Inc. chose for its magazines were simple and easily defined. *Time,* the weekly newsmagazine. *Fortune,* the magazine of business. *Sports Illustrated,* the magazine of sports with lots of pictures. You don't have to do much explaining to the reader. He either wants it or he doesn't. And even if he thinks he doesn't want it, sometimes he comes upon a copy and finds it interesting enough to change his mind.

The strange thing about *Life* is that even in its greatest days when the whole country loved it, we always had trouble defining it, giving it guidelines. (Luce's justly famous prospectus, "To see life, to see the world, to eyewitness great events . . ." is a tone poem, not a definition.) *Life* — the name implies what? It implies everything, which is no definition at all. Over the years many editors and publishers were forced to go through the exercise of trying to define *Life.* Nobody was ever able to say in a sentence or a paragraph or even a whole sheet of paper just what the editor was supposed to be doing — or even what the editor himself thought he should do. In good years this was a problem. In bad years it was far worse. With television as an easy and glamorous alternative for the advertiser, what should you do?

You try everything, both in edit and in publishing.

George Hunt, who succeeded Thompson, was managing editor from 1962 to 1969. A tall, dramatically handsome man, he had been a Marine officer, twice decorated for valor in combat. He was a natural leader and an imaginative and extravagant editor, often carried away by his own enthusiasm and showmanship. "George," Luce told him during his first year as M.E., "you're a goddamned sensationalist."

Hunt ran many pictures at much larger size than in the past, many more full-page pictures and many more single pictures that covered an entire spread. I don't know if he had ever read my memo to Luce about big pictures, but he certainly believed in them and talked often about the impact of "the permanent image." But at the same time, he tripled the number of words in the magazine. He added signed reviews, signed columns and bylined "text trailers." These last were short, signed pieces at the end of a picture story, written by the young reporter who accompanied the photographer and took captions while the pictures were being shot. This was a major break with the anonymous *Life* tradition, but it had the unfortunate side effect of making the reporter think more about his chances for a byline than about helping the photographer get good pictures or about taking proper captions. By far Hunt's most expensive foray into increased text was to create a department of high-priced investigative reporters who spent months and months collecting hidden scraps of information before producing long, intricate articles about malfeasance somewhere in the body politic.

Hunt had been trained as an artist, and he remained a painter all his life. He ran many more art stories in the magazine, and he once devoted an entire special year-end double issue to Picasso. It was Hedley Donovan's favorite issue of *Life*.

But almost everybody else's favorite Hunt issue was Churchill's funeral. It was the greatest news stunt in the magazine's history and could only have been pulled off by an editor who was both imaginative and extravagant. Churchill's grand and gorgeous state funeral (designed in advance by Churchill himself) took place in London on a Saturday, one day after *Life*'s normal closing. The usual *Life* reaction would have been to shoot it in color, send the undeveloped film to New York, develop the film and edit the pictures, lay them out, write the story, close it and send it out to the Chicago printing plant a week later to appear in the following issue.

Instead, Hunt chartered a DC-8 jet and converted the cabin into a *Life* office: a photo lab, an area with layout tables and light boxes, another area with tables and typewriters for writing and editing. During the eight-hour flight from London to Chicago, Hunt's 40-man team developed and edited 70 rolls of film shot by 17 photographers and converted them into a 21-page color story and cover that was on the newsstands two days after the funeral and in subscribers' hands a day or so later. Churchill himself would have applauded. It was his kind of grand gesture.

I applauded too. I have no idea what that stunt cost, but it was worth it because all the dollars spent went straight into the pages of the magazine. It also provided wonderful opportunities for promotion, which were used to the hilt by the promotion department and the ad sales force.

But edit extravagance that doesn't go into the magazine's pages is somewhat different.

Each year Hunt gave a lavish dinner in the ballroom of the Plaza Hotel for his entire edit staff. This event, complete with engraved invitations, cocktails, a three-course dinner with a matching array of wines, speeches and sometimes dancing, became known as the Hunt Ball.

Each year, in addition to their regular vacation, Hunt sent his three assistant managing editors on a one-month "educational" trip anywhere in the world, first class with all expenses paid, and they were allowed to take their wives, also at company expense. (Hunt gave himself and his wife a similar trip.)

Each year during his eight years as M.E. the editorial staff grew and grew in size, even though the number of magazine pages they had to fill grew smaller. This flamboyant style certainly did not give anyone who worked there the impression that *Life* was a magazine in serious trouble. Why should anyone worry? — or work harder?

A deceptively extravagant event took place on the publishing side during this period. Publisher Jerry Hardy, who had moved from the Book Division to *Life,* decided that his ad sales force needed the stimulus of a special sales convention. Not just another Florida trip to Ponte Vedra or Vero Beach. Why not — Portugal? Actually, because Jerry was able to negotiate a good deal on a chartered plane, and because the exchange rate made everything cheap, the Portugal convention probably cost no more than Florida. But it was *perceived* to be extravagant, and perception can matter more than fact.

I went to all the *Life* sales conventions in those years, to show the chairman's interest. Conventions were tough for me. I had to do everything everybody else was doing. I had to play golf and stay up all night playing poker. It's part of the game. And I had to show confidence in the future when I did not have much. Rightly or wrongly, I assumed that the ad salesmen were doing all they could, and that making them feel gloomy would not help.

As chairman I was not involved in George Hunt's editorial budget and did not know some of the details until years later. That problem belonged to Jerry Hardy, as publisher, and to Hedley Donovan, as editor in chief. I don't know what they may have said to him. My own attitude was that we had a $150 million problem, and we were not going to solve it by cutting $1 million out of the editorial budget. I was looking for major solutions.

We constantly tried out different hypothetical equations for the magazine. Somebody would have an idea, and we would run up all the projections, based on the best plausible assumptions. When the figures for that idea did not appear to work — and they usually did not — we would look for another idea and then run up those figures.

We explored the possibility of going from a weekly to a fortnightly. We explored the possibility of reducing the page from *Life*-size to *Time*-size. We explored the possibility of doing both at once. Meantime, to save on production costs, we did reduce the basis weight of the paper, although there was a limit to how far we could go and still reproduce handsome color photographs. We also reduced the "trim-size" of the magazine, shaving an eighth-of-an-inch vertically and an eighth-of-an-inch horizontally, and hoping nobody would notice. Then doing it again a year later. Since weight determined postage, shaving the trim-size and reducing the paper weight cut our cost for mailing the magazine to subscribers.

We tried raising circulation by adding *Saturday Evening Post* subscribers when that magazine failed. Then we tried reducing circulation when it became too costly to sustain 8.5 million subscriptions. We explored and tested the idea of adding special editorial supplements to the magazine, inserts on food and movies for which interested subscribers might be willing to pay extra (they weren't). We explored the idea of changing our editorial approach completely, but the *Post* had tried that with disastrous results: old readers and advertisers resented the changes, and new customers and advertisers were slow to respond.

I never thought a radically new editorial approach would make any difference. We were being killed from the outside by TV, and then when TV went to the 30-second commercial, it was cheaper than a *Life* page and produced far better numbers.

To all magazines, but especially to *Life,* the "numbers" were crucial. One set of numbers was the paid circulation, the total number of people who bought the magazine either by subscription or on the newsstand. This was an explicit, concrete, accurate figure, and *Life* made the most of it with advertisers, because our paid circulation was almost always bigger than our competition's.

The second crucial number was "total audience." This consists of all the people who have seen or read or remembered a given issue of the magazine. It doesn't matter whether they saw it in a barber shop or beauty parlor, in a dentist's waiting room, in an airplane, at a friend's house, or because a neighbor or relative passed the issue along. The average number of "readers per copy" multiplied by the paid circulation produces a magazine's "total audience." This is a far more ephemeral figure than circulation because it is based on statistical sampling, on people's memories and on countless variables. That does not make the figure any less important, because it is what the advertisers believe and use when they are deciding where to place their ads and how much money to spend. Total audience was at the heart of *Life*'s advertising approach — and always had been, ever since the days when Roy Larsen was publisher.

Each year all the country's magazines were studied, analyzed and tabulated by an independent company called Simmons in order to arrive at each magazine's readers per copy and total audience. These "Simmons Figures" were as important to magazine advertising as the "Nielsen Ratings" were to television advertising. *Life*'s Simmons Figures were always at or near the top in both readers per copy and total audience.

Once television became a national phenomenon, *Life* could not hope to match its paid circulation numbers against television viewing numbers. But it could and did try to match its total audience figures against those of television. Our pitch was that more people would see an advertising page in *Life* at a lower cost per person than would see a TV commercial. This was a losing battle — and we lost it.

In spite of its problems as an individual business, *Life* had great value to the company. As I told the board in a report in 1970, *Life* provided $55 million in what we called "deferred income" (D.I.). This was money the subscribers had paid us in advance, and the company could use it for operating expenses instead of having to borrow the same amount from banks at interest. *Life* paid $7 million as its share of corporate overhead, and if it failed, all the other divisions would have to take up that slack. The *Life* name was invaluable to Time-Life Books, Time-Life Records and all the other ventures we were contemplating. I told the board we had no alternative but to press on. And we did.

The outside press and the outside atmosphere were no help. *Collier's* and the *Post* had already folded, and many newspaper and magazine stories predicted — quite accurately, as it turned out — the end of *Look* and *Life*. These reports added to our difficulties because advertisers are much like rats: they leave what they perceive to be sinking ships.

In the final years we changed publishers and managing editors and circulation directors. We hoped that some infusion of new ideas and approaches and cost-cutting might stem the tide. Major stories continued to appear in the magazine. The Astronauts landed on the moon, and our long investment in their first-person stories finally paid off. To worldwide astonishment, Nikita Khrushchev's memoirs, secretly taped in Russia after he was forced from power, appeared in four headline-making installments. (On the other hand, the memoirs of Howard Hughes, fabricated by Clifford Irving, to our great embarrassment, did not appear.) To bring home the Vietnam War in a human way, *Life* ran a lead story in the summer of 1969 called "One Week's Dead." It showed all the American servicemen who had been killed in a single week of combat. The 217 pictures of young men, every picture the same size with no caption or comment except name, age, rank and hometown, ran through 12 pages, row after row, face after face, like a heartbreaking yearbook.

By this time it was too late. We faced an inexorable economic fact: the deferred income that subscribers had paid in advance had become an overwhelming burden of debt to the future. The magazine for which they had paid a low subscription price would eventually have to be delivered at production and mailing costs that had grown far too high. The farther out we looked, the worse it looked.

At last, in 1972, we had to acknowledge that the future was beyond retrieval. Hedley and I and the board made the decision to suspend publication. This was the most painful decision and event of my professional career.

Hedley and I summoned the staff to the auditorium of the Time-Life Building at ten o'clock on the morning of December 8. Because of SEC regulations governing the release of significant information that might effect stock prices, we could not tell anyone in advance what the meeting was about. No doubt some of them guessed. Our announcement to the staff took place at the same time that we were notifying the SEC.

On December 8, 1972, Hedley Donovan and I tell the assembled staff of Life *that we are forced to suspend publication of their magazine.*

Hedley and I had decided that he should be the one to explain the economic reasons for our decision. We hoped that if this came from the editor in chief, the staff would be more willing to accept the decision as an absolute necessity, not just a business-side act to improve the bottom line.

The auditorium was filled and silent.

Hedley had never worked on *Life*, and he was never emotional in public anyway, especially not on a genuinely emotional occasion. Although he later wrote in his memoirs that it was "the most painful day of my professional life," his innate restraint kept him from showing it. He gave a dry, detailed, precise account of the economic realities. While he expressed regret and sympathy, and did so sincerely, no emotion was in his voice.

My speech was shorter and more personal. After all, this had been my magazine for 35 years. I managed not to cry, but I could feel the tears in my voice. This is what I said:

I was hired in '37, six months after the magazine was started, so I can share with you — somewhat, at least — in this painful decision. And however painful it is, I've also been thinking the last few days about the great things that *Life* has done, and I'd like just to remind you of the things that you should be proud of.

Things like the creation of the photo essay, a new form of art.

The coverage of the wars from the Spanish Civil War to Vietnam.

The courage and the talent of the photographers.

The publication of Churchill's memoirs.

A sales force that had the ability to sell three-and-a half billion dollars worth of advertising.

The series on The History of Western Civilization, The Great Religions, The World We Live In, out of which *Life* really created a complete new division, the Book Division.

The publication of Hemingway's *The Old Man and the Sea.*

The contribution that *Life* made by bringing art and science, understandably and interestingly, to the public.

You can go on and on, right on to Lennart Nilsson's pictures of *Life Before Birth.*

So I hope you can join me in taking pride in what has been done. I thank you for all that you have done.

The aftermath of *Life* had some astonishing features.

- The stock market thought we had made a good decision because our stock went up ten points (20%) in two days.
- More than 300 valued employees, many of them long-term, had just lost their jobs in either edit or publishing. We imposed an immediate freeze against outside hiring on all our other magazines and the Book Division, and urged them to take on *Life* staff. Because the quality of *Life's* staff was well known and respected, many requests and offers arrived from outside Time Inc. These were prominently posted all around the walls of a big office where staff members could walk in, read at their leisure, take notes, make follow-up phone calls. Both *Life* edit and publishing created management employment committees consist-

This is how I felt at the close of the meeting announcing the end of Life.

ing of their very best people. They conducted interviews, made phone calls, wrote letters, exchanged ideas about job possibilities for individual staff members. The heroic effort went on for months. Some employees just took their generous severance pay and went off to write novels or climb mountains or build furniture — whatever they had always sort of dreamed of doing. Some took early retirement. But the great bulk of the staff wanted and needed new jobs, and we found them. Virtually every single employee who wanted a job got one.

• We owed a lot of money to *Life*'s subscribers, and we certainly did not want to give it back if we could possibly help it. Instead, we wrote a charming, persuasive letter to each one, offering the chance to convert the remainder of the subscription to one of our other wonderful magazines, whose virtues were fondly and compellingly stated. If the subscriber read to the very end of the letter, it was possible to discover that he could have his money back if he really wanted it. To our delight, a great many subscribers chose one of our other magazines. This had two significant results: (1) we did not have to give back all that money, and (2) the other magazines got a circulation windfall. This meant they did not have to go through the expensive and laborious process of acquiring that circulation on the competitive open market. Thanks to this "free" circulation, our magazines now had the leeway to raise their subscription prices — and did so.

After *Life* and *Look* and the other big magazines were gone, we entered a period where there was less resistance to circulation mailings. Circulation letters got a higher rate of response. I don't think it was because the letters were any better. I can't prove it, but I believe that the absence — the disappearance — of all that circulation pressure from the big mass magazines improved the climate for the survivors. Some 150 million circulation letters vanished. Instead of a flood it became just a river. So response improved, and we could raise prices.

• I felt that the name of *Life* had enormous value if we could only realize it. To give up that name would be like throwing away a gold mine. For the next six years we kept *Life* legally and technically alive by publishing two special issues a year, one on a target of opportunity, the other on the Year in Pictures. But this was not enough to make the name resonate. Finally in October 1978 we brought *Life* back as a monthly. Some of the staff, including the two top editors, Phil Kunhardt and Eleanor Graves, had worked on the old weekly *Life,* but some were brand new. The monthly is now 20 years old. It has 1.5 million circulation and sometimes makes a small amount of money — $7 million in 1997. It is, of course, a totally different creature.

I played almost no role in the six years of those special issues. And I played only a small role in *Life*'s revival as a monthly, although I made the final decision and was happy to have the name restored to regular publication.

But I had been so goddamned tired of the weekly *Life* for eight or nine years, leaning over it all the time, harrassing the publishers, trying to save "my magazine." When we finally gave up, I was happy to turn to all the other parts of the company that needed the chairman's attention.

LIFE WITH MARIAN

◇◇◇◇

MARIAN ALMOST MISSED OUR WEDDING. IT WAS SCHED-
uled for January 30, 1965, to be followed by a week's honeymoon in Caneel
Bay and then a week of sailing around the Virgin Islands. A few weeks before, Marian developed an extremely painful back that got worse and
worse. We joked that it might be a psychosomatic reaction to the prospect
of marrying me. Her doctor told her, "You can either get married or go into
traction, and I recommend traction. You definitely cannot go sailing."
However, Marian is a determined woman. She took lots of aspirin, went
her own way, and her back got better. Backs often do cure themselves.

Our wedding took place as planned, in the living room of her parents'
Fifth Avenue apartment. Only family and a few close friends were present,
perhaps 30 people altogether. Marian's father, Arthur Hays Sulzberger, had
suffered several strokes, but he was able to attend the ceremony. Her remarkable mother Iphigene was emphatically present.

Iphigene was then 72 and would live to be 97. She was very small, even
shorter than Marian, no more than five-feet-two. She had gray-white hair,
was a little plump and very lively. She was a wonderful conversationalist —
and a powerhouse. She never directly exercised her power, but members of
her family simply did not do things they thought she would disapprove of.
No orders were given, no commands were issued, but by and large people
did what they thought Iphigene would want. In addition to marrying the
woman I loved, I knew I was also marrying into a matriarchy, but once
again I was intrigued by the idea of family and of not being by myself. Besides, I thoroughly enjoyed the matriarch.

We did go to Caneel on our honeymoon and we did go sailing without
damaging Marian's back. Our 40-foot chartered sailboat had one object I

A couple of bare-chested friends, myself and my daughter Diane's son James, stroll a beach in Portland, Oregon in 1965.

have never seen on a sailboat before or since: an electric fireplace that produced fake flames.

My apartment at Tudor City was a wonderful place to entertain, but with only one bedroom and only one bathroom that you could reach only through the bedroom, it was very inconvenient. We moved into Marian's 12-room apartment on Fifth Avenue, but she had lived there 17 years with her first husband Orvil. We both wanted to start fresh, with a place of our own.

We would need a large place to accommodate all the children and relatives we now had. I had three children — Diane, Peter and Anne Madeleine — and Marian had three — Jackie, Susie and Bob — and the first of our 11 grandchildren was born soon after we married. By an extraordinary coincidence, we found our new apartment in the exact spot where I had once planned to build the second Time-Life Building.

By the early 1950s Time Inc. had outgrown its old building in Rockefeller Center, and a group of us was shopping around for a new place to build. My friend the real estate magnate Bill Zeckendorf called one day to say he had the very spot for us. He took me to see an area of somewhat disheveled warehouses at First Avenue and 49th Street, way over next to the East River. Bill pointed out that there was plenty of space for a splendid building, and I could have an office on a top floor with a magnificent view of the river. It struck me as perfect, and I notified our team that I had found the spot.

A few days later the team came to my office to make a few points.

"Andrew, how do you expect people to get from Grand Central Station to the office?"

"Walk, I guess." About a 15-minute walk, I thought, if one had long legs and was in good health.

"And how about all the people who use Pennsylvania Station instead of Grand Central?"

Oh-oh. That would be either a very much longer walk or two bus trips. "I hadn't thought about that," I admitted.

Then a third member of the team said, "You realize, Andrew, that if we build there, you will not be able to employ any women."

Since a large part of our staff was female, including all the researchers

and all the secretaries on all the magazines, that would have been preposterous. "Why not?" I said.

"What do you think women like to do at lunchtime?"

One possible answer occurred to me, based on my own experience, but
I suppressed it. "What?"

"They like to *shop*. There's no shopping on First Avenue. It's half a mile
from Saks."

So I called it off, and we eventually built on Sixth Avenue between 50th
and 51st, close to good shopping.

A decade later, after Marian and I were married, I got another call from
Bill Zeckendorf. "I'm building the most magnificent residential building in
New York. Wonderful penthouses! You have to live there."

I told Bill we couldn't afford a penthouse. I was, of course, doing very
nicely as chairman of Time Inc., but I had all the expenses of the Darien
house, as well as child support. Marian, in spite of being one of the four
Sulzberger children who owned the *New York Times,* had little income. Under her grandfather's will, all the income from the paper went to his daughter Iphigene during her lifetime. His four grandchildren were not
permitted to invade capital, so while Marian's income would someday be
substantial, at the time we were househunting, she could contribute little.

But even if we couldn't afford a Bill Zeckendorf penthouse, it would be
fun to look. Bill, in partnership with Alcoa, had built the two United Nations Plaza apartment buildings on the exact site where I had wanted to
build for Time Inc. The U.N. Plaza was not quite finished, but a few tenants had already moved in, and we were told we could visit every floor.

Marian and I arrived at 870 U.N. Plaza, found the office that was conducting tours and selling apartments, and asked the man if we could see the
penthouses.

He looked at us strangely. Then he said, "There are no penthouses."

To Bill Zeckendorf, anything he built was a penthouse. If he built a basement apartment, he would call it a penthouse. But as long as we were there
anyway, we took the tour. We loved it, we decided this was where we
wanted to be, and we picked out a river-view apartment on the 31st floor.
We have lived there for the last 33 years.

Marian and I had a peculiar feature to our marriage. We had to be careful not to tell each other anything about our businesses. Although her family was principally in newspapers, and my work was principally magazines, a conflict of interest was always possible between the *Times* and Time Inc. We were both in publishing, we both bought paper and presses for our products, we both dealt with mailing and distribution and unions, we were both in the marketplace for new acquisitions and start-ups. Our editors were sometimes chasing the same stories and the same sources.

As a Sulzberger, Marian was on the *Times* board, her brother Punch Sulzberger was the publisher, and she knew everything important that was happening at the paper, or that might happen in the future. I was in the identical position at Time Inc. So we had to keep our mouths shut about what was a significant part of both our lives. Marian still remembers once bursting into tears because of the frustration of not being able to tell me something. Neither of us now remembers what it was, but we both remember the frustration.

When we were married, Marian was somewhat active in environmental causes but nothing like what she does now. She took care of our homes, both in New York and Darien. Darien posed a special problem for her. Madeleine had taken her own furniture back to Paris, but she left several chairs and couches that had been custom-made to accommodate my height. Marian is only five-feet-three, so if she sat back in one of these, her legs stuck straight out in front of her. She also disapproved of much of Madeleine's decor. She hated the living room's brown sailcloth curtains covered with sailboats. She hated the carpets piled on top of each other in front of the fireplace. She hated the dining room's pink damask drapes and the cardboard closets in the corners of the bedroom that Madeleine had installed for her clothes. She hated the pink master bathroom. She found the whole look of the house "hideous, gloomy and quite ghastly." It took her many many months to decorate it to her satisfaction — and to mine.

The Darien house has been my anchor all my life. Without Darien I'd be dead. Marian loves it too, thank God. It's just marvelous, so beautiful. I can sit all day in Darien saying, "Isn't this beautiful!" I'm such a bore about it. I even bore Marian, and she likes it as much as I do. The best thing Madeleine ever did was push me into getting that house.

I used to say that the Mediterranean changed me entirely. As soon as I

This portrait of my wife Marian has faced me across my office desk for the past dozen years. It is my favorite picture of her.

got near it, my state of mind would change for the better. Gradually the Darien house on Long Island Sound took over that role. I even call my terrace beside the pool "my Mediterranean," because it's right on top of the water and so peaceful. Unless we are travelling or have some compelling engagement — and it has to be truly compelling — we go to Darien every weekend all year long. It always restores me.

We have more guests in Darien than we used to have. We have more people joining us on the weekends — some family, some friends. Most of the friends are related to our interests in the nonprofit world. Marian likes to have people at Darien more than I do. I don't mind people, I enjoy them, but I see an awful lot of people during the week, so I prefer not to see too many over the weekend. Marian doesn't feel that way. She really likes people. It's not that I don't like people, but sometimes enough is enough.

From the time we were married, I encouraged Marian to play a bigger role in the outside world, both profit and nonprofit. Corporations were just beginning to realize that it might be a good idea to have a woman on their board. The first business board Marian served on was Consolidated Edison, the New York City utility. This fitted in perfectly with her environmental interests. She also served on the boards of Merck and Ford.

I was never on corporate boards. When I was at Time Inc., I knew conflicts of interest would be unavoidable, because our magazines might well do a story on any company where I was a board member. Besides, I find businessmen a little boring. Conversation with businessmen is about what you would expect it to be. They aren't very interested in books or the theater. After all, I did quit business school for a reason: it bored me.

Marian's favorite corporate board was the Ford Motor Company, which she joined as the first and only woman. Henry Ford, the well-known lush and philanderer, was chairman and ran all the board meetings. Marian said that no matter what he had been doing the night before, he always ran the board meeting with skill and authority.

Not only was being on this board a glamorous and fascinating position, but one of Marian's perks was two brand new Fords every year — any model and color she wanted. Each year she turned in the "old" cars for two fresh models.

This became an even more glamorous perk when Ford took over

Britain's Jaguar. By that time, Marian had had to retire from the board because she had reached the age of 70, but her perks were grandmothered. She was still entitled to her two new cars every year, along with a director's pension. However, when she picked out a green Jag, she was told that she could not have it because she was retired. That would have stopped me, but it didn't stop Marian. She pointed out that they were still sending her Jaguar brochures, and she told a good friend who was still on the board about her problem. A few weeks later she got a call from Detroit saying she could have a Jag after all. But like all active directors, if she chose a Jag, she would have to make it last two years, not one. What an imposition!

So far she has had two green Jags, one red and now a blue. She has driven them back and forth between New York and Darien. She is an excellent driver — furious, fast, determined, with some lack of respect for any other driver on the road. I also drive but, by her standards, rather timidly. Her driving makes me nervous, mine makes her crazy. "You could have made that light!" she will cry when I slow down for an amber signal.

Marian has greatly expanded her participation in nonprofit work. She is on the board of practically every organization — state, local and national — that deals with parks. She is a super authority on parks. She is also on the board of the Audubon Society and the Council on the Environment, which she helped to found.

For the past several years her most demanding work has been The New 42nd Street. She is the chairman of this group, which is dedicated to changing one block on 42nd Street from a tawdry, crime-ridden slum to a bright, modern entertainment thoroughfare, with handsome new buildings and refurbished old ones. Her other boards require regular meetings, but 42nd Street is a very busy job with daily activity. The project has been highly successful during the past six years. From her office in the *Times* Building she can look right down on 42nd Street and see everything that happens on her project.

The biggest arguments we have in our life together are over conflicts between our respective involvements. Our evening calendars are terribly full. Dinners, theater benefits, awards, annual fund-raising banquets — always

During a vacation in Caneel, my wife Marian and I wear T-shirts promoting her favorite nonprofit undertaking, The New 42nd Street.

with someone else in tow so that we are rarely by ourselves. Arguments go like this:

I'm always having to go to your goddamn dinners, and you never go to mine. (Often said but not true: we both go to each other's goddamn dinners.) *You're always having to work when I want to do something else.* (Sometimes true.) *You come home too tired to do anything fun.* (Sometimes true, and probably more true as we get older.) *For God's sake, do you have to put everything away every minute?*

This last is my complaint, not Marian's. She is a compulsive neatener. No piece of paper, no magazine, should ever be left lying on a table or on the piano. Pick it up and put it away. Every drawer has to be closed — if it's open one inch, close it. She inherited this excessive neatness from her father, who insisted that his socks be kept rolled up and positioned in a straight line.

I am personally lazy around the house. I can't fix anything. I resent it and I can't do it. So it's just as well to have Marian and our servants, both in New York and Darien, pick up after me and fix things for me. She says I require a lot of picking up after. Marian has enormous energy that she has to consume all the time. She has to be doing something because relaxing is not her style. Relaxing is very much my style, and Marian says I am getting even better at it as I get older.

Fortunately we like many of the same things but not all. We both like good food, although I like it more than she does. I like wine better than she does, but now I'm not allowed to drink much because I have something called peripheral neuropathy, a disease of the nerves that attacks the extremities (hence "peripheral"). The doctor who tried to determine the cause was sure it was alcohol and was very disappointed to discover it was not. However, alcohol does worsen anything involving the nerves, so I'm allowed only one glass of wine a day. I drink two.

Marian likes sports and I don't. I love to read, and I read all the time with great pleasure, but Marian has had to fight dyslexia all her life. When she was growing up, nobody recognized it, so nobody knew how to help her. Reading was a terrible struggle for her, and she kept getting thrown out of schools for bad grades. Her family thought she was simply refusing to work, which made things worse. Marian not only didn't go to college, she never even finished high school. We are the worst educated successful couple that I know.

For presents, I gave Marian a lot of jewelry, especially necklaces, but now she has developed a sensitivity at the back of her neck caused by bone degeneration and cannot wear anything heavy. She can't even carry a camera around her neck, so a hefty Buccellati gold necklace is out of the question. She gives me books and gorgeous wine decanters. I often disappoint her by pouring wine straight from the bottle instead of using a decanter, but as she says, the decanters look decorative even when they are empty.

We both enjoy clothes. I used to buy some clothes for Marian, but now she buys for herself. She enjoys putting on nice clothes and has quite a full armoire of evening clothes, but she is not a clothes-buying junkie. I no longer buy clothes for myself, as I once did. I bought excellent suits, both winter and summer, and I take care of them. Since they never seem to wear out, I have no need to replace them.

Marian loves backgammon, while I refuse to play because I have too many other things to do. Marian won't acknowledge that backgammon is a disease. When we go to Jamaica, she looks forward to long, long backgammon sessions. I used to play bridge fairly well and loved it, but now the occasion never comes up. Somehow we never meet a couple that wants to play bridge. She would rather play backgammon anyway.

She is a passionate walker and keeps careful track of distances. In New York City, 20 north-south blocks make a mile and so do 12 east-west blocks. She adds up every block she walks, and when I come home in the evening, I get a report: "I walked three-and-a-half miles today."

We both love to travel, anywhere and everywhere. Our most adventurous trip was to drive through Eastern Europe in 1968. Few tourists went to Eastern Europe in those Cold War days, but that was part of our adventure. To make things still more sporting, we took Marian's 18-year-old daughter Susie and my 15-year-old daughter Anne Madeleine. I was a bit surprised that Madeleine let me borrow Anne Madeleine for such a reckless occasion.

We plotted our trip with considerable care, because tourist hotels were limited. We knew many of the roads would range from poor to bad, and that gasoline stations were scarce. We rented a big diesel Mercedes — diesel because all the trucks used diesel fuel. Diesel fuel was not very available either, but at least it was more available than gas. We set off from Trieste and drove down the Yugoslav coast through Dubrovnik and all those other ancient cities that have now been bombed and shelled in the Bosnian war. Road signs were a mystery, as they would be all through our trip, and almost nobody we met spoke English, but we got by on my French and German. We drove through Hungary and Czechoslovakia and Poland. The food was pretty bad away from the capitals and not good in the capitals.

In Budapest we made our most "extravagant" purchase of the entire journey, a complete set of the famous Herend china for $330, which we still use in the Darien house. That sum is about what you would pay today for a single Herend serving platter.

We emerged from Eastern Europe through East Berlin and went through the Berlin Wall at the infamous Checkpoint Charlie. Of all the cities we visited, East Berlin was the grayest and the most depressing. To reward ourselves for three weeks of somewhat primitive tourism, we spent a final week of luxury in Copenhagen and Stockholm. Our daughters got along fine throughout the trip, partly because they were new stepsisters and partly because they had no available alternative. Anne Madeleine was so thrilled to be spending this much time with her father that she practically took me over, always walking arm in arm with me, leaving Marian and Susan to bring up the rear.

Marian and I no longer travel as much as we used to, although I go to Rome once a year to visit the American Academy, where I am a trustee, and we tack on occasional side trips to London and Paris. Sometimes we travel to London for a long weekend, just looking around, going to the theater, staying at the Connaught. London is the only city that I love in the rain.

My height never bothers me while travelling. On airplanes I can always stretch my feet out under the seat in front of me, and hotel beds are longer than they used to be. My worst height problem is right here at home in taxis. New York City taxis are impossible. I have great trouble getting into or out of them, and it gets worse as I get older.

Every Christmas we go back to Caneel Bay, where we spent our honeymoon, to celebrate the holidays. Sometimes we bring one or more sets of our children and grandchildren. With the exception of Anne Madeleine I was fortunate to be able to be proud of my children and grandchildren. My

My daughter Anne Madeleine was 15 at the time this picture was taken during our 1965 tour through Eastern Europe.

daughter Diane is a well-known child psychiatrist. Her two grown children are James, a budding author, and Scott, who teaches in the public school system. My son Peter has done well in the brokerage business. He and his wife Didi have two children. Geoffrey teaches in a private school, and Sarah is finishing college. I think — or perhaps hope — that we get along quite well despite a difficult start. Of course Marian has had a lot to do with that. Once Marian and I gave our entire family, all of hers and all of mine, a Christmas present of a full week at Caneel, including air fare. That really breaks the bank.

Marian once had a bizarre accident at Caneel. She was swimming alone, out in the middle of the bay, wearing a white bathing cap. Without warning, she felt a hard blow on top of her head, and as she looked up, she saw a big pelican flying away. This pelican had obviously said to Marian, "You're a fish," and dive-bombed her. At the last moment the bird must have realized she was a no-good fish and turned away after a glancing blow. If she had been hit head-on, it could have split her skull.

As it was, she came back to our cabin where I was reading and said, "A pelican just hit me." Then she took off her bathing cap, and it was as if someone had thrown a bucket of tomato juice. Blood all over the place, her whole head was covered with blood that had been held in by the cap. I jumped to my feet yelling "My God! My God!" Marian being Marian, she said, "Oh, it's nothing," but I rushed her off to a hospital and got her sewed up. She still has a welt. And people still come up to her at Caneel and say, "Oh, you're the woman who was attacked by the pelican."

Now it makes an amusing story, although it could have been serious. What happened to Marian in the spring of 1997 was not amusing at all. She almost died.

We were out at the Darien house having dinner on a Saturday night. Marian said she didn't feel like eating because she had an upset stomach. She went upstairs to lie down. An hour later she had great pain and some swelling. We were in the silly position of never having bothered to get a Darien doctor, but I called two neighbor friends who knew what to do. In a few minutes an ambulance arrived and we all rushed off to the Stamford Hospital Emergency Room. Over the next few hours three or four doctors examined her and gave her various tests but could not figure out what was wrong. Marian was in severe agony with her stomach expanding. I begged the doctors to give her a painkiller but they said it would interfere with the test results. Finally in the middle of the night a senior doctor arrived who was said to know about intestinal problems. More tests but still no answers.

We were told to go home and come back in the morning. I attribute this extraordinary decision to two things: (1) new insurance rules that said you could not book someone into a hospital room without a diagnosis, and (2) bad medicine.

Sunday morning at the hospital provided no answers, so we went back to the Darien house where Marian spent the rest of the day — as best I can describe it — screaming quietly.

Monday morning we drove back to New York. Our internist took one look and said, "She has an intestinal blockage." Off to Mount Sinai Hospital for immediate surgery. By now part of her colon had turned gangrenous. The surgeon had to cut out four-and-a-half feet of intestine. What had happened was that her intestine had wrapped around old scar tissue from a previous operation and locked.

Over the next two days Marian started getting better, with me and her two daughters in constant, rotating attendance. I went home one night, went to sleep, then got a phone call saying that Marian was losing all sense of reality and was being moved to intensive care. Back to the hospital to the Intensive Care Unit. Marian was not dead but she was barely with us. Next morning we learned that a blood clot in one lung had caused a pulmonary embolism. More than two days in ICU. All her systems slowed down, and she was plainly in serious danger. Lots of specialists came in to consult and advise and give medication.

When she pulled out of the embolism and her blood clots dissolved, she was out of danger — but then developed an abscess in her surgical wound. By that time a mere abscess sounded no worse than a bad cold. Indeed it was cured, and she was finally released from the hospital. It took her four months to recover and to be herself again.

All sorts of things go through your mind during a prolonged crisis. I had many, many hours to think about all the good times we had had together — and to wonder, will we ever have any more?

We were lucky. The answer is yes.

This may be the only surviving picture of me with a beard. I grew it in the late '70s during a long vacation in Turkey. Soon after returning to New York, I shaved it off by popular demand.

ANNE MADELEINE

◇◇◇◇

WHAT HAPPENED TO MY DAUGHTER ANNE MADELEINE WAS
the greatest tragedy of my long life. Even now, 15 years later, it is painful to
think about her or to talk about her. She had been such a pretty, loving,
bright little girl.

When my wife Madeleine moved back to Paris in 1961, Anne Madeleine
was 11 years old. After that I saw her perhaps once a year on visits to Paris.
I missed her very much, and I know she missed me. Her life in convent
boarding school was strict, and her life with Madeleine in their apartment
in Neuilly was strict, too. Madeleine's strictness was loving and devoted —
but too much so.

I used to argue with Madeleine that our daughter needed fewer rules and
more freedom to grow, but it was difficult to be persuasive when we were
no longer living together. I am not sure I could have persuaded Madeleine
even if we had still been together. She was convinced she knew what was
best for her only child, and a mother's convictions can be unshakable.

During the years that Anne Madeleine was still in school in France, the
only extended period of time I spent with her was when Marian and I took
our daughters on a month-long tour of Eastern Europe and Scandinavia.
During those weeks she was certainly affectionate with me, even possessive.
I was very pleased to have her with me again.

Marian's daughter Susie, three years older than her new stepsister, has a
vivid memory of Anne Madeleine on that trip: "The most beautiful fifteen-
year-old girl I've ever seen in my life. She was statuesque and looked
twenty-five. The rest of us wore comfortable traveling clothes, but she had
a marvelous navy blue suit and elegant shoes. She also attracted men —
honey in a beehive."

The two girls had never met before, but Anne Madeleine instantly adopted Susie as a full-fledged older sister. She poured out everything to Susie, all her innermost thoughts and feelings, including the fact that she hated her mother. She told horrible stories about her mother and said how much she wanted to escape from her. Marian and I heard none of that, but Susie thinks Anne Madeleine was absolutely desperate for love and friendship. And she adored her "new family."

⤳ Three years later when Anne Madeleine finished her schooling at 18, she came to New York to visit Marian and me. The "visit" stretched on and on. I have to think now that she never intended to go back to France and her mother. And Madeleine never tried in any way to get her back.

Anne Madeleine moved into our guest room at 870 United Nations Plaza and spent weekends with us at our house in Darien. She was tall, five-feet-eight, with dark brown hair. She had a strikingly beautiful face and a beautiful, full-breasted figure. Marian's daughter Susie remembers: "All my boyfriends — *whissht*, right over to Anne Madeleine."

The late 1960s, with all the newly-discovered freedoms concerning drugs, liquor, sex, clothes and anything else you care to mention, was a dangerous time for young people. It was especially dangerous for a young woman who had been leading a sheltered, almost cloistered life. Anne Madeleine became a perfect victim.

At first she was quite pleasant to live with, although the men she went out with and sometimes brought home to the apartment were far less pleasant. *Scruffy* would not be too harsh a word.

When she had lived with us for almost a year, she announced that she was definitely going to stay in America and needed to have her own place. I thought so too. I knew it would be a relief for Marian not to have Anne Madeleine in our life fulltime, and I thought my daughter had to learn to live on her own. At the time I was all for it.

Anne Madeleine chose the most godawful hole in the wall on East 28th Street. She got into weird habits and began to play games with me: *Now I'm here, now I'm there, now I'm gone.* She would come back briefly into our lives, either for a dinner at the apartment or for a weekend in Darien. More and more often she arrived under the influence of liquor or drugs. With the passage of time she made less and less sense. It became an ordeal to have her with us for a meal. She would come to the apartment all smiles and sweetness. Then I would ask her a question — not an attacking question, merely an idle question — and she would turn it into a controversy. First she would gently fly off the handle, then get worse and worse.

She had the idea of becoming a translator at the United Nations and took lessons, but then she gave it up. She tried other things and gave them up.

Madeleine never said she had completely given up on our daughter, but she had. I never realized it at the time. Madeleine came to New York for occasional visits and was always very lovey-lovey with Anne Madeleine, but she never pressed to get her back.

Over time Anne Madeleine grew heavy and then she tried not to eat. She had been big, pleasantly rounded, but now she began to look inflated, not healthy. In an effort to improve her appearance, about which she was vain, she had a breast-reduction operation. She became extremely difficult and argumentative about what she could and could not eat.

She had frightful friends. She had a girlfriend, a close buddy, who was not exactly a prostitute but tending in that direction. She had a terrible man, a minor mobster with a leather jacket and a bare hairy chest decorated with gold chains. He seemed to have her entirely in his power. She would not hear a word against him.

If I objected to her behavior in any way, she screamed at me. Sometimes I screamed at her. I remember slapping her once. She had a great talent for getting my goat. I think she enjoyed making me mad at her. Perhaps it was a way of proving to herself that if I got angry, I must care about her.

Obviously Anne Madeleine was in serious trouble and needed professional help. At various times I managed to get her into medical institutions — one in White Plains, one in New Canaan — to dry out and receive medical therapy. Once she contracted a serious case of liver poisoning with many complications and had to be in a hospital for four weeks. The bill was one of those random numbers that somehow sticks in one's mind: $146,000.

Even in this terrible period Anne Madeleine could sometimes be quite pleasant. In photographs she often looks radiant. She had been beautiful, but as the years passed, she looked more and more coarse. She tried to hide this with heavy makeup. Her face and her whole body grew more and more puffy. She was loaded down with medical problems. Something was always wrong with her. But her psychological problems were even worse than her medical problems.

I finally persuaded her to see a highly-recommended woman psychiatrist on a regular basis. Although I never met this doctor, I talked to her a number of times on the phone. After several months she told me that she was "quite pessimistic" about Anne Madeleine because she was not making any progress. She said she was very worried about her patient. I suppose she was trying to warn me that something bad might happen, although she never actually said so. I now think she was trying to warn me that what did happen might happen.

The worst day of my life began at nine o'clock in the morning. The psychiatrist called to say that Anne Madeleine had not appeared for an appointment the previous day, and her phone did not answer. She said that really worried her. Momentarily I was surprised that she would be "worried," but then I got the drift of what she meant. Maybe it was something in the tone of her voice. Maybe it was just some sense of disaster. I told her I would go down there right away.

Anne Madeleine was now living on East 22nd Street in the Stuyvesant Town housing complex. I had no key to her apartment. The security guard at her building said I could not go in without official permission.

I spent a desperate hour making phone calls to the police and to other officials who might help get me in. Each time I called someone I shouted, "It's a matter of life and death!" I had an image of Anne Madeleine having taken an overdose. I thought she could be dying right now while I was trying to get into her apartment.

The police finally arrived and told the security guard that I should be allowed into her apartment. A policeman came with me to the apartment door. He stayed at the door. I went inside.

I was aware of a slight smell of incense. The living room was dark. The shades were all drawn, so there was little light. I walked on into the bedroom.

Anne Madeleine was on the bed. She was lying there quite peacefully. She was dead. It was a sight I will always remember.

I don't think she had been dead very long, perhaps a few hours, perhaps a day. There was no sign in the apartment of violence or disorder or disruption of any kind. She was not bruised. She bruised easily because her flesh was so puffy, and she often had bruises because she liked to be beaten up. Now there were no bruises. She was just dead.

I called Marian at her office, but she had not yet returned from a meeting in Detroit. Her daughter Susie was there and offered to come down and help me. Susie is extraordinary about death, very very good about taking care of things. She arrived quickly and made all the necessary phone calls. We waited together in the kitchen, talking, until the people from the funeral home arrived and took away my daughter's body.

No autopsy was performed. The psychiatrist said she thought she could arrange it so that there would not have to be an autopsy, and somehow she did. I still don't understand how that was possible, since the police had been present at the scene, and the cause of death of this 33-year-old woman was unknown. From a coroner's point of view she could even have been murdered.

I don't think so. Given the way she lived, I have to guess that she died of an overdose of drugs. And I have to guess that she did it on purpose.

Does one have a wiping machine that wipes out things you don't want to remember? With Anne Madeleine, I sometimes have trouble remembering what happened — or why it happened.

INVENTING *PEOPLE*

◇◇◇◇

STARTING A SUCCESSFUL NEW MAGAZINE IS DIFFICULT AND expensive. Even at Time Inc., widely considered the preeminent magazine company, we had not launched a new magazine in eighteen years. With *Life* at first dying, and then dead at the end of 1972, we urgently needed new magazines to make up for the tremendous loss of *Life's* revenues.

The story of creating *Money* and *People* is as great a contrast in style, method and result as one is likely to find in publishing.

Compared to our weeklies, we found it difficult to make a real financial success out of monthlies. They tended to be too small in circulation and advertising income, and too large in staff costs and overhead. In 1971 we started an experimental department to explore a fresh approach.

We thought we might solve the economics of monthly magazines by starting four little ones, with a circulation of perhaps a few hundred thousand each. We would spread the overhead across all four magazines: ad sales, circulation, promotion, finance, business management, everything except edit, which had to be separate. By combining all these publishing functions, we would save a lot of money and make monthlies profitable.

Accordingly, we created dummies for four magazines: *Well* (about health), *Money, View* (about movies and TV) and *Camera Month*. They quickly became known around the office as Health, Wealth, Flicks and Pix. We tested all four, both for advertiser response and for circulation response. When the test results came back, it turned out that the most promising one was *Money*. So we went ahead just with that, thereby defeating the whole argument in favor of joint economies of scale. This is typical of the kind of rationale that magazine publishing is based on. I.e, it is not rational, nothing is rational.

Money was duly launched in October 1972, two months before the end of *Life*. It had a hard birth. Somehow the editorial idea and the promotion for the magazine were completely at odds, almost 180 degrees apart. What the editors were delivering was not what the circulation promoters were selling. Subscribers were confused. They thought they were buying one thing, but they got something completely different. It took a long, long, painful, costly time to get the two halves together. At the end of its second full year, we gave serious thought to killing it.

Money was really directed at middle income people, mainly younger people who had little knowledge about how to handle money or invest it. It finally worked out well, especially after Marshall Loeb became managing editor. Loeb is what you might call an editor-packager. He is not a fine-tuner searching for just the right word, but he has an extraordinary sense of how to package a magazine. The reader grabs it because it has been presented so clearly in terms of his interest. Today, several managing editors later, *Money* makes a pile of dough for a monthly.

↪ After the death of *Life*, I kept reaching and scratching for a good, big idea that would restore the company's health. Over the years I had been aware that the "People" page of *Time* was the most popular department in the magazine, the one many readers turned to first. And I knew that the "People" columns and the gossip columns of the newspapers were also popular. It didn't take an enormous leap of genius to go from there to the thought that we should create an entire magazine about people.

Most successful ideas in publishing are not leaps of genius. But someone does have to think of an idea and then be in a position to do something about it. For the latter, it helps to be the chairman.

When I thought of this magazine in the spring of 1973, I said to myself it has to be called *People*, it can't be called anything else. That would almost certainly cause legal problems — somebody was sure to own that title — but I remember thinking that if we could not get that title, we should not publish the magazine. With any other name we would lose half the value of the idea. We would have to spend an enormous amount of money over a number of years trying to explain what the magazine was all about. Even *Life*, as famous and successful as it once had been, was not really explained by its title, and we could never find a single phrase or sentence that defined it to our readers and advertisers. *Time* was obviously "the weekly news-magazine," but what was *Life*? We never could answer that question. When *Life* fell into trouble, the lack of a clear, succinct definition only added to its problems.

The person to whom I told my new magazine idea was Otto Fuerbringer, the head of Magazine Development. One day in the hall outside my office, I saw him heading toward Hedley Donovan's office. I said to him, "Hey, Otto, why don't we do a magazine about people? We'll call it *People*."

Fuerbringer had been managing editor of *Time* for eight years. Former managing editors are like former presidents of the United States: it is diffi-cult to find a suitable job for them. But this was not true of Otto, who moved straight from *Time* to the field of newspaper acquisition and then to Magazine Development. A former St. Louis newspaperman of German extraction, he was a commanding, black-haired figure, known as the Iron Chancellor from his authoritative *Time* days. He was tall enough so that he and I could almost talk eye to eye. We stood in the hall outside my office.

"Here's how I see it," I said. "Instead of starting with last week's news, we start with last week's people and see if we can't tell the reader quite a lot about what's going on."

For someone who had edited *Time*'s "People" page for eight years, this was an easy concept to grasp, and Otto was a quick study.

"But," I said, "it must not be serious. It has to be fun." I told him a few of my other thoughts.

"Fine," Otto said with his smile. He has one of those smiles that is diffi-cult to read with accuracy. He said his group was busy on a couple of other items, "But then we'll get to work on it."

Did he really mean it? Or was he just brushing me off?

Since I knew what I wanted, it was just a question of getting it. I wanted the magazine to be lighthearted and gossipy. It would be fast, breezy, irrev-erent and never, never solemn. Lots of pictures, but they would not have to be the size of *Life*, because *Life*'s page size was one of the things that bank-rupted it. *People* would be standard size.

It would be all black-and-white because there are very few occasions when you need to photograph people in color. If you want to do fashion or nature or art, you need color, but if it's strictly people, then you don't. That would be a great economic advantage because black-and-white is much cheaper than color. The advertisers would provide the color — at their own expense. If the magazine was successful, it wouldn't look black-and-white because many of the ad pages would be in color. In edit terms, only the cover needed to be in color.

I waited a couple of weeks, somewhat impatiently, to hear from Otto. I wasn't sure what his real reaction was, but he had sounded interested.

Finally, I went downstairs to his office and stood in his doorway. "Hey, Otto, what's happening with my new magazine?"

Otto looked up from his desk and said, with his smile, "You'll have a memo tomorrow."

So at least he had been thinking about it. And indeed, next day his memo arrived. It was only a page-and-a-half long, not a full prospectus and outline, but what it said certainly sounded right:

> Not slick, but on paper heavy enough for good reproduction, since pictures will be a large part of edit . . . color cover and color ads, but black-and-white edit. . . .
>
> Flexible in makeup; that is, not standard departments in the same place every week. Standing features, yes; but only when they can be filled with credit. Let each week's topicality dictate the content and flow of the magazine. Nothing to impede the progress of stories and items of people in action — people in action physically, mentally, socially, artistically.

Now you're talking, Otto!

I was certain we could tell the news entirely through people — big people, little people, medium people, men, women and children. I thought we should mix famous people (whose names would sell the magazine) with a lot of other people that the reader ought to know about.

I discussed the memo with Hedley Donovan, who was not enthusiastic. Hedley was always careful about anything new. Years earlier I had suggested to him that we do a column in *Life* called "The Presidency," and that Hugh

Sidey in our Washington bureau would be perfect to write it. Hedley rather liked the idea, but he wanted to make sure it would hold up on a weekly basis. He made Hugh Sidey write ten columns, week after week, none of them published, before he finally agreed it would work.

A major question raised about *People* was, were there enough people to fill a weekly magazine? And were there enough famous, interesting people to put on the cover every week? I said, "Oh, for God's sake, of course there are." The one thing I was sure of was that if there was anything we had enough of in the world, it was people. Just the same, we went through several weeks making lists of people who might be in that week's issue and on the cover. It seemed to go reasonably well. It was only much later that I learned from the business manager Tony Cox that some of the publishing side hated my idea. He told me, "If you hadn't been chairman, the damn thing would have been killed right away."

Well, I *was* chairman, so eventually we went to the dummy stage. Magazine Development had inherited two *Life* assistant managing editors who would now play major roles in creating *People*. Both Phil Kunhardt and Dick Stolley had worked at *Life* for their entire Time Inc. careers, some 20 years each. They knew pictures, they knew how to tell picture stories, they had imagination and drive.

Kunhardt had been the most accomplished picture editor on *Life*. He had grand, spacious story ideas. He was an immensely strong, red-headed six-footer, one of the best armwrestlers in the building. He was also an author and a devoted family man, with six children and a house perpetually filled with litters of Labrador puppies.

Stolley came from Pekin, Illinois. He was one of the few Time Inc. top editors who had actually gone to journalism school, but it did him no harm. He had spent years in the *Life* bureau system, where his most famous coup was to get the Zapruder film after the Kennedy assassination. He was an experienced reporter. He was also a good athlete, a daily jogger, a marathon runner. His stamina would soon stand him in good stead.

Kunhardt put together a first paste-up issue for internal study only. Stolley was busy on another project and did not take part in this. Kunhardt had the help of some former *Life* colleagues and some extra writers that Fuerbringer borrowed from our other magazines. In order to avoid the cost of typesetting and printing, they used typewriter type with uneven, ragged lines that could simply be cut out and pasted onto the page. I thought this looked wonderful — breezy, fresh, informal, different — and I decided that if we ever reached the real magazine stage, we would stick with the typewriter type. It was the worst single idea I ever had for *People.* What I thought looked breezy, everybody else thought looked cheesy.

During the period when we were noodling *People,* I called Clare Luce and told her about it. I wanted her views because she was smart and always had ideas, so I took her to lunch in the elegant, dark-paneled Edwardian Room of the Plaza Hotel. The ceiling is high and the tables are far enough apart so that you can hear each other talk. It is a perfect setting for a woman as elegant and beautiful as Clare. She was enthusiastic, and as usual, she had a lot to say.

"It has to be very chattery, very gossipy," she said. "Then women will love it. Tell us whether Liz Taylor is gaining weight or losing weight this month, and how much. I'll love it — and so will my maid and my hairdresser. That's important, because Time Inc. doesn't have a magazine that appeals to women as women. I've never understood that. I was never able to get Harry to do a thing about it."

We had quite a few lunches and teas to discuss the magazine, sometimes in restaurants and sometimes at her apartment in the Waldorf. She was helpful with her enthusiasm and her own gift for gossip. She would mention a woman who might make a good *People* story and then reel off tidbit after tidbit of gossip about her. She had nothing to do with inventing the magazine, as has been reported, perhaps with some encouragement from Clare, but she did help, and I always enjoyed talking to her about it.

To my surprise, since she had once been an editor herself, Clare had almost no interest in the structure of the magazine, only in particular stories and tidbits. A magazine needs a structure, a framework, something that makes readers say to themselves, "Oh yes, I'm comfortable with this. I know what this is." You can surprise the hell out of the reader with this story or that picture, but you have to keep inside the familiar framework.

After several paste-up dummies, we decided for the first time in Time Inc. history to print a test issue. In the past, we had done only mail tests, but this time we wanted to find out if we could actually promote and sell the magazine before we went to an expensive all-out national launch. If we failed, the cost of a test issue, though high, would be far less than a national launch, and the failure would be less noisy and embarrassing.

Sure enough, we learned there was a legal problem with the title. A local newspaper in the midwest owned the name *People* and refused to sell out to us. We finally had to call our magazine *People Weekly.* That distinction was enough to clear us legally, and the word *Weekly* has always been quite tiny on the cover. Try to find it. Nobody except the lawyers has ever called it anything but *People.*

We picked out 11 market areas, representative geographically and demographically. Since this was a single test issue, there were no subscriptions. Every copy had to be sold on the newsstand. That was fine with me. A big newsstand magazine was exactly what I was aiming for. The profit margins on newsstand copies are far greater than on subscription copies, where you have not only the weekly cost of mailing the issue but also the perpetual cost of soliciting and renewing subscriptions, a hideously expensive process.

I insisted on the low price of 35 cents, well below the average copy cost for magazines. We did test in one city at 50 cents, but that was only to protect ourselves against my low-price hunch. If 50 cents did as well as 35 cents, we could launch at the higher price. (It didn't.)

The test issue would get the same kind of promotion — TV spots, radio spots, newspaper ads — as a national launch, but only in the chosen 11 cities. It was a sizable, expensive test requiring an enormous amount of complicated planning and coordination just for that single week. We had to coordinate promotion and distribution, make sure that everything was going to work just right, and then make certain that we could measure the results with confidence. It took far, far longer to arrange all this than it took to produce the test issue itself.

Phil Kunhardt edited the test issue, which had Elizabeth Taylor on the cover and a number of show biz stories inside. His notes for August 1973 say:

> I closed the test issue on Wednesday night, August 8, and left for Maine
> the next day without seeing a make-ready [advance copy] or anything. I

was utterly exhausted when I arrived in Maine, felt we had done an acceptable job but didn't want to think about it for a week at least. Otto called on Friday and said Heiskell loves it. No more word until the following Saturday when a copy of the magazine arrived in Maine. Sandra [14-year-old daughter] devours it. Even Katharine [wife] likes it.

Returning to the office the next week, Kunhardt was in for a shock: "I got in Monday morning only to hear that our office has had nothing but abuse for the past week — people inside Time Inc. either calling or appearing to say how dreadful the thing is. Hugh Sidey [Washington *Time* correspondent] thinks it's a cross between *Women's Wear Daily* and *Silver Screen*. Tim Foote [former *Life* senior editor] says, 'It violates everything Luce stood for. It has no redeeming social or educational qualities whatsoever.' "

Kunhardt was stunned. Otto said, with the confidence of a longtime managing editor, "I was shocked in a way, but I figured they didn't know what they were talking about."

I was not shocked by the criticism. My skin is thick, and I was determined we would show up all those guys. I knew we were on to something good, and I was going to bull it through. Period. And I did.

This kind of attack on a new magazine always happens at Time Inc. When *Life* was first published in 1936, it was decried by *Time* and *Fortune* people as cheap, trashy and a disgrace to the company. When *Sports Illustrated* was first published in 1954, it was decried by *Time, Fortune* and *Life* people as a shallow, inconsequential, unworthy magazine and a disgrace to the company. It was known around the building as *Muscles* or *Jock* or *Sweat*. When *Money* was first published in 1972, *Time, Fortune, Life* and *Sports Illustrated* people said it should be called *Greed* and decried it as a disgrace to the company. Now it was *People*'s turn to be the new kid on the block and therefore beneath contempt.

Fortunately, the people in our test cities felt differently. Not only did they buy the issue, but they told us they would buy it again or buy it regularly. We had a hit with the public. One incident from the test launch made this clear. The Safeway supermarket chain was upset by one story that Kunhardt and Fuerbringer daringly included. It was a two-page picture act on a *very* bare-breasted young woman on the beach at St. Tropez. They justified it as a *People* story because this well-endowed creature was the girl in the Chiquita Banana commercials. Safeway, which considered itself "a family store," hit the roof. Headquarters sent immediate word to all its stores in the test cities to take *People* off the racks. "Too late," the word came back. "It's already sold out."

Somehow — I can't remember how I got there — I got stuck on the idea that we could launch a weekly newsstand magazine with a circulation of one million by the end of the first quarter. It seemed like a nice round number, much more impressive than 750,000 or even 900,000.

The great Italian director Visconti once staged a new version of *Tosca* that called for the heroine to smash a Venetian goblet into the fireplace during her scene with Scarpia. In spite of the dramatic effect, it upset management that Visconti chose to use authentic antique Venetian goblets. He was destroying a very expensive object at every performance. Couldn't he use a cheaper modern goblet? Why did he have to use a costly antique? Visconti's answer: "It sounds better."

I had the same answer for setting *People*'s first-quarter circulation goal at one million: "It sounds better." In fact, one million sounds twice as good as 900,000. I am now older and wiser, and I know this was a preposterous goal. Anybody in the publishing business, including me, could tell you that it was impossible to start off that high that fast. But having settled on a million, we had to do a *pro forma* analysis of how much money we would have to invest in *People* before we could break even. How much were we going to gamble? These exercises are always optimistic. For instance, nobody ever estimated that *Sports Illustrated* would lose $32 million dollars (which is more like $100 million today) over nine years. If we had had the benefit of that estimate, even Harry Luce would have decided against it. Nobody estimated how much *Money* would really lose before breakeven six or seven years after launch.

The *pro forma* on *People* came up with a possible loss of $25 million before breakeven, which would take place after three years. (In the end, we invested only $17 million and reached breakeven in 18 months. By the time you read this page, *People* will have made a total profit of more than $1 billion, a *very* splendid return on a $17 million dollar investment.)

After the test issue, I had a philosophical debate, first with myself and then with a few others, including Hedley Donovan and IBM chairman Tom Watson, a close adviser and board member. My question to myself, and to them, was whether or not it was appropriate to ask our board of directors to vote on the decision to launch a new publication. Quite clearly, they had absolutely no competence to judge. I was not being rude, I was not trying to put them down, but directors are not chosen because they can recognize a great publishing idea. I finally put it to the directors that it would not be relevant for them to vote on *People,* unless some of them thought they knew something. So it turned out that the most successful magazine we ever published, the most successful magazine in the world history of publishing, was never formally approved by our board.

The critics inside the Time-Life Building were not the only ones who hated *People.* Madison Avenue thought the test issue looked terrible for advertising purposes. "Do you expect me to advertise my fine product in that crummy magazine?" They thought the typewriter type was too cheap even for those cheap, gossipy stories — "And by the way, it's obvious that with Liz Taylor on the cover and all those other entertainment stories inside, it's a show biz magazine and therefore not for us."

Again, I was not terribly surprised. Advertisers are slow to come around until they can place a magazine in what they think is its proper niche. Since *People* was a brand new creature, it had no niche. But because of this poor advertiser response, we decided that before we launched *People,* we better put out a second "test" issue. This would not be a real test like the one we had promoted and sold to the public. This one would be designed solely to persuade and reassure Madison Avnue. It would correct some of the perceived faults of the original test issue, including my disastrous typewriter type.

This second issue, dated October 22, 1973, would be created by a new editor-publisher team. Phil Kunhardt, who had edited the dummies and the first test issue, had had a heart attack four years earlier. He thought the intense pressure of editing and closing a weekly magazine could hardly be the best thing for his health. Besides, while he thought from the start that *People* had strong possibilities, his greatest interest was in trying to revive *Life,* first as a twice-a-year publication, later as a monthly.

Kunhardt's diary reports:

Heiskell got wind of my reluctance to edit *People* on a permanent basis. He came down to my office and closed the door. His message was, 'If it's not fun, quit!' He didn't mean quit the company, he meant quit the project. 'This magazine,' he said, 'is only going to go if the fun the editor is having putting it together shows through.' Andrew said that he had spent the weekend with Scotty Reston [James Reston, former *Times* columnist and Washington bureau chief]. He told Reston that he was going to try his hardest to keep 'the clean hands' of people like Scotty off his 'new dirty magazine.' And by 'dirty,' Andrew said, he didn't mean 'smutty,' he meant 'fun,' he meant 'non-serious, non-causy.' The way Andrew summed up his notion of *People* to me was, 'Just plain fun to read.'

Kunhardt continued: "At a late hamburger supper at '21,' I told Otto Fuerbringer, 'If I were an officer of this company, I would not make the mistake of putting me at the head of *People*. Dick [Stolley] would be a better editor of *People,* and I would be a better editor of *Life.*' "

Hedley Donovan agreed with Kunhardt's reasoning and with his health concerns. On Otto's recommendation he appointed Dick Stolley managing editor of the new magazine. Stolley had a good news sense, he liked solving problems, and he was good at managing people. All would come in handy now.

The publisher was Dick Durrell, who had been the last ad sales director of *Life*. More important in terms of *People,* his first job at Time Inc. in 1949–1951 had been to oversee newsstand distribution and sales in Minneapolis–St. Paul. There he learned every trick, dodge, lie and excuse that distributors use to explain why the right number of magazine copies are not reaching the right newsstands on the right day. This experience proved fantastically useful at *People,* where reliable newsstand distribution meant everything.

The two Dicks, Stolley and Durrell, would work closely and happily together for the next eight years. They were as fine an editor-publisher team as the company ever had. Actually there were not two Dicks but four. Stolley's deputy editor was Dick Burgheim, and Durrell's ad sales director was Dick Thomas. An inordinate number of phone calls began, "Hello, Dick. This is Dick."

Stolley and Durrell went to work on the issue that was supposed to convince Madison Avenue of our good intentions. No more typewriter type — out with it! For the cover, Stolley chose Billie Jean King and her new tennis-playing husband Larry. (This was long, long before Billie Jean acknowledged that she was gay.) This cover was designed to establish several things: we were interested in couples, we were interested in people who were not in show business, we were interested in sports, and we were interested in marriage.

When we showed the new issue to Madison Avenue, it definitely helped — but not nearly enough. To the advertisers it was still a new thing and therefore untrustworthy. They were slow to buy pages in *People*. We were also hurt by the fact that right after we announced we were going to publish, the Arab-Israeli War broke out. And not only was the economy in recession, but it was the time of those endless, infuriating gas lines. It was probably the worst climate in which to launch a magazine since Luce started *Fortune* at the height of the Depression.

Nevertheless, the magazine was launched on March 4, 1974, at a price of 35 cents. Mia Farrow was on the cover because of her movie *The Great Gatsby*. The cover also carried a long list of names of other people who appeared in the first issue. The early issues of *People* sold like crazy — 80% to 90% sales on newsstand, which is considered a technical sellout in this quirky business. But it was a resounding flop critically. Everybody said how awful it was. The criticism came not just from inside Time Inc. and from the press but from the ad agencies. Their position was, "Oh, we would never recommend that magazine to our clients." The response in the academic community was especially frightful. The magazine was denounced in faculty lounges across the country — although a lot of the professors seemed to have read a fair number of the stories.

I had no difficulty staying cheerful. Despite all the adverse commentary, the magazine kept on selling and growing. However, some weeks before the end of the first quarter, I was told that a publishing delegation needed to see me to make an important presentation. I was asked to set aside two hours for this event.

Right on the dot the four men trooped into my office: Art Keylor, the head of the magazine division, his deputy Kelso Sutton, Gary Valk of Magazine Development and Bruce Barnet, the young circulation manager of *People.* (Publisher Durrell was off on a sales promotion trip but had given the others his proxy.) Sutton and Barnet were carrying thick manila folders filled with papers.

My office originally belonged to Harry Luce. It had broad sheet-glass windows looking north to Central Park and west to the Hudson River and New Jersey. One entire wall was covered by a map of the world. In front of the map stood a long polished-wood conference table surrounded by armchairs. I sat down at one end, and the delegation took their seats around me.

"Andrew," Keylor said, "I'm sorry to say we are not going to make one million circulation by the end of the first quarter. We want to show you our plan to make one million by the end of this year, but we can't make it by the end of this first quarter. We can't even come close."

I looked around the table at them. Giving direct orders is not my management style. I prefer to urge, persuade, convince. But now I made an exception. I stared at them coldly and said, "Oh yes, gentlemen, you will."

I told them how they were going to do it. "You will print and distribute many more copies. I don't care how many, just make sure it's enough. Get the magazines onto more newsstands. A lot more newsstands. Increase the number of racks at the supermarket checkout counters, and I don't care what it costs you to convince them to do it. Spend whatever you have to spend on newspaper ads and TV promotion. You are going to do whatever has to be done to get there, regardless of cost. But get there."

The meeting that was scheduled for two hours lasted ten minutes. Sutton and Barnet never got a chance to open their folders and make their presentation. Bruce Barnet, who still remembers that meeting today, says, "It was a perfect example of passion, commitment and decision at the corporate level. I've never seen anything like it since."

They had their marching orders on how to get to the magic number. All they had to do was get there.

They did, and we came close enough — just a hair short — so that we could claim our million. One of the many curiosities about magazine publishing is that if we had not met our announced goal, everybody would have said, "Aha! You see? It's a failure." Even though 900,000 would have been a whopping success for a brand new magazine, our competition and the press would all have jumped on us and said we had failed. And all the ad agencies would have said, "See, that's why we didn't recommend it to our clients." As I have said before, it is not a rational business.

After six months, circulation was so strong that we were able to raise the cover price to 40 cents. But the advertisers did not really accept *People* until the first audience numbers came in. Circulation is the number of copies sold, but audience tells you the average number of people who see or read each copy. Independent firms calculate audience numbers for all the magazines. The figure for *People* was fantastic: eight readers per copy, far better than any other major magazine. Readers were picking it up on airlines, in barbershops, in beauty salons, or just borrowing it from their neighbors.

The readers per copy coupled with our low page rate for advertising made *People* at last irresistible to the ad agencies, even if they still didn't quite approve of the product. They flocked in, and we went into the black after only 18 months. From then on, the line went straight up, 45 degrees, practically continuously. Durrell and his troops insisted on raising the cover price frequently, pretty much over my dead body. I always thought we should keep the price low so that the magazine would be accessible to everybody, but they turned out to be right.

Dick Stolley is the editor who really implemented and shaped the magazine. He deserves most of the credit for making it a non-schlocky magazine of reasonably high quality. I would have made it schlockier. He never ran a nude or a near nude or a bare breast, which everybody would have assumed we would do. In fact, he ordered the elimination of nipples from show-through blouses with an airbrush.

But he did have some special quirks. Having been born a twin, he took particular personal interest in every conceivable twin story. When he left *People,* his colleagues reported that during his eight years as managing editor, he had published 44 stories about twins.

Managing editors do have quirks, to which I suppose they are more or less entitled, under the divine right of kings. John Billings, my first boss at *Life,* could never resist any picture of a train, especially a locomotive. On the other hand, he was bored to death by pictures of Indians. The staff used to talk about setting up a picture of a big, gleaming locomotive with an Indian in full regalia seated at the throttle. What would Billings do when confronted by this dichotomy? Unfortunately his staff never got around to testing him.

Dick Stolley had substantial impact not only on the content of the magazine but on its philosophy, if that is not too ponderous a word for my fun magazine. He enlarged the notion of doing stories on people you never heard about who had done something interesting. The only thing that had to be a famous person was the cover. The cover person had to be instantly recognizable because that was what controlled newsstand sales. During Stolley's years Elizabeth Taylor was the most frequent cover subject. In the post-Stolley years it was Princess Diana.

After some years of experience in choosing *People* covers and paying close attention to the resulting newsstand sales, Stolley learned a lot about what works for *People* and what doesn't. He arrived at the following formula: "Young is better than old, pretty is better than ugly, television is better than music, music is better than movies, movies are better than sports, and anything is better than politics."

Stolley kept his edit staff thin, not just to save money but to make everybody feel needed and important. He was determined not to have a big staff because he thought totally dedicated people would do a better job. Nobody should have any spare time. This is known as the theory of being "optimally undermanned." The theory says that you want just enough people to get the job done without total exhaustion, but you want so few people that everyone thinks, "If I don't come to work today, the whole place will fall apart." Stolley worked his staff to death, including godawful closings until dawn. Sometimes he looked as though he was killing himself. I think he may have carried undermanning beyond the optimum.

Dick Durrell turned out to be a crackerjack publisher, simpatico to editorial problems, a savvy judge of quality, a good promoter and an incredible, indefatigable salesman. He personally visited supermarkets in his own neighborhood or wherever he traveled around the country. He wanted to make sure that *People* was there at the checkout counters. Because many more women bought *People* than men, the supermarket checkout line was the crucial sales point. Durrell was not satisfied merely to find that *People* was on sale. He also wanted to make sure that the magazine was in the top-choice eyelevel rack. If he spotted anything wrong, anywhere in his travels, he called headquarters to get remedial action.

My sister Di and I share a vacation moment in Paris.

In the wake of all the criticism they received, the two Dicks both made a number of speeches explaining the editorial philosophy of the magazine. It was not really, they claimed, a gossip magazine, because gossip was nothing more than hearsay and might be inaccurate. *People,* on the other hand, checked its facts and took great pains to be accurate. *People* wasn't gossip, it was "personality journalism." I'm not sure how many listeners they convinced.

I know one they didn't. *People's* huge success and the severe criticism it continued to attract was terribly embarrassing for Hedley Donovan, the editor in chief. The product embarrassed him, even though it was a hell of a lot better magazine than everybody was saying. Hedley never really liked it and made that clear to me in private. But at least he never said so in public.

Intellectual criticism of *People* never bothered me. One day at lunch during the magazine's early weeks, Otto Fuerbringer was giving me a gloomy report about the attitude of his former colleagues at *Time.*

I interrupted him. "Otto," I said, "if the editors of *Time* like it, then we have failed."

THE SUCCESSION — ALAS

◇◇◇◇

MOST PEOPLE BLAME EVERYTHING THAT WENT WRONG AT Time Inc. on the merger with Steve Ross and Warner Communications. This is an error. Most of what went wrong happened before the merger was even discussed. *Fortune* conducts an annual survey of top business executives and financial experts, a very tough jury. In 1980, the year I retired, Time Inc. ranked eighth among the most admired companies in America. In 1988, the year *before* the merger, Time Inc. had dropped to 223rd. Time Inc. had already lost its heart and soul before Steve Ross appeared on the scene.

↪ Choosing a successor is a difficult task. Sometimes, of course, there is a single outstanding candidate, whose quality, talent, experience and judgment are apparent to all — even to the board of directors. But the existence of such a superb candidate is a rare and fortunate event. I had no such luck.

Under Time Inc. rules I would retire on my 65th birthday in 1980. Hedley Donovan's retirement as editor in chief would come a year and a half before mine, so both church and state would come under new management at about the same time.

On August 2, 1972, eight years before my retirement, I sent Hedley Donovan a confidential memo. It began, "And now let us begin a serious discussion about succession." In the course of the next two pages, I mentioned 18 men on the business side of Time Inc. who I thought were possible candidates for top management. They currently held jobs at various levels of authority, and I said they would have to be moved around during the next few years to gain more experience and to give me a better look at what they could do.

The main purpose of my memo was to force myself to put down on paper the names of all the principal players, so that I could begin planning their future training. It may seem strange that I addressed this strictly business-side document to the editor in chief, but Hedley and I discussed everything. I found it natural to talk over my own succession with him and to get his judgment on the candidates.

Five years before my retirement, I began talking to our board about it. I saw no need for a succession committee and didn't have one, but I wanted the board to know what I was doing and how I was thinking.

I made the decision that Jim Shepley, the president and chief operating officer, would not succeed me. He was almost as old as I and would have had to retire two years after taking over. But having decided this, I had to tell him. I knew he wanted the job and probably expected to get it. His close friend Arthur Temple, our vice chairman, thought Jim should succeed me and had told him so.

I admired Shepley and thought he was terrific — very tough, very driving — but he was too explosive, too irascible, to be in complete charge. I put it off and put it off. I wasn't trying to prepare arguments because I had already made up my mind. I only tried to prepare myself emotionally to say it and get through it.

Finally one morning I called him into my office and asked him to shut the door. He sat down across the desk from me. I guess he could tell from my manner that this was something unusually serious, because he sat very stiffly with his fingers clasped and his shoulders back.

"Jim," I said, "the only way I can say this is straight out. When I retire, you will be sixty-three. That's too old to become chairman. You'd have only two years in office. What we have to do, you and I, is put in place a management that can have a long run. That means looking for people under fifty."

Jim said in his rather harsh soldier's voice, "In two years I could train someone to take my place."

I shook my head. "That's not the right way to do it."

"I think it could be."

"I've thought about it a lot. Believe me, I know it's right."

He opened his mouth to say something else, but then he closed it. He nodded his head sharply twice. The good soldier: *I accept.*

Over the next years Shepley and I moved my candidates around from one job to another, giving them broad experience and new challenges. Year by year I winnowed the group down to a smaller number of possibilities for the top jobs. The names that surfaced most regularly were Ralph Davidson, Dick Munro, Kelso Sutton and Nick Nicholas. There were occasional others. One was Gerald Levin, who is today the chairman of Time Warner. I knew Levin was smart, but I didn't really know enough about him. His principal experience was limited to Home Box Office, and he had not been at Time Inc. long enough to run it. I thought he was a generation away from the top — a generation being about five years.

Ralph Davidson was an extrovert with a long and successful career in sales and publishing. As publisher of *Time,* he had the biggest and most important line job in our magazines. He was a fine speaker, a tall, athletic man distinguished in manner and presence, and he had had a lot of experience with Washington. He would be instantly accepted in any *milieu* in the U.S. or anywhere in the world. He was as much at home in London or Paris or Bangkok as he was in New York and Washington. I liked him immensely, and we shared a number of *bon vivant* tastes. But I also thought he had some weaknesses. He didn't like to spend much time on details, on figures, on the nuts and bolts of profit and loss, and he didn't care too much about social issues like equal employment.

Davidson liked competitive action — in his private life (tennis, mountain climbing) and in his professional life. Sometimes his eagerness to compete got him in trouble. When he learned that *Newsweek* would announce a European edition in three days, he quickly consulted with managing editor Henry Grunwald, then announced *Time's* own European edition one day ahead of *Newsweek.* But he neglected to tell his boss Art Keylor, group vice president of magazines, who read about it in the *New York Times.* The world's reaction to Davidson's press release was rather ho-hum, but Keylor's was not.

A handsome white-haired man with a keen sense of authority and a deep respect for red tape, especially his own, Keylor was furious. He arrived in my office to demand that Davidson be fired for insubordination.

I tried to cool him down. "Art," I said, "sometimes people have to make decisions rapidly, and I am sympathetic to that."

Keylor was not sympathetic. "I can't run this division if one of my publishers can take a major step without even telling me."

He stormed out just as sore as when he stormed in, so I knew I had to do something about it. I was more annoyed at Davidson for sticking me in the middle like this than for his competitive decision, but I couldn't ignore Keylor's anger. I called Ralph on the phone and told him to come see me.

When he walked in, I looked at him and shook my head. "Keylor has told me all about your actions." Then in the iciest voice I could summon up, I said, "The telephones work around here. I suggest that next time before you decide to launch a new magazine, you use the telephone."

"Yes, sir!" He didn't quite salute.

The incident made Davidson somewhat of a hero to his fellow publishers, not only because of his foolhardy courage but because Keylor was so furious at Davidson that for several weeks he did not have time to be furious at anyone else.

Davidson told me much later that he had deliberately failed to inform Keylor. As he explained it: "That would have led to weeks of study and projections and budgets and assurances that it wouldn't fail, because Art couldn't stand the idea of approving something that might not work. So I just went ahead."

Since from time to time I had quickly approved things that might or might not work, I found this reasoning attractive.

Dick Munro had a fine record, working up to a successful run as publisher of *Sports Illustrated*. In 1975 we had turned over to him what I called "the four dogs"— namely, our four efforts at getting into the "new" TV. They were (1) Home Box Office, the first pay-cable venture; (2) our cable systems, consisting mainly of Manhattan Cable and a 10% interest in the American Television Corporation; (3) hotel television; and (4) Time-Life Video. In reasonably short order after Munro took over, HBO — thanks to cross-country satellite transmission — became a big success. We also rode cable systems from rags to riches, as cable caught on everywhere across the country. We got out of hotel cable (all the hotel customers wanted was pornography), and eventually we disbanded Time-Life Video.

Munro had taken four dogs, turned two of them into great successes and got rid of the other two. In hindsight I can guess that Levin and Nicholas, the managers of the two successes, may have deserved much of the credit, but since Munro was their boss, he was entitled to take the bows.

Munro was somewhat of a Boy Scout, a populist whose dress and manner said, "I'm one of the boys." Dick Munro making his way through the lobby of the Time-Life Building was an all-out display of political democracy. The lobby has four elevator wells, each with a uniformed security guard to check ID cards and passes. At one side of the lobby is an escalator down to the concourse with a long, solid rail protecting it. At lunchtime people line up against this rail to wait for their friends because "Meet you at the escalator" is a common telephone understanding.

And at lunchtime here comes Dick Munro. He steps briskly out of the elevator, trim, athletic, light on his feet, of medium height, with thinning light brown hair. Because he has a business lunch outside the building, he is reluctantly wearing a suit jacket, but it is the only reluctant thing about him. He has been chatting with his fellow elevator passengers all the way down to the ground floor, and now it is the lobby's turn.

To the elevator security guard: "Hi, Charlie, how's it going?" Then he bounces through the lobby and past the contingent along the escalator rail. An occasional handshake but more often a friendly pat on the shoulder. "Hey, Bill . . . Hello, Sally . . . What d'you say, Marge? . . . How's the baby, Sam? . . ." He genuinely likes people and has an astonishing memory for their first names. From his cheery lobby demeanor one would never guess how much he would prefer to be lunching in the company cafeteria, having a bowl of soup and a sandwich, sitting in his shirtsleeves and again greeting everyone by name.

Munro was a former Marine with distinguished combat service in Korea. He was a strong believer in equal employment, which happened to be a special cause of mine. He and I were much less close personally than Davidson and I. To a former Frenchman, Munro's lack of interest in good food and wine and the outside world were deplorable, although he probably knew the U.S. better than Davidson did. Munro and Davidson were not pals at all, not interested in the same things, but they respected each other and got along fine.

Kelso Sutton had been *Time*'s business manager and later the head of corporate circulation for all our magazines. He was short, stubby and round-faced, given to smoking cigars that were much too big for him. He always made the short list but he never made the Number One or Number Two slot. I thought very well of him at that time and thought he had a real future. Maybe he did. You have to have the right qualities, but everything also has to work for you. The river has to flow your way to bring out your qualities in the best possible way, and for Kelso it never did.

Nick Nicholas was as good as anybody I've ever known at making the river flow in his direction. He was a tough manager, good at cost controls. He liked to say, "I can cut the costs anywhere, I can make it work." He could always come up with the right figures to prove his case — any case.

A neat, trim man with black hair and a lean face, the son of Greek immigrants, he had come from Harvard Business School to our financial department and later turned Manhattan Cable around, from failure to success. If it hadn't been for Manhattan Cable, it is possible that no one would ever have taken Nicholas seriously. Jim Shepley told him, when he gave Nick that job, "You're just a little son of a bitch who doesn't get along with anybody. Now we're going to put you in charge of something, and it'll either make you or break you." It made him.

Nicholas was a snappy dresser, and he had a push-button smile that he turned on at will. He was terribly smart, but I was not comfortable with his brand of smartness. It had a sharp edge, it had no philosophical context. It was purely operational — namely, how effective will this action be in the short term?

Nick Nicholas making a presentation to the board of directors was a demonstration of supreme clarity and total conviction. He stands at the front of the board room in his dark suit, alert and sincere. Onto the screen comes a series of neat, numerical charts. He speaks in a clear, firm voice.

Here are the current costs.

Here is the trend line.

If we don't change, here is where we will be in three years. This is not acceptable.

Now, here are the areas for cutting costs.

Here are the potential savings.

Here is what will happen to the P and L in three years under this program.

Therefore the following actions are recommended.

"What is the alternative?" a director asks, as directors are supposed to do.

"Alternative?" Nick asks in a slightly surprised tone. "There is no alternative. These are the numbers."

It sounds like a contradiction, but Nicholas could make generalities with figures and draw broad conclusions from them.

Having been CEO and having been both the headman internally and the chief ambassador externally, I had already begun to wonder whether my job shouldn't be divided in two. One part would be inside and operational — in effect, running the company. The other part would be outside, representing the company to the public, to Washington and to the world.

The demands on my own time as CEO were enormous, especially during the last years. If you are the head of Time Inc., you are much more in demand than if you are the head of Bethlehem Steel. Bethlehem makes the same piece of steel every week, and this does not create much news. Time Inc. makes many different products every week in the form of new issues of magazines, and each one of them makes waves. The magazines are quoted constantly in newspapers and on radio and television. Somebody in government or business or society or the entertainment world is always furious about something one of our magazines has just said. Because of this widespread, constant attention and interest, the CEO of Time Inc. is really a public persona as well as an operating executive. He has to appear all over the place because everybody is aware of Time Inc. I thought the division of responsibility would fit the characters of my two final candidates, Davidson and Munro.

Munro ate hot dogs and hamburgers and peanut butter sandwiches, hated to wear a jacket, never traveled abroad, wanted to go home to Connecticut at five rather than to black tie dinners. For a man with his experience in the Marines and in business, he was strangely naive, almost innocent. Davidson knew the map of the world and the big players, spoke well, had an instinct for promotion and public relations, and had an excellent church-state record with Henry Grunwald, the managing editor of *Time.* He was a worldly, sophisticated man. It did not take long for me to become enamored of the idea of Davidson as chairman and public persona, with Munro as president and CEO to operate the machinery. To me Munro *looked* like a leader. He *looked* like a man ready to take charge.

Two years before my departure, I pulled Davidson and Munro out of their regular jobs — publisher of *Time*, group vice-president of video — and installed them on the corporate floor. I assigned them to a small group with the three executive vice-presidents for administration, finance and forest products and told them to learn everything they could about the company. I also added Davidson to the "Lunch Bunch," of which Munro, as a group vice-president, was already a member.

Davidson remembers the months before the succession was finally settled as "A limbo period of time, because it was so ill-defined. It was pretty apparent that Dick Munro and I were the ones who were in the race, but neither of us got much direction. As we got closer to the date of Andrew's retirement, we were no closer to knowing what was going to happen."

But I knew. I tried out my plan for the new structure — Davidson as outsider chairman, Munro as insider president and CEO — first on the board of directors and then on the two men. The structure was not typical for a large corporation, but I did not invent it. Other companies have had similar arrangements for their two top executives.

The board asked me a number of questions. Arthur Temple wanted me to promote his good friend Shepley to my job and let him run it for a couple of years before creating a more conventional management. The businessmen on the board would have been more comfortable with a chairman who was CEO and a president who was COO. In my plan the chairman Ralph Davidson would run the board meetings rather than the CEO Dick Munro, and that made them uncomfortable. But how do you run a board meeting? You do your best to get away with whatever murder you can, that's about all. If you want to call that "running a board," fine, but I don't take that aspect of a board too seriously. In the end, the directors accepted my plan.

When I tried out the idea on Munro and Davidson in separate, private talks, they seemed a bit bemused, but each said he thought it could work. (Years later, in his book *To the End of Time*, Richard Clurman quotes Munro's true feeling: "It was hard for me to tell Heiskell that's not acceptable. I wouldn't have got the job.")

Davidson says today, "I was naturally disappointed, but I wasn't so disappointed that I thought it was an unworkable management team. Like a lot of us in that generation, Time Inc. was my whole life, my identity. We worked hard, we played hard, but what came first was Time Incorporated ahead of any personal ego. My ego was the company. So I said, 'Fine, let's get on with it, let's make it work.' "

Several directors suggested I stay on the board after retirement. I was against this as a general principle, even though I had been very grateful to have Roy Larsen around after I became chairman, still on the payroll and still there in the office. I wasn't being nice to Roy, I just wanted him there for continuity and for consultation and because I loved him. But now I was worried that if I stayed on the board after retirement, whenever the new management made a report to the board, every head would swivel to look at the former chairman. *What does he think?* I have never understood how at IBM they had *three* former chairmen on the board.

I decided to ask Munro what he thought about my staying on the board. His vehement negative response surprised me. He told me bluntly, "They should never have asked you." He made it clear that he thought I should leave. He made this clear right away, during the transition process. In retrospect, I think he did not want to have to be compared to me on a regular basis. Perhaps he didn't have enough confidence in himself. But if I had stayed on the board, I might have helped him avoid the church-state collapse that was about to occur. At the very least I would have made sure the new CEO and the new editor in chief talked to each other.

My second early surprise from Munro came soon after the public announcement, when he stated that he would retire in ten years at age 60. Before even establishing his own authority, he was inciting the start of a succession race. I was aghast. He had not told me of his plan. If he had, I hope I could have talked him out of announcing it.

↪ Hedley Donovan had conducted the search for his own successor in a very different way. Unlike me, he never had a long list of possible candidates. Although he and I often talked about other top editors in one context or another, his list consisted of two men. During his final years he had both of them working right next to him on the 34th floor.

Henry Grunwald had, for eight years, been a brilliant, autocratic managing editor of *Time,* the only place in the company he had ever worked. He and publisher Ralph Davidson had built *Time* into a formidably successful magazine. Grunwald, an owlish-looking man with heavy horn-rimmed glasses, had risen from copy boy to become the company's preeminent intellectual. His breadth of interest and knowledge was extraordinary, at least if you kept off the subject of sports. Born and raised in Vienna, his childhood was as European as my own. He read widely and voraciously. In his capacity as managing editor of the world's foremost newsmagazine, he interviewed heads of state all over the world. He knew everybody and everything. But he was an indifferent manager. His inability or unwillingness to make timely decisions created poor morale and heavy cost overruns.

Ralph Graves had been the last managing editor of *Life,* having previously filled a wide variety of positions on the magazine. He was unassuming but greatly respected by his colleagues. He was particularly "people-oriented" and devoted the year after the end of *Life* to getting his staff placed in new jobs inside or outside the company. I thought he would be an ideal editor in chief, not only because of superb journalistic judgment but because he understood the importance of the appointment process, the selection of the right person for the right job.

Hedley and I talked about his choice off and on at great length. Since he had to retire a year and a half ahead of me, he had to make his decision well before I did. Obviously it was his call, and Grunwald got it. Now that I look back at what went wrong, I realize that Munro-Grunwald was the first step in the breakdown of Time Inc. management. What had always worked as church *and* state was to become church *versus* state. With a different editor in chief, Munro might have got along better. With a different CEO, Grunwald might have got along better.

↬ The jockeying for position on the business side started soon after the appointment of Munro and Davidson. Munro recognized his own limitations in financial matters and turned to Nicholas for guidance. Nicholas leveraged this strength into becoming Munro's alter ego.

Davidson remembers that meeting after meeting would end with Munro saying, "Let's see what Nick thinks." It doesn't take corporate executives long to catch on to this kind of situation. "Pretty soon," Davidson says, "everybody was asking, 'What does Nick think?' "

Within a relatively short period of time Munro was not making any decisions of his own but was being propelled by Nicholas. After a while I began to wonder, who the hell is Dick Munro? What have I done?

A failure. My big failure.

The only consolation I could find was from something Tom Watson had told me years earlier, after he retired from IBM because of a heart attack. He said, "Listen, kid, once you're retired, that's all you are. You're retired. There isn't anything you can do about it, so there's no use getting in a sweat about it. You're not going to like it, but don't pay too much attention to it."

Maybe Munro did not really have the instinct to make decisions. He certainly seemed indecisive after becoming CEO. Some good people get better and stronger in new jobs, some don't. Maybe I had been taken in by the fact that good, strong decisions were made in his video areas, but perhaps they were made by his lieutenants, Gerry Levin and Nick Nicholas.

In retrospect I had not asked myself a crucial question about Munro. He appeared to have so many of the right qualities on the basis of his record, but I never really asked myself: does he have the culture to run this company? I don't mean culture in the way it's used these days, "the Time Inc. culture." I mean culture in the broader sense. I guess Munro read books because he thought reading books was the thing to do, but I don't think he ever read books because they would do something pleasurable and important for him. When you finish a wonderful book, you say, "I never realized that. I never realized that's what people think, or how they act. This is the way life is!" That's what great books do for you, but I doubt that Munro ever had that kind of reaction.

The first victim of Nicholas's drive for power was, of course, Ralph Davidson. In order to further consolidate his position, Nicholas started a campaign to disparage the previous management. He preached the management gospel of strong financial controls and derided the "paternalistic" management of Time Inc. in previous periods.

I had envisaged Davidson's job as deputy headman. While his primary responsibility was external affairs, I expected him to participate in all major management decisions. I had discussed this at length with Munro and Davidson and thought they were in agreement. But Nicholas's campaign for power resulted in Davidson being frozen out of the decision-making process. Davidson found that he had no power base from which to draw support for things he thought should be done. The fact that he did not participate in deriding his predecessors did not help him. Before long, the staff managers came to realize that their futures depended on Munro-Nicholas. Davidson was left with the shell of a job.

Another victim of this feud was the always fragile relationship between church and state. It works only if the editor in chief and the CEO both want it to work and both participate individually and jointly in making it work. Implicit in the church-state separation is that both sides recognize that in a journalistic enterprise, both sides work together to enhance the success of the effort. But both sides also recognize that ethical boundaries are involved, and that church is the final arbiter of those boundaries.

Donovan and I instinctively understood this relationship. I always discussed major business policies with him, and he talked over major editorial decisions with me. Actually there was one time when I failed to do so. The matter itself was so insignificant that I have forgotten what it was. What I *do* remember — and this is the true measure of the importance of the relationship — was the terrible sense of guilt I felt as a result of my unintended misstep.

But by and large Donovan and I were in and out of each other's office several times a day. I valued his advice, and he paid attention to my views. When we had differences, we knew the two of us had to find a solution, since there was no further court of appeal. We certainly were not about to appeal any difference to the board of directors.

Grunwald was perhaps more of an intellectual than Donovan and certainly a man far less interested in the often-unwelcome affairs of state. Even after he became editor in chief, his overwhelming interest was still *Time,* where he had spent his entire career. He had none of Donovan's background as a business writer and editor of *Fortune.*

As for Munro, he was no intellectual. He was awed by Grunwald's intellectual capacity and reputation. Munro did not deal with abstractions. I have always been convinced that people do improve as they go along, but sometimes they need help. Grunwald could not be bothered to help Munro improve. Nicholas was interested only in improving himself. Munro stayed away from Grunwald, who, having no use for small talk, never left his office to chat with Munro. As Davidson faded, an enormous gap developed between business and edit. And then when serious operational problems occurred, the gap became a chasm.

TV Cable Week was the worst example. Watching the success of *TV Guide* and the rapid growth of cable, the magazine publishing team was hard at work on what they boasted would be the most profitable magazine ever —even more profitable than *People*. This was not a Grunwald project. The proposed new magazine had only barely perceptible editorial content. It was purely an elaborate service tool for the cable-connected viewer who would be buying it (supposedly) at the urging of his cable system. Unlike *TV Guide,* the new magazine would carry listings and brief comments for all cable programming, as well as for conventional over-the-air programming. Therefore it would become indispensible to all the new cable subscribers across the country.

TV Cable Week was budgeted for an expensive $50 million launch, but the promised return thereafter would be fantastic. Munro, Nicholas and Sutton (who was now boss of magazines) had no doubts about it. But not quite everyone agreed. Graves, who had become editorial director and Grunwald's deputy, wrote a memo warning that the predictions of *TV Cable Week*'s huge success were based on far too many variables, too many gambles, and that we had to win not just some of those gambles but every single one. "This is like Russian roulette," he concluded, "where we have to keep pulling the trigger and all the chambers have to prove harmless." The warning was ignored.

With immense fanfare *TV Cable Week* was launched in April 1982. It was supposed to put *TV Guide* up against the ropes. The publicity was terrific. The fanfare was so great that it looked at first as if it might be a hit. But all too soon disturbing sounds were heard. The cable companies that were supposed to be partners in selling it did not seem to be promoting it — and with good reason. It turned out that the cocksure Time Inc. management had never consulted them. Had they done so, they would have known that the cable companies saw nothing in the scheme that they liked. They had little financial incentive to push it, and they certainly did not want smart-ass New York writers telling their customers why tonight's cable movies weren't worth watching.

The extraordinary thing about *TV Cable Week* is that nobody in charge — Munro, Grunwald, Sutton, whoever — wanted to talk to the cable companies who were going to distribute the magazine to their viewers. That's as if we had started *People* and decided that the distributor didn't really matter very much. The distributor *always* matters very much. You wish he didn't, that I understand, and I understand that they wished the distributor would do just what they told him to do. But that's not the real world. For *TV Cable Week* we had a middleman between us and the customer, and we didn't pay him any attention.

It is very, very difficult to launch a magazine. Most magazine launches are bad, but we had the reputation of sticking with a new magazine until we got it right. This time no such hope existed. Soon the $50 million launch money was spent, and the magazine was losing a bundle every week. At the end of six months it was buried. There remained only the matter of finding a scapegoat. He was close at hand: Kelso Sutton, head of the magazine division and prime architect of the fiasco.

The only winner was Christopher Byron, a staff member who wrote a scathing and funny book about *TV Cable Week* called *The Fanciest Dive.*

My vantage point for observing all this was nowhere. I had been invited out to White Plains one day to see the new headquarters being built for *TV Cable Week,* but aside from that courtesy visit I took no part in the thinking or planning, on this or anything else. After 20 years as chairman, I was once again an outsider. I never heard from any of my old directors on the Time Inc. board. I was not a member of any team.

Every few months Munro and I had breakfast in the spacious main dining room of the Dorset Hotel. This was virtually our only contact. He sat with his jacket draped on a chair, his shirtsleeves rolled up, his tie flipped over his shoulder. Even before the disaster of *TV Cable Week* he said to me, "Oh, Andrew, you have no idea how hard this job is!"

I concluded he was not enjoying himself. Instead of growing in the job, which most people do, he was shrinking into it. Plainly he did not enjoy his job. I had always enjoyed my job — every job I ever had — even when

I had to face one disaster or another. I think I always managed to convey my enjoyment to everyone around me. If you don't enjoy your own job, people working for you won't enjoy theirs, either. And then you have trouble.

It also struck me as odd that Munro should say that I, who had had to cope with downsizing the company by one-third after *Life* folded, would have "no idea how hard it is." This in a booming decade.

The booming '80s started Munro and Nicholas on their merger kick, with ultimately disastrous consequences. They kept looking over their shoulders and seeing takeover signals — all of which proved imaginary. Since the '80s were a time of takeovers and mergers, their paranoia had some excuse but no supporting evidence. They concluded that only by growing through merger could they remain independent. They courted CBS (whom I had turned down in the '60s when they courted us), ABC, Gannett, the *Wall Street Journal* and perhaps others. They were wasting their time because in each case the courted party wanted the same thing they wanted: to remain independent, to be the boss partner. As to the fear of takeover, no trace has ever been found of real money being put on the table by any devouring piranha. Not until Munro and Nicholas put the company in play by trying to merge with Warner did any takeover attempt ever emerge.

↬ Like most retiring chairmen of large companies, I was given a modest office in the Time Life Building at company expense. This is such a common practice in American business that a chairman would practically have to be convicted of fraud or child abuse before being deprived of this courtesy. I had many continuing business affairs in the nonprofit sector, so my office was a great personal convenience.

However, in the midst of one of the company's cost-control frenzies, Munro appeared at my door one day to inform me that I would either have to vacate the premises or pay for them myself. The cost, including all services, was about $50,000 a year. It was inconceivable to me that this was Dick Munro's own idea. He could only have been the messenger.

My wife Marian was outraged in my behalf. Without telling me, she sent Munro the following letter:

In the Plaza Hotel ballroom Marian and I celebrate my retirement from Time Inc. in 1980. I am dancing better here than I can dance today.

Dear Dick,

This is the 100th letter I have written and not sent since I heard the news. Andrew tells me to be compassionate and that I should feel sorry for you. I do. I feel sorry that you made so many promises and that you then proceeded to make a complete about face. I am deeply disappointed and hurt. How can you ever have told me not to worry and that Andrew was like a father to you? (I sure would not like being your mother if this is the case.)

Can't you (Time Inc.) remember what Andrew did for the company? Are you all so short-sighted and unfeeling that you'd toss him out after all those years of service and leadership? My god man. Ask your board of directors what they've done with their retired CEOs and don't bother telling me about the ones who were gently eased. I'm talking about a man whose record was good all the way.

I'm afraid you've become so engrossed in what you consider the major problem of the day, "take over," that you've lost sight of what makes a good company. It's *people*. People who enjoy this work. People who will do anything for you because they know they've got the support of their CEO. People are more creative when they are happy and not constantly worried about what the next day will bring and I gather that there is a lot of worry in your shop. Your fears have taken the heart and drive out of a lot of people. The sex appeal of working for Time Inc. is fast disappearing. Now to prove how "lean" you all are, you're about to kick out the former CEO under whose leadership Time Inc. grew to the great heights it reached. Yes, I do feel sorry for you. You've nearly broken Andrew's heart.

Sincerely,
Marian

I decided to pay for my office. I still do.

↪ With *TV Cable Week* out of the way, a magazine project sponsored by Dick Stolley was revived. Stolley, the very successful original managing editor of *People*, proposed a magazine to be called *Picture Week*. It assumed that a lot of good newsy pictures were available "out there" and could be captured and arranged into a lively, inexpensive, weekly magazine. It was to be black-and-white, very much like *People* in format. Grunwald, who was caught up in his own dream of a quality magazine called *Quality,* showed little zest for it, although he took an active part in discussions and designs and layouts.

I was asked for an opinion. I found it hard to believe that all those good newsy pictures were lying around "out there." I also thought that if it did succeed, it would do so at the expense of *People,* both in circulation and advertising. The project kept surfacing and resurfacing, with new designs, new layouts, new dummies. Grunwald fiddled with all of them. After many months *Picture Week* lingered into death at a cost of $15 million.

What disturbed me most about this project was not the cost or the concept but the way that top management came down on both sides of the issue over and over again. It was an endless display of terminal indecision — with nothing to show for it.

The unstated conclusion was that Time Inc. had lost its creative touch and, in the wake of the *TV Cable Week* disaster, its nerve. Instead, at Nicholas's insistence, management bought existing, successful publishing outfits — *Southern Living, Sunset,* etc. These were essentially financial transactions with no role for our own editors, who shortly would have not even a supervisory role over them.

Even more unstated — but even more important — was that the company had reached the end of the road as far as the creative interplay between church and state was concerned.

The church-state corpse was to receive another blow as a result of the Sharon Trial in the winter of 1984–1985. *Time* reported — on the basis of a secret Israeli document it had never actually seen — that Defense Minister Ariel Sharon had implicitly encouraged a Lebanese group to take revenge for the assassination of its leader, thereby leading to the massacre of hundreds of villagers in refugee camps. Sharon sued *Time* for libel, stating that the secret government document contained no such charge against him. Grunwald and Managing Editor Ray Cave refused to back down and were too stubborn or too proud to arrive at satisfactory wording for an apology. Therefore a trial took place, where it would be revealed that what *Time* had printed was a monstrous error.

A parade of *Time* editors, writers, correspondents and researchers took the stand during a supremely embarrassing trial. Some shabby journalistic procedures were made public. And it turned out that the secret Israeli document did *not*, in fact, contain the published charge against Sharon. In the end, the jury cleared *Time* of libel on the narrow grounds that actual malice was not proved. But the jury added, in deliberate criticism, that *Time* had "acted negligently and carelessly in reporting and verifying the information." No monetary damages were awarded — only massive damage to *Time*'s prestige and reputation and to the standing of journalism itself.

Time's posture and defense in the Sharon Trial had been orchestrated entirely by the editorial side. The Time Inc. directors, among many others, were horrified by the result. The jury verdict and the public reaction to it allowed Munro and Nicholas to vocalize their outrage about an independent editor in chief. The traditional independent role of the Time Inc. editor in chief was for all practical purposes eliminated.

Munro and Nicholas were determined to put down Henry Grunwald, and Henry bears considerable blame for it. In one sense he asked for it. He had shown virtually no interest in the business side of Time Inc., as Hedley Donovan always had. He had practiced total editorial independence, and now there was the Sharon calamity. Munro and Nicholas clearly wanted an editor in chief who was not going to be strong. They were in awe of Grunwald and diffident about approaching him, and of course he is not an easy person to deal with. Even in my day, lunch with Henry was not a friendly conversational gambit.

But if they were in awe of Grunwald, they did not intend to be in awe of his successor. Ray Cave, the managing editor of *Time*, and previously a top editor at *Sports Illustrated*, was unacceptable to them because he was a very strong man. He could be difficult, disagreeable, impossible, outrageous, but at least he had strong views. There was massive pressure not to have Cave as the next editor in chief.

Grunwald, who was scheduled to retire at the end of 1987, dithered about picking his successor until the last possible moment but finally chose *Time*'s Jason McManus. McManus was a former Rhodes Scholar (like Donovan), a very popular, charming man who preferred compromise and negotiation to anything approaching confrontation. He liked to work

Carl Mydans took this picture of Aaron Shikler painting my retirement portrait for the 34th floor reception area. The new Time Inc. management decided to get rid of it, so my portrait now hangs in the New York Public Library.

things out. Much as he was liked and admired by the editors, there were fears that he would not be a strong editor in chief. The fears were justified.

↬ In July 1986, Munro became chairman as well as CEO. Nicholas was named chief operating officer. In everything but title, he was already the company's executive officer. Davidson was demoted to the empty job of chairman of the executive committee. Less than a year later he left with an extravagant negotiated settlement, including the fees for his lawyers.

A system of lucrative contracts was installed for top executives on both the publishing and editorial sides. These contracts spelled out the most extraordinary conditions and limitations which, if not immoral, were certainly improper for anybody in the publishing business to sign: namely, you are not going to say a word about the company that could possibly be construed as negative. If you do, you forfeit a lot of money you otherwise have coming to you.

Time Inc. had died in all but name. It had become just another company.

All this happened before anybody proposed the merger with Steve Ross and Warner.

I was personally made aware of the passing of Time Inc. by Munro. He appeared in my office one day and sat down across the desk from me, shirt-sleeve-casual as always, friendly and earnest.

"Andrew," he said, "We're going to give you back your portrait."

I was more than astonished. At the time of our retirements, the company had commissioned Aaron Shikler to paint official portraits of Hedley and me. They were part of the 34th floor ambience.

When you got off the elevator, the first thing you saw in the elevator well was a hundred cover plates from our magazines hanging from the ceiling. You could pick out the first cover of *Life,* the Fort Peck dam, and many others. This was impressive even when you learned that these were only plastic copies, because the ceiling could not have supported the weight of the original metal plates.

When you walked out of the elevator well into the spacious reception area, you saw a great semicircular arc of bookcases, every shelf filled with the bound volumes of all our magazines. Between the cover plates and the bound volumes, you were witnessing a lot of history.

And then you became aware of the two portraits, facing each other across the room. Hedley and I are both in shirtsleeves, our informal at-work uniform. Hedley leans slightly forward with the stern expression that all his editors knew well. I am leaning back in my chair with my hands behind my head, my glasses tucked in my shirt pocket, with a benevolent expression that I hope was equally recognizable. I must say I thought rather well of these portraits, and I liked the concept of Hedley and me standing guard, each in his own way, over our company.

"We're redecorating," Munro explained, "so you're welcome to it. We want you to have it."

"What about the portraits of Luce and Donovan?"

"Yep, they go too," Munro said.

I thought this amounted to something more than redecorating. I sent him a memo saying so:

> You came to my office to tell me you were remodeling the 34th floor reception room and that the Donovan and Heiskell portraits were to be

taken down. Furthermore, you said there would be no other place in Time Inc. where they could hang. You added that Henry Luce's picture would also go. I believe you said something like, "This is a different world, you know."

Indeed it is, and what management does with today's Time Inc. is obviously its responsibility.

However, Time Inc.'s history belongs to the corporation, not its current management. And rewriting history is not part of *our* company tradition.

I hope and trust you can find a way of accommodating these elements of Time Inc. history and heritage.

My memo won that round, but it was not the last round.

A year later, as chairman of the New York Public Library's board of trustees, I was conducting a board meeting when I was asked if there could be an interruption. I agreed. In walked Dick Munro and Nick Nicholas and a handful of others to make a special presentation. Time Warner, said Munro, was contributing $500,000 to the Library. Since this gift had been under discussion for months, I was not surprised, but naturally everybody was delighted.

Then Nicholas, with a gleam in his eye that he made no effort to conceal, said, "Andrew, we are also presenting your portrait to the Library."

Applause all around the table. Nick had won the last round.

My portrait now hangs in the New York Public Library. Hedley's portrait was given to his children, who in turn gave it to his college, the University of Minnesota. Luce's boardroom portrait is still in the building.

I don't know what became of Time Inc.

↬ Actually I *do* know what happened to Time Inc. It got devoured in the 1989 merger with Warner Communications and Steve Ross. After all the searching around that Dick Munro and Nick Nicholas and Gerry Levin did to find a suitable partner for a merger, the end of the chase was that they got involved with that awful man.

Ross was smart as hell. He had started in the funeral business and then the parking lot business and then the office cleaning business before, after multiple acquisitions, he got into movies and music. One of his projects was the Westchester Theatre, which turned into a scandal with charges of skimmed box office receipts, stock and tax fraud, bribery and obstruction of justice. Three of his aides and colleagues were convicted, but nothing happened to Ross himself.

When the merger with Warner Communications became a serious possibility, Dick Munro and Nick Nicholas consulted me. Perhaps they hoped to neutralize me by asking my opinion. I said that it was a bad *human* fit for Time Inc., with its excellent reputation, to merge with such a dubious partner. Hedley Donovan as former editor in chief flatly opposed the merger.

Munro and Nicholas and Levin went ahead anyway. The original plan was to merge the two companies by a stock swap. That would have avoided the huge expense of having to buy Warner Communications. But once the merger plan was announced, Paramount Pictures in the person of its CEO Marty Davis took the position that Time Inc. was now "in play." He offered to buy Time Inc. for $175 a share, almost 40% above the market price. This was also far above the price that would have applied to the stock-swap merger with Warner. The Time Inc. stockholders would have made a marvelous profit, but it was not to be.

Because of the Paramount offer a stock-swap was no longer possible. Munro's only alternative was for Time Inc. to *buy* Warner Communications outright. In the end that is what Time Inc. did — at a total cost of almost $15 billion. Even so, a court decision was necessary to say that this was a legitimate act on the part of Time Inc.'s board. The purchase of Warner stock enriched Steve Ross and his friends beyond anyone's wildest belief. And Steve Ross became chairman.

But the resulting company, Time Warner, has been in monstrous debt ever since. The poor stockholders didn't do very well either. During eight years of stock market explosion, the price of Time Warner stock stayed flat for eight years before a rise in 1997.

However, salaries did not stay flat. Early in the merger talks it was noted that Steve Ross paid himself and his top executives at Warner far, far more than Munro and Nicholas and Levin were paid at Time Inc. Whatever in the world could be done about that? The answer was easy. Munro and Nicholas and Levin got vast increases in salary, bonus and options.

Nothing else in the next decade was easy. Steve Ross died of cancer. Munro retired. Nicholas took over as chairman of Time Warner but was overthrown by Levin in a surprise coup that took place while Nicholas was out of town.

Ted Turner, whose Cable News Network and Atlanta superstation WTBS were merged into Time Warner in 1996, wound up as the new vice chairman and the owner of 61 million shares of Time Warner stock — by far the largest holding. Turner told the Time Life Alumni Society in a talk on June 25, 1997 that he had promised Levin, "I will never sneak up on you in the night, the way it happened to Nick." He also told the alumni that for Time Inc., "The Warner deal was horrible. They got cash, and Steve Ross got to run the company anyway." He also said in the same talk that, long range, print was headed for a continual decline. "The future for print," said the vice chairman of America's largest magazine publisher, "is not good, but it's not so bad that we have to bail out of it."

⤲ Today Gerald Levin, the chairman of Time Warner, gets $1 million in salary, $6.5 million in bonus and $300,000 in "other compensation," along with generous stock options. When I retired after 20 years as chairman of Time Inc., my salary was $250,000 with a bonus of $200,000. I thought that was quite good. I left my company in good shape — financially, spiritually, ethically. Its reputation was splendid.

Times change.

WORKING FOR "CHARITY"

◇◇◇◇

DURING MY TIME INC. YEARS AND EVEN MORE AFTER MY retirement I have spent a large part of my life working for what is loosely called "charity." It is an unfortunate word. To me, "charity" is a 15th-Century term meaning "to give alms." I prefer the word "nonprofit."

Nonprofit organizations do indeed depend on fund-raising and contributions from many, many people, but that is not their most important characteristic. The core fact about most of the nonprofits I have worked for is that they are large, complicated institutions. Although they rely on generosity — the giving of alms — they rely far more on creative ideas and on financial, managerial and political skills.

A big nonprofit organization is harder to run than a Fortune 500 company. The Enterprise Foundation, where I have worked the past ten years, has helped build *$3 billion* worth of housing for low income families. Harvard University and the New York Public Library, where I have also been closely involved, are both huge, complex institutions.

The nonprofit world is an American phenomenon, with very little of it anywhere else in the world. Yet it is vastly misunderstood in this country. It is considered marginal and not quite respectable compared to business and government. But it is probably 15% of our national economy and growing fast. It includes half of our college education system, half of our medical schools and hospitals, and most of our libraries, museums and arts, as well as thousands of smaller enterprises.

Because the nonprofit world is not properly respected, its employees are often poorly paid. A good nonprofit executive measures his skills and stature and responsibility against those of business executives, but his pay is only a fraction of what business executives get. When Harvard decided to set up its own in-house investment team to manage its endowment, it created an instant problem for itself. It had to pay its investment managers more than full professors or even the president himself. The differential was so great that Harvard had to move the investment group out of sight —away from Cambridge to downtown Boston.

Nonprofits have a similar problem when they try to get good trustees. *Trustee* is no longer just an honorary label. Trustees must give, get and work. Attendance at meetings is a problem. If a person is on the board of a business corporation, he gets paid maybe $40,000 a year. If he has to choose between collecting this fee from a corporation and attending a non-profit board meeting where he is not only not paid but is asked for money and told to help on some difficult task, his decision is not hard to make. I have often thought that nonprofits should pay their trustees — until I think of all the editorials that would condemn this foul act.

What goes on inside a business corporation is largely cloaked from the outside world. But in the nonprofit world every move, every decision, has to stand the test of public examination. How does the president's salary compare with the mayor's? Are you taking risks with your investments? You are considered reckless if you do and stodgy if you don't.

In a private business, if some fungus creates a minor health problem, you just deal with it. But if the same fungus appears in a branch library, we announce it broadly and wait for the press and politicians to find fault with our inadequate fungus control. In fact, one is lucky if a law isn't passed to prevent any future repetition of what has now been termed gross negligence.

Why would anybody spend as much time as I have in this world? I was not attracted to the nonprofit world for its own sake but rather because of specific causes. A lot of satisfaction for people like me comes from setting a goal and achieving it. Still more satisfaction comes if you believe you have done something good for a lot of people.

◡ I got into the Enterprise Foundation in a roundabout fashion over a period of years. That is perfectly normal in the nonprofit world, where one thing invariably leads to another.

Two of the magazines Time Inc. owned were *Architectural Forum* and

House and Home. They were small and always lost money but had great prestige in the housing world. Because I was chairman of the company, some of that prestige rubbed off on me, even though at that time I was no expert on housing.

In 1954 a group of people interested in housing problems formed a non-profit organization called ACTION — American Council To Improve Our Neighborhoods. Our goal was simply stated: to achieve "decent housing" for everybody in America within ten years. But within ACTION there was a deep philosophical split about the best way to achieve that goal. Half believed it should be done through public housing, and the other half thought it should be done through the private sector. Since I was neutral, and since I had the windfall prestige of *Architectural Forum* behind me, they picked me to be chairman. ACTION did not, of course, come anywhere near meeting its ten-year goal, but we had real influence on federal housing policy, and we managed to raise public interest in urban housing.

ACTION was hampered by the fact that we were somewhat poverty stricken. Fortunately another nonprofit organization called the Taconic Foundation was trying to improve the esthetic appearance of our cities through better housing, and Taconic was supported by buckets of Mellon money. In the early 1960s we merged into a single organization called Urban America, and I became chairman of that, too.

We tried to get important people in big cities involved in the housing problem. The deeper we got into it, the more we realized that the housing problem was in many ways a race problem. American had segregated its poor minorities in ghettos. So we got involved in the larger issue of trying to make the public and the government face the fact that we must end segregation. Obviously many other people were attacking this same problem at the same time in different ways.

Then, in 1966 and 1967, one city after another went up in the flames of race riots. Watts, Detroit, Newark — city after city. The National Guard was called out. Blacks were shot. Stores and homes were looted and burned. It was close to civil warfare, as blacks tried to break out of their poverty ghettos. Suddenly the whole country was asking, "What are we going to do about this?"

Everybody urged me as the chairman of Urban America to mobilize the

American system, the American structure, to do something that would both calm the country and give hope to the ghettos. All along we had met with individual mayors to discuss the problems of their cities. Now we realized we had to make a truly national gesture.

We called a meeting of 1,200 leaders of the U.S. in Washington, D.C. on August 25, 1967. It was an extraordinary meeting because we brought together people from government, big business, labor unions and minorities, many of whom had never met before, much less sat down to confront a common problem. Our executive committee had such people as Walter Reuther, Henry Ford, George Meany, John Lindsay, Whitney Young, A. Philip Randolph, Roy Wilkins, David Rockefeller.

They wrote a document calling on the 1,200 leaders to work together on a program. The problem was far too large to be handled by any one sector of the country. We must all work together in an Urban Coalition. At the big meeting we read this platform, it was discussed, amended, voted and passed. This made a tremendous splash on the front pages of the *New York Times* and the *Washington Post*. Everybody was talking about it. We felt a great sense of exhilaration that such a large, diverse group of leaders could agree on a national program.

The next day everybody went home — and I suddenly realized that as chairman I was left holding the bag. Nobody else had been given any specific responsibility. We had simply agreed on the program, and here was little Andrew supposed to execute it with no funds or personnel or anything. The budget of Urban America was only around $700,000 and our staff was only 25 people. Besides, I had a fulltime job as chairman of Time Inc.

Panic and dismay set in immediately because I had no idea how to handle the situation. I phoned my friend McGeorge Bundy, head of the giant Ford Foundation, and asked, "Mac, do you ever give advice instead of money?" He said, "Yes, sometimes. Come on over Saturday morning." "You work on Saturday?" "Yes, sometimes."

We talked for several hours and agreed that the key was to find someone with real stature and competence to run our new Urban Coalition as a fulltime job. We went over a whole series of names, most of which didn't impress me much. I finally said, "Look, if I find the right man, will you fund this operation with five million dollars?"

"Yes."

Now all I had to do was find my replacement.

A week or so later I read that John Gardner was resigning his cabinet post as Secretary of Health Education and Welfare. I called my friend Scotty Reston, the Washington bureau chief of the *Times*. I said, "Scotty, I know John Gardner somewhat, and I admire him immensely, but I think you know him quite well. Could you find out what he plans to do with himself now?"

Scotty said sure. Next day he called back and said, "John thinks he should get involved in the urban scene."

Well, my God.

I called him and went down to Washington to have lunch with him at HEW. It was one of the worst lunches I ever had, a piece of stringy pastrami and a cold potato. That was lunch in the bureaucratic world — horrible. But the meeting was wonderful because John said he was cautiously interested.

I pursued him by phone and letter. I got him to meet with Mac Bundy, who repeated his promise of Ford Foundation support if John took the job. John didn't say yes and he didn't say no.

A week later we met for a drink in New York's Regency Bar. I was talking quite loudly, trying to persuade him. The man at the next table finally leaned over and said, "Excuse me for interrupting, but I've been overhearing your conversation. I think the Urban Coalition is the only thing that can save the country."

I said, "John, honest to God, I didn't stage this."

I'm not sure John believed me, but he finally took the job.

Gardner is a tall, light-built man with a strong nose and penetrating eyes, an enormously thoughtful man who has devoted practically every minute of his life to the public good. He never had any money, and he never made any money. The only form of money he enjoyed was having a car and driver when he was Secretary of HEW. At the Urban Coalition the only thing he wanted was a car and driver — that was his total extravagance. Harry Luce liked to convince people by vigorous argument. John likes to convince people by gentle persuasion, logical but gentle. He never raises his voice.

Under his leadership we eventually organized some 30 Urban Coalitions in 30 cities. Over the next two decades we accomplished many great things. We broke down many racial barriers. We gave the minorities, the depressed, the poor, a place to go in Washington where they could get help, and we taught them how to go to their own city halls for help. We opened doors for them. The local Urban Coalitions also broke down barriers, getting people to talk to each other, getting people to agree that certain things had to be done, and in many cases getting them done. It's a slow, slow process, and there is no arithmetical way to prove how much we achieved.

Today I don't think many Urban Coalitions even exist. Most of them have metamorphosed into something else. All too often these nonprofit organizations get started for a good reason, but often there comes a time when they continue only because the staff wants to keep their jobs, or because somebody wants to be chairman.

One of the forms into which the Urban Coalition metamorphosed was the Enterprise Foundation. Its founder was Jim Rouse of Baltimore, a close friend and mentor whom I had known since ACTION days. He was a housing evangelist, an eloquent and persuasive speaker who could talk anybody into anything, very much including me.

As a builder, Rouse had made a fine fortune out of The Rouse Company. From scratch he created the brand new city of Columbia, Maryland, one of the greatest building gambles of all time. He also created the Faneuil Hall complex in Boston, the New York City Seaport and the Baltimore Waterfront. He was both a genius and a success, but you would never guess it to look at him. He was small, slightly heavy, quite bald, and his round owlish face was, to be blunt, unprepossessing. But he was charming and amusing, a lovely person.

When he retired from The Rouse Company, he decided to devote his time, energy and money to housing for the poor. Because we had worked together so often and so happily, he crooked his finger at me and said, let's go to work. In 1982 he started the Enterprise Foundation, which was a logical development of all the housing initiatives we had gone through before.

In ACTION we had been babes in the woods, trying to address the housing problem without knowing how. In Urban American we got involved in housing esthetics and learned a lot. In the Urban Coalition we

Jim Rouse was my mentor and good friend throughout my many years in the housing world, from Urban America and the Urban Coalition down to the Enterprise Foundation, which he created and where I am still active today.

learned that we could not impose solutions on communities. In Enterprise, Jim said that the way to take care of lower income people was to enable them to participate in their own salvation. Healthy communities must be created by the people who live there because that is the only way to have a lasting effect. What they want may not be what we want them to want. Everything has to be localized, community by community, because each one is different.

In Enterprise we took the position that housing was the best entry point to the totality of the poverty problem. If you don't improve housing, your efforts in other areas are frustrated. For instance, you can't expect to achieve educational goals for children if their housing is so bad that reading and homework are out of the question.

Rouse knew that Enterprise would require very big bucks. He devised something called the low-income housing tax credit and got it through Congress. This allows companies, particularly banks, to invest large sums in low-income housing at an excellent rate of return, but with the crucial proviso that the money has to stay there for 15 years. It is up to Enterprise to make sure those investments do not fail — and poor communities are always a risk. Enterprise is the intermediary between the investor and the community. We protect the investor's commitment by helping the community to succeed. Our failure rate, I am happy to say, has been small.

We work with what are called Community Development Corporations — CDCs. A CDC always starts from within a community, frequently through a local church. A CDC always starts small, and it is always run by their people, not our people. Sometimes they hear of Enterprise and come to us, sometimes we hear of them first and offer our help. Our main job is to provide housing — so far $3 billion worth in 700 CDCs all across America. But we also help them establish their own goals, we give them advice, we show them how to make things work, we try to be useful when they get in trouble, as they often do. But it is their show, not ours. As they progress, we also help them set up programs for employment and child care. Enterprise also develops special housing for the elderly and persons with medical problems such as AIDS.

In New York, where I am chairman of Enterprise's advisory board, we have helped build more than $600 million in housing. Our executive director Bill Frey and a staff of about 20 are helping 70 CDCs achieve their goals. Here is one example:

The Aquinas Housing Corporation grew out of the Aquinas Catholic Church in the West Farms section of the South Bronx. Aquinas started small by co-sponsoring a low-income housing project under another organization's leadership. When they decided, a decade ago, that they wanted to be independent, they got in touch with Enterprise. They wanted to build a 19-unit housing development for the elderly. I have said that CDCs start small, and you can't start much smaller than 19 housing units. Aquinas had some funding from the State, but there was a gap between what the State would pay and what the development would cost. Could we help? We did, by arranging a low-income housing tax credit investment that closed the gap.

Since that time Aquinas has built 1,000 housing units. Much of this is rehabilitation of old buildings, but some is brand new. With encouragement and advice from Enterprise, they have branched out into job training, health care, child care, safety programs. The Aquinas Housing Corporation is now far larger than its founder, the Aquinas Church. Its area of interest and development is roughly 15 blocks, a large size for a CDC. The population is about 75% Hispanic and 25% black.

The most important person in this institution is its executive director, Meagan Shannon. She is white and Irish. She is an attractive woman in her early 30s, of average height, average weight and average brown hair, but she has terrific energy — and a smile to match. It is fascinating to walk through the Aquinas territory with Meagan Shannon. Everybody knows her, everybody stops to ask her a question or to tell her something. When she visits a new housing rehabilitation project, the building contractors ask her questions and so do the tenants. Everybody counts on her, and she is on duty all day long every day.

I like to get out in the field to see firsthand what Enterprise is doing. I like to watch people like Meagan Shannon at work. I like to visit other community leaders like Abdur Farrakhan in the Brownsville section of Brooklyn, and I am pleased that he now trusts me enough to have promoted me from "Mr. Heiskell" to "Brother." I ask a lot of questions. Sometimes I have suggestions. I prod people. Have you thought of this? Have you thought of that? This worked somewhere else, so maybe it will work

During an Enterprise Foundation tour of the Aquinas Housing Corporation in the south Bronx, executive director Meagan Shannon and I take a park-bench break.

here for you. I tell them that if they want to start improving a neighborhood, the very first and very cheapest step is to sweep your streets. Then you can use a bucket of paint here and there. We can help you get a machine that will eliminate graffiti.

I love to take people from midtown Manhattan on a tour of the South Bronx or Brownsville or anywhere else that Enterprise is engaged. Many successful people want to help in some way, and I like to show them what Enterprise is doing.

My great friend Jim Rouse is now dead, but his last grand adventure, the Enterprise Foundation, is very much alive.

⤺ I first went to work for Harvard because of my experience in urban affairs. (As I said, one thing leads to another.) Harvard asked me to chair several committees dealing with urban matters. I must have done it reasonably well because one day I was approached by a Harvard friend, Bill Rothschild, the retired CEO of Abraham Straus. He was a Harvard graduate and a member of Harvard's Board of Overseers. This is a prestigious group of 30 individuals who are proposed by the Alumni Association and then voted on by the alumni.

Bill said to me, "Why don't you run for Overseer?"

I had an excellent answer to that. "I never even went to the college. I only went to the Business School for a year, and I hated that."

"That doesn't matter," Bill said. "You'd find it very interesting."

"How could I even get elected? I mean, there's not an alumnus who ever heard of me."

"Don't worry, you're fairly well known. You just might get elected, and it wouldn't do you any real harm if you didn't make it. Why don't you let me put you up?"

So I agreed. Each year the Alumni Association proposes a slate of ten candidates, and the top five vote-getters become Overseers. So once you are on the slate, you theoretically have an even chance of being elected.

"Now look, Andrew," Bill said, "there's one thing you have to make sure to do. When you send in your picture for the ballot that goes out to the alumni, don't have a picture that makes you look like a stuffy old banker. Wear an open-collared shirt."

So I sent in a casual picture taken by my wife Marian. I was the only one of the ten people on the ballot in an open-collared shirt. I came in fifth, I'm sure on the strength of that shirt, so I became an Overseer with a six-year term ahead of me. It started my long, long career at Harvard.

The Overseers met five or six times a year. They tried — very badly — to address various problems, and they spent a lot of time arguing. Indeed, they were a structural mess. One major problem was that they didn't know what they were supposed to be doing. Power is distributed very broadly at

Wherever I am, I spend a large part of my life on the phone. This phone booth is at Harvard, and I am checking back with my office in New York.

Harvard. As Harvard people like to say, "You can't even find out where it is." The Overseers were just one branch of government. The faculty had its own branch. The deans of the graduate schools had their branch. And then there was a mysterious thing called the Corporation, which from the Overseers' point of view seemed like a secret society — a much smaller group that met much more often and appeared to deal with much more substantive matters. (When I eventually joined the Corporation, I found that all these suspicions were reasonably correct.)

One reason the Overseers were such a mess was that many of them considered themselves representatives of a special interest, be it women, or the church, or minorities. Instead of talking and thinking about what's good for Harvard, they talked and thought about "the woman issue at Harvard," or whatever their favorite issue was. So there was no cohesion whatsoever.

They were also unruly and indiscreet. Derek Bok, the president of Harvard, hated to address them. He knew that if he told them all the truth, it would immediately leak out, but if he didn't tell them, they would probably find out anyway and complain publicly about not being informed. It was such a dilemma for him that he tried to avoid coming to meetings. The Overseers were not helpful to his cause.

I think if Bok had had his way, he would happily have disbanded the body. But since it had been created 350 years earlier, originally composed of the leading ministers in Boston, he couldn't quite do that. Besides, the structure of Harvard is embodied in the state laws of Massachusetts, so you can't change anything without going to the legislature. And if you ever went to the legislature, would they ever have fun with Harvard! Once you let them in the tent, they would think of many, many things to change. So for fear of that, the last thing anybody would ever do is try to change any legal aspect of the structure. So Bok was stuck with the Overseers.

When I had been an Overseer long enough to have some influence, I decided we had to elect members who had more discipline and more sense of cohesion. By fair means and foul I persuaded the Alumni Association directors to propose candidates who would be acceptable colleagues and work well together. I talked to the head of the Association, to the Secretary of the Corporation, to anybody who had power in this area. I convinced them it was important to reform the body and give it the kind of muscle that would help in the huge capital campaign that Harvard had just announced. The campaign was a handy tool for my purpose, and I used it to the hilt.

A strange fact about the alumni who bother to vote for the Overseers is that they tend to be the older ones, who would presumably be more conservative. Not at all. They inevitably vote for a woman or a minority or a radical. While I did not exactly pack the slate of candidates, I tried to ensure that those who were proposed thought of themselves as representing the interest of the university rather than of their particular sector. I also loaded the slate with businessmen, first because we needed them for the capital campaign, and second because they were trained to operate in a committee structure. Most of them had been on a lot of boards, so they didn't take advantage of being elected to the Overseers by expressing every view in the world.

In my fourth year I was chosen president of the Overseers. By that time I knew all the players from Derek Bok on down, and we all had the same goal: to make the Overseers function better. We did this chiefly by establishing half a dozen committees, each with a reasonably clear purpose. The full Board of Overseers, with 30 members confronting an entity as vast, disparate and uncoordinated as Harvard, cannot address the university as a whole. You have to break it up into small component parts — the committees. Ultimately we got the Overseers to function quite well, and to realize that they were *not* running the university, and that that was *not* why they were there. Their role was to oversee the different functions of a university with 15,000 students and 14,000 employees. But oversight does not include actual authority, and that always bothered them.

In 1979, my sixth and last year as an Overseer, Derek Bok took me aside. "You know John Blum is retiring from the Corporation, and I would like you to take his place. I realize it might cause you considerable problems. It's very demanding in terms of time, but I'd like to have you as a Fellow."

The Corporation has only seven members: the president, the treasurer and five Fellows. It is really the management council of the university. It meets every two weeks and requires an immense amount of homework.

I had to think hard about this. I was still the full-time chairman of Time Inc. Could I spare that much time away from the job I was paid to do? But

President Derek Bok is first row center in this picture of Harvard's seven member Corporation, where I served for ten years.

I thought I had my management succession pretty well in hand, and I thought maybe the wisest thing might be to distance myself a little bit so that my successors could learn the trade while I was still around to answer questions and give advice. And it appealed to me to be on Harvard's small management council and to work closely with Bok. I told him I would do it.

Derek Bok was an enormously thoughtful man. His capacity for work, ranging from the intellectual to fund-raising, was extraordinary. He could do in a day what would take most people two weeks. Every year he wrote a major paper on a different academic subject, often criticizing some particular part of the university. One year he criticized the sainted Business School and infuriated all its wealthy graduates. It takes a lot of courage to do that. He wrote excellent letters to the deans of the college and the graduate schools, prodding them gently but firmly in the direction he wanted them to go. He was a proponent of innovation. He was very good at administration and handling budgets. Because he recognized that he could not run Harvard single-handed, he spent perhaps a third of his time on appointments, carefully selecting the exactly right man or woman for the right job. I have the greatest admiration for him as a man and as a president. But he is not a genuinely warm person. He is really quite distant. You never get closer to him than three feet. And yet he and I had a wonderful relationship, and still do.

I had become accustomed to the fact that when I joined the Board of Overseers, it was a mess. I couldn't believe the same thing was true of the Corporation. Yet when I joined it, I found that the agenda for our meetings was slapped together by the handful of administrators who composed the Corporation staff. They piled up stacks of paper on various problems, an incredible amount of reading on subjects that had not been thought through or studied or digested in any way. This pile was plunked on us on Friday. When we arrived in Cambridge for the Monday morning meeting, we were expected to discuss each item intelligently.

I complained repeatedly about this system, but the words of the newest Fellow had no effect. Then one Monday morning after a year of this, I achieved a certain amount of fame when I said, in exasperation, "I'm sick and tired of being tossed a bowl of untreated sewage to consider for the next meeting." That stopped everybody cold. At last I had got my point across because I had used the term "untreated sewage." You can express a view in ten different ways, as I already had, but if you can find exactly the right words, it stops everybody. "What do you mean, untreated sewage?" I said, "This is no way to run an organization like this."

We then settled down to thinking about how we *should* operate. We came up with a scheme whereby we laid out the entire year's agenda, so that we knew that over a three-year period we would cover every unit and every kind of problem that the university faced. We allowed one hour at each meeting to discuss recent events or crises, but after that we followed an organized plan. So we did improve the system, and we did cut down on the sewage.

The Overseers made a lot of noise and achieved not that much. The Corporation made no noise at all and achieved a fair amount. Anonymity was the name of the game for the Corporation. We were always anonymous, it was part of the job.

During my ten years as a Fellow, the Corporation dealt with everything imaginable — and with some things that were unimaginable. My favorite, in terms of sheer complexity and horror, was the new power plant. It began while I was still an Overseer and continued throughout my career as a Fellow.

The Harvard Medical School has 11 associated hospitals, practically a whole section of Boston. The central power plant was antique, expensive and inefficient. During the oil crisis of the 1970s, somebody dreamt up a creature called "co-generation," a power plant that provides electricity, air conditioning, heat and chilled water, all at the same time — greatest thing ever. So we decided to build a nice $50 million ultra-modern co-generation plant in the center of Boston.

Before Harvard began construction, the environmentalists took us to court, charging that the oil fuel for our plant would produce carcinogenic agents. Although we were able to proceed with construction, it was not until February 6, 1987 — 13 years later! — that the court procedures ended. After millions of dollars in legal costs we could go ahead.

Meantime over these years our nice $50 million plant became an $80 million plant, became a $100 million plant and eventually became a $350 million plant, at a time when the budget of the entire university was about $1 billion. We borrowed a lot of money, we capitalized the interest, which in those times ran as high as 18%, and we were forced to learn how to manage our finances.

The power plant crisis was happening at the same time we were starting a massive capital campaign. If you are in a capital drive, you need a good reputation for handling your finances, because nobody likes to give money to an institution that is financially irresponsible. While we were raising tons of money for the university, we were trying to drape dark blankets over the co-generation plant so that nobody could see it.

We did fulfill our campaign drive, and the power plant finally functioned. But it's not the way to run a railroad — or a power plant either, for that matter. In 1997 Harvard gave up and sold it to Commonwealth Advanced Energy Systems for a price less than the debt Harvard was still carrying on the plant.

I finally left the Corporation in 1989 when I was 73. No one is ever asked to resign from the Corporation. Once you are chosen, you are there for good, but you are expected to resign at age 70. I was asked to stay on until 73, which was very flattering.

At a Harvard Commencement I doff my top hat to the graduates as I follow President Derek Bok to the dais.

Looking back on my long experience, I believe that Harvard is a combination of people and time and reputation, the three all go together. Over a long period of time you build up a reputation, and then the reputation helps you attract people: good professors, good assistant professors, good instructors, good students. Over time you develop in a number of directions, not only a great college but great graduate schools. You attract and pull together some of the best minds in the country, and best minds like to be with other best minds. It's a continuous process that builds and builds and builds — if you are doing it right. The price of being Number One is that you are extremely visible, everybody pays attention to what you do. You have to operate by consensus. You know that any time you are about to make an important decision, you have to take time to talk to everybody and build that consensus. Half of your reputation depends on protecting it from ill-advised proposals.

In 1978 when I first signed on to help the New York Public Library, it had almost no reputation left to protect. During the 1970s New York City came so close to bankruptcy that it had to cut back on everything. It cut back savagely on funds for the Library because in those days the Library had no political clout. It had no constituency except scholars, children and ordinary citizens who like to read.

The Library is a semi-public, semi-private institution. Basically the city supports the 83 branch libraries scattered throughout the boroughs. The branches get some help from private funds, but they run mainly on city money. On the other hand the research libraries, including the main building at Fifth Avenue and 42nd Street, are supported mostly by private funds but also by city and state money.

In the 1970s the city cut back so hard on the Library that some of the branches were open only eight hours a week. Some librarians had to scurry from building to building trying to service three branches in one week. The marble inside the main Fifth Avenue building, the one with the great sculpted lions guarding the broad front steps, was so filthy brown that you would never guess it was marble. Inside this building were more than three million books, many of them extremely valuable, gathering dust and crumbling away in stacks that were not air conditioned. The Library had begged the city for air conditioning for 20 years, but nothing happened. The Library had a weak board of trustees and no management worth mentioning.

Richard Salomon, a friend of mine who lived a floor above me in my apartment house, was the chairman of the Library. He had worked hard but was getting tired and discouraged. He knew I was close to retirement from Time Inc., so he asked if I would join his board. His thought was that if it interested me, I would succeed him as chairman. If it didn't, I could just quietly withdraw after a year. (This is an excellent way to recruit people; I've used it myself on others.)

I joined the board and spent a lot of time looking over this rather sizable enterprise. I visited the branches, and I went through the stacks, and I talked to people, and I looked at the finances. It was a sad, dismal picture in every way, big and small. If it had not been for Brooke Astor's mammoth gift of $5 million several years earlier, the Library would have slipped over the edge. Even after her gift, the Library was broke. The chandeliers and lighting fixtures all through the main building were dirty and had only two or three bulbs in each. The beautiful Celeste Bartos Forum, now the Library's most important meeting place, had been turned into a warehouse. The gorgeous Gottesman Exhibition Hall had been divided by masonite partitions into tiny offices for personnel and accounting. The only decent room in the entire building was the board room, but even there the tall curtains fell apart if you touched them.

The picture was so bleak that I had only two choices: (1) I think I'll get out of this one, or (2) the Library is so essential to the future of the city and to all the other institutions in the city that maybe a really big effort should be made. When I retired from Time Inc., I chose the second option. But with one condition: I would have a lot to say about picking a new president.

We set up a search committee and hired a search firm. We saw a number of characters, adequate but not sparkling, not the kind of people who would turn a nearly defunct organization into a lively and vibrant one. Then, out of nowhere, a new candidate appeared.

Vartan Gregorian, an Armenian and an historian, had been provost of the University of Pennsylvania. Faculty, students and a number of trustees had expected him to become the new president. I don't know exactly what happened, but I can guess. One trustee probably said to another, "I don't think Philadelphia should have an Armenian as president of the university. An Armenian who doesn't even use articles when he talks!" That sort of thing probably went from one Philadelphia trustee to another, and he ended up not getting the job. He was furious, to put it mildly, and suddenly on the market.

Instinctively I knew he was it. Here was the man who could do the job, and the search committee agreed. We told the search firm, "Okay, no more. Just make sure we get him."

Vartan Gregorian, called Greg by me, was 46. He had good academic credentials and great energy. He speaks seven languages. He is a funny-looking man, small and stocky with bushy gray-black hair and a strong Armenian accent. Over his years at the Library he gained 30 pounds because he had to go to a working breakfast, lunch and dinner every day, sometimes two or three dinners. At Penn he had already proved he was a good administrator, and I had a hunch he was also a good salesman. And he had to be good with people if the Penn faculty and students wanted him for their president.

When you bring somebody into New York City from outside, the first problem is not salary but housing. Somehow the word got out that we were talking about spending $500,000 to house this new man. Many people with good intentions and bad judgment started screaming. How can an organization that's practically bankrupt spend that kind of money on housing? In fact, of course, all the big nonprofits provide housing for their presidents — universities, hospitals, churches. It is not a question of misspent money but of getting the right person to save the institution. We solved the crisis by getting my predecessor Dick Salomon to give the money for this explicit purpose. He stated publicly, "I would not give this money if it were not for this purpose." That took all the rest of us trustees off the hook.

Greg immediately did the same thing I had done, but even more thoroughly. He examined every cranny of the whole enormous institution. We had 2,600 employees, an operating budget of $52 million and an endowment of some $75 million. (In 1998 the budget is $175 million and the endowment is at the $400 million level.) But the Library had been spending the endowment just to keep afloat, which meant we now had less of the endowment income on which the Library depended heavily. Greg realized it was a perilous job. A huge amount of work would have to be done at great cost over a long period of time before we could turn the monster around.

Staff morale was terrible. They had been hit so often, there had been so many firings, that they practically had their arms up over their heads, waiting for the next blow. Greg and I made a major decision. We told the staff: *No more talk about what's wrong with the Library.* From now on we will say only what's good about the Library — even if you can find only one small thing.

This sounds funny, but without having achieved anything substantive during the first year, just stopping the bad talk and spreading the good talk made a difference. It also made a difference that this character Gregorian immediately got embraced by the entire city. Or perhaps he embraced the entire city, I'm not sure which. Within six months he knew Mayor Ed Koch and Philanthropist Brooke Astor better than I, who had lived in this world for years. He sold the importance of the Library: why we needed the money, what would happen if we didn't get it. He sold this to the city, to the state, to the feds and to private citizens.

Greg and I realized that the Library's long-term health would depend on creating a professional management. Like most nonprofits we had highly competent specialists who had been asked to take on managerial tasks for which few were fitted. In addition to attracting paid talent for specific jobs, we tried to fill out certain areas by inviting highly-qualified people to join the board.

While our main function was collecting books and documents and making them available to the public, we were also in the real estate business. We had close to 100 buildings ranging from mini-library size to the 700,000 square foot main building. Many were crumbling. Like other nonprofits the Library was living off what is called deferred maintenance: don't spend any money fixing things because you need that money just to stay alive. We needed a person with a clear sense of real estate value, someone who understood the proper use of space and who had the savvy to oversee repairs and reconstruction.

We asked our board for suggestions. One came up with the name of

Library President Vartan Gregorian and I stand in front of a sculpted lion that guards the front steps.

Marshall Rose, a young fellow who owned his own real estate firm. Greg and I called on him, liked him and asked him to join us. He demurred because he was terrified that we would ask him to raise money, a prospect that often frightens first-time trustees. When we finally convinced him that we wanted him for his real estate expertise, he said he would try.

At virtually the same moment that he agreed to help us, we were faced with the prospect of selling a garage at 87th and Broadway. People often leave us strange things in their wills, and somebody had willed us this garage. It was valued at $150,000, and a buyer stepped forward. Since we had no use for a garage at that location, we certainly wanted to sell. But just for the hell of it, I asked this new guy Marshall Rose to take a look. He reported back: don't sell it, something is happening up there. Sure enough, the garage was at the bottom of a building that was about to be demolished to make way for a high-rise. We eventually sold the garage for $3 million.

We turned over all real estate to Marshall, put him in charge of all construction, and later made him head of the executive committee. (Ten years later he became chairman of the Library.)

We hired John Masten from the city's Office of Management and Budget, a fellow as tall as I am. The minute we had him we solved many of our problems with the city, because he knew how the city operated. He knew where the money was and what pockets to look in. Even more important, the city officials knew that he knew. That stopped the kind of game-playing that had gone on before, where officials pretended that they were helpless to help us.

From the Metropolitan Museum of Art we borrowed, part time, an architect named Arthur Rosenblatt to help us begin reconstruction. Arthur later claimed there was so much work that he was doing two fulltime jobs, one for the Met and one for the Library. He was shocked to hear that we were planning to ask the city for only $600,000 for our capital building budget. He pointed out that the Met gets $10 million and that even the Brooklyn Museum gets $6 or $7 million. He said we should ask for something so big that even if the city cut it way down, it would still be a lot of money. In the end we got $4.7 million.

As part of our building campaign, Arthur Rosenblatt and a colleague took photographs of every horrible scene and detail they could find in the

Library and put them all in a slide carousel that they called "The Ugly Show." They showed it to board members, city officials, potential contributors — anybody they could persuade to sit down and watch.

Ultimately so much reconstruction work had to be done that within five years we were running over 100 reconstruction projects in the research libraries and in the branches. Fortunately it was all reconstruction, not new construction from the ground up. That meant we did not have to deal with the construction unions and the Mafia.

Where did we get all the money? We were not like other big nonprofits. The Metropolitan Opera is supported by people who go to the opera and love opera and can afford to pay $150 for an orchestra seat. The Metropolitan Museum is supported by people who love paintings and who are often wealthy enough to collect paintings. Harvard has its 220,000 alumni, a rich source of contributions. We at the Library would have to create our own base of support.

In Greg's and my third year we made what is called a needs assessment for the entire Library system — every single thing that needed to be done. The total came to a billion dollars. Well, we knew we couldn't possibly raise that, so we rather arbitrarily cut out this or that need and got it down to $475 million. When we asked an outside firm for an evaluation of what was possible, they estimated we could raise $300 million, half in public funds, half in private money. We cut our shopping list again.

So how do you get $300 million when your only alumni are schoolchildren who borrow books from the branch libraries and authors researching exotic subjects? Greg and I went to the board and said, "This is what we recommend. But it will only happen if the board itself puts up a sizable amount."

Now you are getting on very dangerous ground!

"What do you mean by sizable?"

I said, "Forty-five million."

At that time we had perhaps 35 trustees, and six or eight of them were academics with no money to give. But the board voted that it should put up the $45 million before going public with the campaign. A gallant statement of support.

The whole trick on this kind of drive is to set the right level of giving.

The first big contribution is called "the lead gift." It pretty much determines what everybody else is going to give. It's extraordinary to what degree it does. The level of the lead gift means more than the name of the donor. But if the first donor also happens to be prominent, really connected and therefore setting a clear example, that is all to the good.

In our case Brooke Astor, Mrs. Vincent Astor, head of the Vincent Astor Foundation and our most prominent trustee, was obviously the lead gift. She would set the level for good or bad. If she ended up giving $2 million, then everybody else would give proportionately and we might as well forget the whole thing.

It was a long and arduous courtship. Not that she didn't want to give. On the contrary, she did, and she knew she had to. But her foundation had already given away so much money that if she made a big gift to the Library, it might be the last substantial gift she could make. Naturally we — Greg, Dick Salomon and I — talked to her as sweetly as we knew how.

It took six months. Time went on and on, and we could not ask any other trustees to give until Brooke set the level. With some discreet detective work we finally got a good fix on how much money she had left in her foundation. We figured $40 million. But because the foundation had already made a number of commitments to other institutions, how much did we dare to ask for?

We finally designed a package for her that came to $7.8 million. Our package described in detail exactly what that sum would accomplish. It was the most we could hope for. More time went by.

One day she said, without preamble, "I'm going to give you ten million." Period. No conditions, no nothing. "That's it as far as my foundation is concerned. This is my last big gift."

She has been marvelous. Today she is in her mid-90s, but she regularly attends meetings of the executive committee and comes to all the Library's showcase events. She visits the branches. She writes poetry and books. She's *seriously* interested in the Library. When we have our Christmas party open house, attended by more than 10,000 people, she is standing there in the receiving line.

After Brooke's lead gift, we eventually fulfilled our capital goal from both public and private funds. Raising money consists primarily of having a clear view of what you want to do and being able to articulate it. You make it absolutely clear that you have the people to implement it so that the donor's money won't go down the drain. Then you have to be smart and guess that such-and-such a person might give you a special gift for lighting or for a particular new book collection. Most people don't want to give just money. They want to give money for something specific. They don't necessarily want to have their name on it, but they want to give for something that is real, something they can see and touch. You try to match the donor with the object.

Of all the Library packages that I thought I would never sell to anybody was the $1 million needed to dust 88 miles of bookshelves. They had not been dusted in 75 years. Because we never had air conditioning, all the windows had been open every summer for decades. All the dust and dirt of the city was inside the Library. But who in the world would want to pay us to take down each book and dust it off?

It turned out that Hannish Maxwell, chairman of Philip Morris, loved books. He thought dusting books was just the greatest thing he ever heard of, so his company gave us the million. When one of the young ladies brought me the first installment, a check for $250,000, I said, "This will clean twenty-two miles of books!" She was amazed at the thought, asked a few questions and then told somebody else how the cleaning was done. It wound up as a full column in the *New York Times* about Russian emigres whose profession it is to clean books.

Today the New York Public Library is an institution the whole city can be proud of. After eight fantastic years as president, Greg went on to become president of Brown University. I remained chairman for two more years after Greg left. Today I am still a trustee, and I remain part of the Library's kitchen cabinet: the president Paul LeClerc, the chairman Marshall Rose, the chairman of the executive committee Sam Butler and me.

I will leave it only when I die.

↝ I have told the stories of three nonprofits — Enterprise, Harvard, the Library — where I have spent the most time and had the greatest personal satisfaction. In another chapter I will tell the story of Bryant Park, which was perhaps the greatest satisfaction of all because it was my longest and most frustrating project. Not only did these undertakings overlap with one another in time, but I also worked for many other nonprofits. In no particular order over the years I have tried to help:

People for the American Way

Common Cause

Lincoln Center Theater

Bennington College

Brookings Institution

Institute for International Education

American Academy in Rome

For a while during the Reagan years I was also chairman of the President's Committee on the Arts and Humanities. This was a government body rather than a nonprofit, but its aims were similar to the nonprofit world. It was an advisory group founded by friends of the Reagans from Hollywood days. They wanted to protect the National Endowment for the Arts and the National Endowment for the Humanities, both of which Reagan had promised to eliminate during his election campaign. It had only a small staff and budget, and its declared purpose was to review what the endowments were doing, promote private giving to the arts and humanities and recommend policy to the President. The committee cleverly named Nancy Reagan to be chairman. Like most honorary chairmen her principal role was to serve as a figurehead, but it would be difficult for the President to eliminate NEA and NEH when his own wife was playing that role. They asked me to chair the committee because I had had a lot of experience and because they thought it would look better if the chairman was not a personal friend of the Reagans.

Shortly after becoming chairman, I hired the two key staff people, one to handle the administrative end and one to handle the programmatic end. The one I picked for the latter was Joe Krekora, who had been running a ballet company in Chicago. I persuaded him to work for us, to leave

Chicago and move to Washington. Two weeks after he arrived, somebody fired him because he was not a Republican.

This act meant that I had no authority as chairman, so I had to do something about it. I asked to see Mrs. Reagan at once. The White House thought it had a great excuse: the Reagans were leaving for California tomorrow and would be gone a week. She would have no time to see me. "That's all right," I said to their surprise, "I'll come to California. Make an appointment for me out there."

I flew to Los Angeles and showed up at the giant Century City building, where the Reagans had two full floors of offices. After I sat for a while in one of the meeting rooms, White House aide Mike Deaver came in to see me. He obviously hoped that he could take care of my problem, whatever it was. We chatted a while but I told him nothing. Then Chief of Staff Jim Baker, soon to be named Secretary of State, joined us. More chat, but still I told them nothing.

At last Nancy Reagan appeared and sat down with us. Now it was time for me to talk.

I explained that if the White House wanted to fire the man I had just hired, if the White House wanted to maintain that prerogative, that was fine with me. I certainly understood it to be their right. But I would have to bow out as chairman. I said, "Please make up your minds rapidly, because this story is going to blow. It will be quite embarrassing because I haven't been chairman very long, and everybody's going to want to know why I quit. And of course I'll have to tell them. So please let me know by Monday what you want to do."

I said goodby and flew back to New York.

The White House called me first thing Monday to point out that this was Columbus Day, a holiday, and they could not reach the right people. Could they please have one more day to deal with this? I generously said yes. They talked to the right people and called me on Tuesday. Joe Krekora was reinstated.

More recently I had another successful experience with the U.S. Government, this time with the State Department. I had just become chairman of the executive committee for the American Academy in Rome. Heading the executive committee of a nonprofit allows me to be "inside" the organization. You deal continuously with staff and key trustees. You can guide the long-range direction of the venture. And you don't have to be chairman of the entire organization, presiding at formal affairs, making speeches and performing ceremonial functions, all activities that I can cheerfully forgo.

I had tried hard to avoid the American Academy in Rome. The paid president, Adele Chatfield-Taylor, came after me in 1989. I have always been vulnerable to a charming, persuasive woman, but I told her, quite truthfully, that I had no space in my calendar. The more she told me about the Academy the worse her problems looked.

Wealthy Americans, including J. P. Morgan, had founded the Academy in 1894. Each year it brings gifted Americans, chosen by juries, to Rome to study and to complete important projects. The 25 or so Fellows, who are on total scholarship with all expenses paid, including a stipend, can be classicists, architects, poets, composers, authors. This is quite an elitist thing, it's as elitist as anything can be. But if you don't cultivate the elites, where will your civilization be in the next generation?

The Academy had 11 buildings on the Janiculum, overlooking Rome and the Tiber. But the Academy had been poorly managed, its endowment had shrunk. As usually happens when an institution runs short of money, repairs and maintenance had ceased. I was relieved to be able to say no thanks to Adele.

Six months later she came back for a second try, bringing with her Elizabeth McCormack. She was a former nun and the former president of Manhattanville College. She resigned both roles to get married and to enter vigorously into the outside world, including the board of the Academy. She was about five feet tall, brilliant and packed with energy.

While I had been able to resist one charming, persuasive woman, I could not resist two. Between them they squeezed me into taking over the executive committee.

It did not take me long to discover that the administrators and academics wanted to preserve all their authority and expected the trustees to stay out of their way. This is a common attitude at academic institutions. It was most vividly expressed to me by an academic at the Brookings Institution: "The trustees should rustle up the money and leave it on the stump."

Since we had architects on the board, we already had excellent concepts about how to restore and repair the crumbling old buildings. But we had no money to carry them out. I learned, however, that one of our buildings was rented out to the U.S. State Department for their Vatican Embassy at the trifling price of $85,000 a year. This was a ridiculous rent for an imposing building in a magnificent location, suitable for splendid diplomatic entertaining.

I said we had to do two things and do them simultaneously: we had to sell the building, and we had to notify the State Department that we were going to throw them out, and they would just have to go hunt for another embassy. Since one can no longer build anything new in the city of Rome, one can only improve or expand or renovate what is already there. The State Department would be in a bind.

We found an Italian businessman who was willing to buy our building for $6 million. We paraded this news in front of the State Department, which thought hard about how much work and money would have to go into buying another building in an inferior location and then fixing it up for offices and entertaining. After they thought about it long enough, they caved in and settled. They rented our building for 20 years at $500,000 a year, rising to $750,000 a year. Most important, they paid part of this rent as a $3 million advance. Now we had enough money to go to work on the Academy's other buildings.

A few days after the settlement, our would-be Italian buyer was thrown in jail for corrupt business practices.

⤳ No account of life in the nonprofit world would be complete without a story of failure. Mine is Bennington College in Vermont. A friend at the Ford Foundation who had helped me raise money for an urban world project said he thought Bennington needed somebody just like me as a trustee. It was blackmail, but so what? I said yes. This was in the early 1960s when I could still use the company plane for my associations of this kind, saving me a five-hour drive from New York.

Bennington was founded as a woman's college, very liberal, very arts-oriented. It had had some success, both in its graduates and its faculty, but it was in a perpetual financial bind. The main reason was that at commencement they told the graduating class, "We've done everything we can for you, you've got everything you can out of Bennington, so go on your way, God bless you, and you don't have to think of Bennington again." So of course they didn't. The school did not even have a complete list of its graduates. They did not even hold reunions. This is totally different from, say, Dartmouth. At Dartmouth commencement they say, "We've done everything for you, now you've got to do everything for Dartmouth." And by God, they do. They contribute enormously. And every Dartmouth graduate hears from Dartmouth every year.

I am convinced to this day that a lot of Bennington graduates are wealthy because they came from wealthy families. But very few came back to the college, and very few gave money. No private college can survive without contributions from its graduates.

Bennington is a long way from anywhere. Everybody lives within the college community, constantly seeing each other and practically nothing else. By the time I became a trustee, it was slightly coeducational but not very.

The first big job I got involved in was picking a new president. For some reason I and various other trustees thought it would be a great thing — in part because the place was so isolated — to pick a married couple, the wife as president and the husband as vice president. We picked a couple from Harvard, and brought them to Bennington, but it didn't work out at all. Nothing went right. After a while the chairman of the board of trustees quit, and then the president herself quit, so we had to start all over again.

Because of constant financial crunch and endless deficits, being president of Bennington wasn't much fun. One president, told by the board to cut costs by 20%, wound up having to fire a sizable number of tenured professors. Since Bennington was still mainly a woman's college, many of the trustees were understandably women, but two-thirds of them had no business experience, no fundraising experience and no academic experience beyond their own college years. Uphill all the way.

I got deeply involved in a major building project. In those days a college could borrow quite large sums of money from the government at only 2% or 3% interest. Bennington was an arts college with no great studio, no great dance center, no great facility to attract students and faculty. We decided to build one. Even though it was a financial risk, we felt we had to do *something*.

We hired a good architect. Plans were made and remade. Finally we got to see little cardboard mock-ups. They looked fantastic, so we began to build.

Well, my God! By the time it was finished, it was far bigger than anything we had visualized from looking at those little cardboard mock-ups. In retrospect, I still think the decision was right to create an art center, but I sure was wrong about the heating bills. This magnificent place has rooms 30 and 40 feet high. Vermont is very cold. The only thing that spared us from disaster on heating fuel was that Bennington has a non-resident winter term, so they can shut down from December to March. But even today I hear people say, "The reason Bennington is in trouble is because of that goddamn building." That's not the only reason, but the building didn't help.

   In raising money for nonprofits I am not embarrassed by anything. I am absolutely ruthless. If people see a letter signed by me, they run like hell. Every day I ask somebody for money, sometimes quite a large piece of money. Sometimes I don't actually ask but simply describe a need and the cost, leaving it to the person to decide whether or not to help. In all my asking, in all my different ways of asking, if one out of three says yes, I've made it. Many people hate to ask for money, even for a fine cause, because they are afraid of being turned down. Sure, you get turned down. Just go on to the next.

When I was at Time Inc., I believed firmly in corporate giving. I also believed in staff participation. I set up a generous matching grant program to encourage the staff to contribute to the public good. Each dollar given was matched by three dollars from the company. I personally used the matching grant program to the hilt: when I made a $2,500 personal gift, it became a $10,000 gift. Retirees were included in the program, but soon after I left, retirees were dropped — a sad money-saving decision.

When I retired, I took a lump sum rather than a pension. This was a fortunate decision because the combination of the market boom and an excellent financial manager made it possible for me to live well and still be generous, even though my top salary was only 1/20 of the current chairman's.

Personal giving is an intensely personal matter. Some people like to make large capital gifts. Some — a few — like to give away their personal fortune while they are alive to enjoy the results. Some plan to give and want to give but worry about what might happen in their old age if they give away too much too soon. Then they forget to write gifts into their wills, thereby enriching only Uncle Sam through estate taxes. Some like to spread small gifts among many different causes.

Having been involved in so many nonprofits, I know that the most difficult money to raise is for what is known as the annual fund, the money that covers annual operating deficits. So the bulk of my own giving to my nonprofits goes to cover operating losses. I try to gauge the amount I give in relation to what I plan to leave in my will. In other words, the income a nonprofit will receive from my legacy will in effect perpetuate my annual giving. I have left my Darien house to Harvard and my New York apartment to the Library. Both will be sold to benefit the two institutions.

One of the many things I have learned about fundraising is that it is often a waste of time to ask people who have just struck it rich. Many people have just struck it rich these last few years, especially on Wall Street. I am convinced that people with new money like to look at it for a while. Just look at it. They want to make sure it's really, really theirs and to revel in that fact. After they get used to being rich, then they might become prospects. Maybe.

Now that I am in my 80s, I am trying to cut down on the number of nonprofits I work for. It is much harder to escape from a nonprofit than to join one. I spend an enormous amount of time on this work. My estimate is 40 hours a week, and this does *not* count the time I spend attending nonprofit dinners, receptions and award banquets. I also don't count the time I spend reading to keep abreast of my fields, or the time I spend merely thinking about solutions: Where can I find the money to fix this particular problem? Who might be the right person for this particular job?

My assistant Barbara Widmayer, who has the task of arranging all my various meetings, thinks 40 hours a week on nonprofit work is a low estimate. Whatever the correct measure it is a full-time job. I probably work harder at it than I did as chairman of Time Inc.

Now when I am badgered to join a new undertaking, I try to say no. But I always give the person who is badgering me another name to try in my place. I don't want anybody who is working in this marvelous and essential field to go away empty-handed.

It is always flattering to be asked to help some good cause, especially when you have had as much experience as I have had, and when you can see the possibilities of what might be done.

I consider it citizenship.

BRYANT PARK

◇◇◇◇

HERE, FACING FIFTH AVENUE, GUARDED BY ITS PAIR OF STONE lions, occupying half the entire block between Fifth and Sixth Avenues, stands the main building of the New York Public Library, which we are trying to rescue.

And here, right behind the Library, occupying the other half of the block, not guarded by lions or by anything else, stands Bryant Park. It is theoretically owned by the New York City Parks Department, but it is actually owned by drug-pushers and drug-users. In 1980 when I became chairman of the Library, the druggies were in total control of Bryant Park. If you did not want to sell or buy or use drugs, you would never dare walk into Bryant Park except between noon and two on a bright sunny day — and even then, keep your hand on your wallet or pocketbook.

The pushers operated not just in the park but all around the Library building. The broad front steps are always a busy, populated area, with many people walking in or out of the building or just sitting on the steps to relax and talk. The drug-pushers would stroll around the steps, offering their goods to any likely-looking customer — and sometimes to unlikely-looking customers. One day when we were having a meeting at the Library, a pusher offered his product to Mrs. Brooke Astor, our leading benefactor. That's not exactly the image the Library wanted to project.

I realized that if we were to save the Library and make it the institution it deserved to be, we would have to do something about Bryant Park. So I set out to fix it. It took 12 years.

Bryant Park was named for William Cullen Bryant. He is remembered now as the poet of "Thanatopsis," but he was the editor of the New York *Evening Post* for 50 years. A large, brooding bronze statue of Bryant looks out over the park. It was in such frightful shape that we had to remove it and repair it — more than $300,000, one of those little extra costs that one encounters when something has been neglected over a long period of time.

The park was originally laid out in the mid-1880s but did not become a disaster area until 1934, when Parks Commissioner Robert Moses decided to do it over with WPA money. Moses was a great builder but sometimes a great wrecker. Bryant Park was one of his most notable wrecks.

Moses raised the park's ground level three or four feet, which meant that nobody, including patrolling policemen, could easily see into the park from the surrounding sidewalks. He added many bushes and shrubs around the perimeter, creating many hidden areas, and the lighting deteriorated over time. His new Bryant Park was designed for crime, and sure enough, crime rose to the bait.

The management of the Library had enough work to do without worrying about Bryant Park, so I set up a separate entity called the Bryant Park Restoration Corporation and, with a gift from the Rockefeller Brothers Fund, hired a 26-year-old executive director named Dan Biederman. I chose him because he had been chairman of Manhattan's Community Board 5. Every geographical area of the city has an advisory board made up of neighborhood people who are appointed by borough presidents or by city council members for that area. Board 5 covered most of midtown, home of the Library and Bryant Park.

The Community Boards have an advisory role in all planning of physical development. Whenever you want to do something, you have to appear before your neighborhood board. The board does not have the authority to say yes or no in any legally binding way, but if it says no, you will later have a lot of trouble with the Planning Commission and the City Council. Since we would have to take our Bryant Park plan to Board 5, I figured that its former chairman would be a major asset.

Biederman and I collected much advice from people who were knowledgeable about parks. Vartan Gregorian, the Library president, and Marshall Rose, our real estate trustee, joined many of the talks. So did Parks Commissioner Gordon Davis, who was friendly to our intentions.

Our plan was to "privatize" the park, to take it away from Parks Department ownership and management. No one had ever privatized a public park in such a visible location, and no one had ever tried to do it in such a difficult location, only one block away from what was then one of the worst downtown areas in America, Times Square. We planned to run it as a B.I.D., a Business Improvement District.

B.I.D.s were a fairly new concept. You have to get 51% of the businesses in the area not to object to paying slightly higher taxes to support a neighborhood improvement project. You have to go around building by building to persuade them. In our Bryant Park B.I.D. it would be five extra cents a square foot, which would bring in $400,000. The higher taxes are deductible as a business expense. When a B.I.D. works right, everybody wins. Thanks to the additional funds, the district itself improves, a city's problem area turns into a success, the businesses that contributed prosper, and more businesses and customers are attracted to the improved district, which leads to more tax revenue for the city.

We hired the landscape architect Laurie Olin to create a new version of Bryant Park. A key feature of our plan came from a theory set forth by William H. (Holly) Whyte, the great urbanist and author. He said that the only way to make a street safe is to have "eyes." Somebody must always be watching, because you will never have enough police to cover an entire city. To a considerable extent, said Whyte, a city can police itself. The "eyes" can be shops or stores or delicatessens or fast-food establishments, preferably those that stay open until midnight. Above all, the people who use the space provide eyes.

When we talked about what would make the best "eyes" for our new park, we decided on a good restaurant that would open early and close late. We cast around, we checked out a number of restaurateurs and finally chose Warner Le Roy, who had made such a success of his Tavern on the Green in Central Park. He designed for us a grandiose Crystal Palace sort of restaurant to be set against the back wall of the Library, an area we called New York's biggest latrine because that's what it was used for. (This restaurant was one of many elements during the 12-year Bryant Park project that was destined for trouble.)

Besides the restaurant our plan had many other features:

- A beautiful garden and open pathways.
- Attractive concession facilities for a coffee shop, a flower stand, a pasta takeout, all in the same style.
- Public restrooms.
- Better access to the park through shallower, more inviting entrances.
- Excellent security.
- Excellent lighting, so that our park would not go back to its old ways at night.
- A perimeter that allowed full visibility into the park. This would mean getting rid of bushes, hedges, ugly newsstands, phone booths and other excrescences.

Because of the nature of our proposals, we had to provide an environmental impact statement. That takes six months and costs about $120,000.

When our plans were at last complete, Gregorian and I had to begin the process of getting approval. The first step was to appear before our local Community Board, Board 5, which met in the basement of St. Malachy's Church on 49th Street. Arthur Rosenblatt, our borrowed architect from the Met Museum, and Dan Biederman, our executive director, came with us, along with all our drawings and charts. On the same night, five other supplicants for lesser projects also appeared.

The board took great delight in making us wait till last while it heard the other five proposals. The fact that the other proposals were simpler did not mean that they were necessarily briefer. We waited hours.

Board 5 had some 50 members. These are people who don't like to go to movies or to stay home at night and watch television. They like to go to community boards. Many are well-informed and have diverse interests, but others are not very sophisticated. A few people with no judgment or experience become terribly important, especially in their own eyes. Many resent authority, wealth and power. All like to ask questions and argue.

At Board 5, and at every other board, council, department or commission we visited over the years, there was invariably at least one person who was antagonistic or suspicious or didn't understand what we were trying to do or what we were asking for. Often there was more than one.

The result of our Board 5 meeting was excellent, in part because we were last on the agenda. After they had kept us waiting in a depressing basement room, listening to all the other supplicants, the board members began to drift away, one after another. When our case was finally called after ten o'clock, only a few board members remained, and they were anxious to go home. They asked us a few questions, some of them mildly unfriendly, but they adjourned without voting any objection to our plan.

Our Board 5 meeting was step one in an interminable process. Of course we had to win the approval of Mayor Ed Koch and Parks Commissioner Gordon Davis. But in addition we had to appear before the following agencies and win *their* approval:

- The Parks Department
- The Landmarks Preservation Commission
- The Art Commission
- The Department of Environmental Protection
- The Planning Commission
- The City Council
- The Manhattan Borough Board
- The Office of Business Development
- The Police Department
- The State Historic Preservation Office
- The State Legislature
- The State Comptroller's Office

These were just the official groups. We also had to appear before various esthetic groups, whose support was highly desirable:

- The Municipal Art Society
- The Parks Council
- The Landmarks Conservancy
- The Fine Arts Federation
- The City Club
- The American Institute of Architects
- The Women's City Club
- The American Society of Landscape Architects

Round and round and round. On and on and on. It is an endless, slow-motion obstacle course, one big fence after another, and each time you are not certain that you can get over the fence. After you clear one, it may be three months before the next one is scheduled, and nothing happens in between. Some boards are linked: you have to get through number one and number two before you can apply for a date with number three, so any delay kicks in another delay. It's like trying to climb up a waterfall.

I blame this on all the reform movements that have created laws saying you can't do this, you can't do that, you can't do anything. The sole purpose is to prevent something that might be *bad*. But the effect is to prevent anything *good* from happening. Candidates get elected by taking credit for laws they have passed preventing something, or by promising to pass some preventive law if they get elected. The overriding principle in city government is to prevent anybody from doing anything wicked, not to encourage anybody to do something good. What rules the system is that nobody must do anything that might embarrass the mayor.

Gresham's Law is that bad money drives out good. Heiskell's Law is that we must use the good to drive out the bad. A good new Bryant Park must drive out the bad old Bryant Park. But given the negative attitude that governs all activity, it was uphill all the way.

Dan Biederman remembers that whenever he and I had lunch during this dreary, endless period, I would say to him, "You're lucky you're a young man, because you'll live long enough to see this park. I won't."

Sometimes we encountered so fierce an objection to some aspect of our plan that we had to go back to the drawing board and modify it, then resubmit the proposal. Sometimes we were asked to provide a surprise piece of irrelevant information that we did not have, and then we had to go dig it out and come back for a second meeting.

One awful complication was that the players kept changing. As just one example, Gordon Davis was Parks Commissioner when we signed our first agreement with him and Mayor Koch on what we planned to do. But while we were working out approval from all those boards and councils and commissions, we got a new Parks Commissioner, Henry Stern.

Henry Stern is bright and unpredictable. He had been a Councilman and was therefore an experienced public official. Public officials hate to make decisions and will do practically anything to avoid making one. The longer you postpone a decision, the longer you postpone criticism. It's only when you make a decision that the brickbats start flying. That's why public officials don't make decisions, and they are very good at not making them.

As soon as he became Parks Commissioner, Stern said that no restaurant by Warner Le Roy was going into the new Bryant Park. He said he had a dispute with Le Roy about his Central Park restaurant, Tavern on the Green, and until and unless that was cleared up, he could not even consider Le Roy's Bryant Park restaurant.

The restaurant had other opponents. The Parks Council raised questions. The staff and some of the board members objected to the commercial aspects of our plan. Their theory is that you should never remove a single bush or tree and that every park should be kept pristine, clear and clean. Any changes we planned to make were therefore bound to be bad, and a restaurant was the worst. If I had ever been able to lock up the Parks Council in Bryant Park for 24 hours, they might have had a different view. My wife Marian almost resigned from the board of the Parks Council because they were so nasty about Bryant Park.

At one point I found myself standing in the Mayor's office at City Hall and screaming at Ed Koch. I spent 20 minutes screaming at him that Bryant Park was getting nowhere, that he wasn't giving me proper backing, that his Parks Commissioner was screwing up everything. Everybody present was amazed that Koch didn't scream back. He *always* screams back. In fact, he usually screams first. Somebody was actually tugging at my jacket to get me to sit down.

After two years of delays and pot shots, Warner Le Roy said, "Almost nothing ever depresses me, but this does. It's never going to happen." He withdrew.

After that we went through a series of potential restaurateurs, including Smith & Wollensky and a Japanese group. Each time we were able to get a restaurateur to join us, we had to submit architectural plans to all the appropriate boards. When we obtained approval, we then had to go to the banks for financing — a slow process. Then if for one reason or another the restaurateur pulled out, the process would start again from scratch. And the bank loan for Restaurant A was no good for Restaurant B.

In spite of all that, we finally did get our restaurant. It is the Bryant Park Grill and Cafe. The Grill is a 200-seat year-round restaurant owned by Ark and designed by Hugh Hardy. In the good-weather months the Cafe can add outdoor and rooftop seating for another 600 people. That means that in good weather we have 1,600 "eyes" to police our park, and even when the outdoor Cafe is closed, we still have 400 indoor "eyes." But we were a long, long time getting there.

Everything I get involved in, especially in the nonprofit field, reaches a point where it all seems impossible, so unlikely to be successful, no realistic hope of making it work. I get to the point of wanting to quit. Sometimes you *should* quit. Perhaps we should have quit on *Life* sooner than we did.

But usually I get a second wind and decide to persevere. Energy is the biggest thing you have to carry you. Some talent, but a hell of a lot of energy. You have to keep saying, it can be done, it can be done, and finally you convince everybody else that it *can* be done, and then it gets done. So much of management is not just making a reasonable number of intelligent decisions and having a bit of imagination. It's the conviction that carries it through. That conviction that you transmit to others adds up to a critical mass of conviction that carries the project to success. Having a good idea isn't worth a damn unless you have this conviction, the willingness to put yourself totally behind it so that everybody else feels it is okay to put himself behind it. Some people do this by scaring people to death, and some do it by energizing people around them by making them part of a team, and some do it through the incentive of financial reward. You can't do anything by yourself. You have to get other people to work with you.

Enthusiasm can be communicated to other people and implanted in them. Getting people to go along with you is a mixture of many things: persuasion, conviction, the way you conduct yourself, the way you have conducted yourself in the past, how good your reputation is.

Through all our negotiations with all the groups, both governmental and private, we needed lawyers to research rules and regulations and precedents and to prepare documents complying with them. Those documents were sometimes an inch thick. Legal bills and environmental impact statements were big expenses. Altogether I raised $1.6 million in private funds. This money was totally separate from the money we were raising during the same period for the Library. I felt I had to keep the Library and Bryant Park separate. But then something happened that brought the two together in a strange and exciting way.

Bryant Park had now been reviewed by every civic group in the Western hemisphere — and by some of them twice. We began to prepare for construction, when suddenly we heard that a Spanish company wanted to build a garage under Bryant Park. This might have seemed preposterous except for the fact that the company was represented by a law firm that had, among its partners, former New York City Mayor Robert Wagner and former New York Governor Hugh Carey. They were formidable advocates.

I was horrified. I went stamping all over town. All those cars belching fumes into our new park. We had had to provide environmental impact statements on everything we proposed to do, and here was a truly noxious impact, not to mention how much it would add to midtown traffic congestion. I said it could easily destroy the whole idea of a new Bryant Park. I raised so much hell at City Hall and everywhere else that the proposed garage went away. But it left us an unexpected legacy.

Marshall Rose, the Library's expert on real estate and space, had a brilliant idea. If it was theoretically possible to build a garage under Bryant Park, why not use the same space to build stacks for books? We were already far out of space for books. New collections came in and new books were published, but we had no place to put them. We had talked, reluctantly, about creating a whole new subsidiary location, perhaps some giant remote building in New Jersey. That was superseded by Marshall's underground idea. If it had not been for Wagner and Carey, we would never have thought of putting the stacks in a cavern under the park.

Now we needed a design for our cavern. More architects, more engineers. The final design had two floors of stacks, each floor covering one-and-a-half acres, connected to the main building by a tunnel.

Once we had a design, we had to get approval to excavate and then to build the stacks. That meant going back to many of the previous groups that we already knew — and who already knew us. More hearings, more lawyers. The stacks would cost $20 million. This was public land, so no bank could give us a mortgage, because if we failed, the bank could not foreclose public land. Because we could give no guarantee, we could not get

Bryant Park, once a dangerous drug center, is today one of the gems of New York City, safe for everyone. In the background are the Library and, at its base, the park restaurant. Bryant Park is my proudest achievement.

a mortgage. Instead, we had to lobby a $20 million bond issue through the state legislature and persuade Governor Cuomo to sign it. Which they did and he did.

When we went back to the Landmarks Commission to get approval of the underground stacks, we no longer had a restaurant design because Le Roy had dropped out. The restaurant situation was in transition, so we did not know what the next design might be. We said to Landmarks, "Give us approval to redesign the park. Here's a design. And give us approval to put the stacks underneath the park. Here's a design for that." They said they would not give approval because they did not know what the restaurant would look like. We said, "You're going to get another crack at that when we come up with a new restaurateur and a new design. But we want to get going. We have the money for the park, we have the money for the stacks. We need to start. We'll come back in six months with a restaurant design." They refused to approve us, based on a totally nonexistent issue. But fortunately for us, this being public land, Landmarks had only advisory power. The Art Commission had final power, and they approved it.

We had a terrible mess in the park for two years. We had to blast a hole 30 feet deep through solid rock. We faced enormous hazards. We had to make sure that our blasting didn't damage any of the buildings around the perimeter of the park, including our own Library. A subway ran through one corner of the park, and we didn't want to blast any of its trains off the rails. We were terrified that somewhere in the hole we were excavating we would run into serious underground water — a spring or a stream. That often occurs in deep excavations, and it would be a major problem because dampness would damage the books we planned to store in that hole. We also had a transportation problem: getting rid of all that rock as we blasted it loose.

Almost everything worked. No buildings fell down. We did not cause a single subway problem. We did encounter underground water that has delayed the construction of the second full story. But we completed one story that now holds 1.6 million books, and we are working on the other.

We were lucky. Sometimes that happens. I have always believed that if you are not lucky, you should not be in business.

The opening ceremonies for Bryant Park took place on April 21, 1992. It was a beautiful sunny day, Bryant Park looked beautiful, and I was beaming inside and out. The governor and mayor were there and a goodly crowd of well-wishers. I can only remember saying to the crowd, "Well, it really has happened. This is now your park — once again."

Bryant Park taught me more about dealing with public authority and the bureaucracy than the Library ever did. Most of our Library improvements were inside the building and not subject to all those rules.

Bryant Park is probably the only time in my life that I have been able to take on a problem, live through it, survive it, live long enough to come to the end, to see it work, to be able to say, that's fine, it's all over, it's done — and then turn it over to somebody else. And also be able to say, yeah, I did it.

Usually whatever you do, it's like pushing spaghetti. You do push it around a bit, but you can never really say that you completed the job. Bryant Park is the only clear case where I can say, I started it and I finished it.

Others thought so too. The main entrance to the park is a broad ramp at the corner of Sixth Avenue and 42nd Street. On the left as you walk into the park, on a low stone parapet, carved in discreet three-inch letters are the words "ANDREW HEISKELL PLAZA." You might not notice it, but it's there. I always notice it, and I smile.

AN INFORMAL INDEX OF PEOPLE AND PLACES

◇◇◇◇